# *I Rode with Tupper*

by J. Patrick Shannan
as told to William Bicket

Printed in the United States of America

Published by:

Founders Publishing Company
Eustis, Florida
(904) 483-0700

Second Edition

# TABLE OF CONTENTS

This is the story of a man believed by many to be a true hero of the modern age.

A decade ago F. Tupper Saussy of Sewanee, Tennessee was the most beloved writer and speaker on the Constitutional research circuit. Without benefit of media coverage and the shelves of corporate bookstores, his *Miracle on Main Street* sold over 100,000 copies. Later as editor of *The Main Street Journal*, he provided Americans with monthly truth on insider information reminiscent of Thomas Paine of Revolutionary days. Then he was attacked by the IRS.

For his beliefs, which mirror those of our country's founding fathers, he was persecuted, prosecuted, and persecuted some more until he was finally forced underground in 1987, fearing for his life. Saussy's anxiety proved to be well grounded a year later when the motor home in which the non-violent misdemeanant was living in Placerville, California was surrounded by a twenty-man SWAT team wearing full combat regalia and carrying high-powered, automatic weapons.

Although Tupper Saussy narrowly escaped, many people still wonder what plans were in store for him had he not. Starting over in Seattle with some clothes from Goodwill and fleeing from hideout to hideout, he kept in touch with his old friend, Pat Shannan, but then that communication suddenly stopped. Did he leave the country? Had he died a natural death? Recent actions by SWAT teams from various U.S. agencies have now led thousands to wonder if Saussy has not been finally found and quietly silenced forever.

Here Shannan tells of the encounters and adventures of his friend, the author, ad-man, songwriter and Grammy nominee, editor, lecturer, and fugitive, Tupper Saussy. Shannan describes Saussy's battle with various government forces, his flight from capture, and his life on the run. Shannan also takes a ride through history, shedding new light on old facts for even the most knowledgeable American.

Within the dictators of every era is found a shrewd insight into the potential power of books. Whenever tyrants and authoritarian regimes have wanted to suppress opposition and kill ideas, their first thought, almost invariably, has been to destroy books of contrary view, and oftentimes their authors. Conversely, they have cunningly turned to their own advantage, to bolster their grips on the people, certain other books; e.g., Adolf Hitler's *Mein Kampf*, Karl Marx's *Das Kapital,* and the voluminous writings of Lenin and Stalin. No one realizes better than the despot the enormous explosive forces pent up in books. Books are dynamic and powerful instruments and tools—the weapon of Truth. However, as Voltaire warned before our nation's founding, "It is dangerous to be right when government is wrong."

During the very early days of this nation, the Sedition Act took about as blatant a head-on flight into the First Amendment as any attack since when it made illegal the publishing of "false or malicious criticism" of the government or to "inspire opposition to any of its acts." Some two dozen arrests were made, ten people were actually convicted, and countless more were censured or intimidated into silence. Thomas Jefferson said that the Act "attempted to crush all political opposition" by making criticism of federal officials or policies a crime.

In the first week of Jefferson's presidency, he began pardoning every victim of the Sedition Act because, he said, "...it was as contrary to the spirit of American freedoms as if Congress had ordered us all to fall down and worship a golden calf." By 1802, none of the Alien and Sedition Acts remained on the books. However, the same sort of restrictions of liberty began to surface in the federal judiciary during the late twentieth century under the various labels of "Conspiracy."

Two thousand and thirty-seven years ago Cicero pointed out that murderers are less to be feared than traitors. An enemy at the door is less formidable for he is known, and he carries his banners openly. The traitor moves freely among those within the gates. He works secretly and unknown in the night to undermine the pillars of a city. The traitor "rots the soul of nation ... and infects the body politic so it can no longer resist."

F. Tupper Saussy discovered the traitor behind the walls of Washington, D.C. and began to sound the warning, and he was not the only one. Through the exposure to Saussy and further research of my own, I have gotten to "know" many people whom, regrettably, I never had the pleasure of meeting personally. While Lee Harvey Oswald, James Earl Ray, Bruno Hauptmann, and Sacco & Vanzetti will certainly never be listed in the annals of history as American heroes, anyone who knows the truth of their lives has to be saddened by the fact that these men have been unjustly perverted into villains by those writers of history.

There are many more. Most readers today upon reading Chapter Three of Pat Shannan's account will be reminded of another horror story of their own or their neighbor's. We knew of many more too, but space prevented us from giving you the details of the attacks upon law-abiding people such as Charles Reily, Dick Viti, Paul Quillan, Gary Rickman, John Voss, Irwin Schiff, Bill Benson, Dan Gibson, Richard Leineke, Red Beckman, Paul Robinson, Grant McEwan, Paul Morris, Robert MacElwain, and a thousand others. Most of these men never knew one another, yet their true tales of federal tyranny are as bone-chilling as any fiction Charles Dickens ever created. Christians, Jews, and agnostics, the only common bond in their lives was a love of liberty and a willingness to stand up for it, to go to jail for it, even to die for it, if necessary.

Each time I learn of a new one, I am reminded of an incident in the life of Henry David Thoreau who a century-and-a-half ago was a political prisoner more often than most of us go to the beach today. This time, in jail for some incidental challenge at government for its infringement upon his freedom, he was visited by his friend and fellow writer-scholar Ralph Waldo Emerson.

"Hello, Thoreau. What are you doing in there?" asked Emerson with a denigrating tone indicating his attitude toward the folly of his friend's actions.

"Hello, Emerson. What are you doing out there?" replied Thoreau.

Just as in every war, there are heroines in this one, too. I wish we had known about Gail Sanocki at the time we were compiling Chapter Three's atrocities. She was a professor of Microbiology at the University of Southern California who was dramatically arrested in front of her students in the college classroom and hauled away. She spent much of the next year in a Los Angeles jail without a conviction on a federal charge of failing to file some government forms—forms that the filing of which even the government admitted was "voluntary." Between the filing of numerous handwritten motions from the jailhouse, she spent hours per day scrubbing the lines in the tiled walls and floor of her cell with a toothbrush to alleviate the boredom. She refused to take a lawyer to speak for her in court and eventually beat the case on her own. There surely must be an underlying, ironic message in the fact that her husband—who had been charged along with her—hired an attorney, lost the case, and received a five-year sentence in federal prison.

Then there are Vivian Kellums, Lucille Moran, and Claire Kelly; and we must mention again tough ol' lovable Peggy Christiansen, Pat Shannan's favorite from Chapter Eight. These women did far more for the cause of freedom in this nation than did the simple flag stitchers and wavers such as Betsy Ross and Barbara Fritchie.

Vickie Weaver of Idaho made the ultimate sacrifice. Seconds after hearing the shots that wounded her husband and realizing her home was under siege, she ran to the front door with her suckling baby in her arms to investigate. Lon Horiuchi, a Special Operations Group marksman with the United States Marshal's Service, stood with a high-powered rifle less than fifty yards away and seized the opportunity to shoot the unarmed woman through the head. What manner of free nation are we that this man can not only commit such a dastardly murder with impunity but remain on the federal payroll, presumably to someday do it again?

Drifting, as Pat Shannan might, to the world of music, I lean on the words of Cole Porter:

> The world's gone mad today,
> and good's bad today,
> and black's white today,
> and day's night today ...

Indeed, Bob Dylan, The Times, They Are A Changin'.

To the above-named American heroes (of whom you probably never heard) and to the little known, nondescript, misunderstood, faceless man or woman in your town (even though I have not yet heard of them, either) who had the courage to say, "I'm mad as hell and I'm not going to take it anymore," and then went up against all the might and legal power of the *federales*, whether they won or lost, Pat Shannan and I dedicate this book. If America is looking for heroes, this is where you find them today.

— WILLIAM BICKET, January 1, 1995

Evil men who wish to rule the world have a pattern which has not changed since the days of the Tower of Babel. That pattern has always been some form of collectivism; a somewhat varying but always ubiquitous and formidable method of enslaving many to a few. The current, nefarious scheme of usury was initially tested by The Bank of Amsterdam in 1609.

Collectivism by any other name is simply the collectivization of people versus the sovereignty of individuals. Human liberty, as expressed by the Christian ethic, cannot exist in collectivism because human liberty (and the sovereignty of the individual) is death to collectivism. Hyper-individualism is totally frustrated in a collectivist system.

People do what they are told for many reasons. Habit and tradition may be the most common. We stop for the red light because we have always stopped for the red light, and we alway wait for it to turn green even though the intersection is deserted at 3:00 a.m., and it is no more unsafe to cross there at that time than it was a century ago when there were no automobiles or stoplights at all.

Self-preservation plays a part also. We attend to the boss's desires because he is the boss. It is not prudent to disregard him. Underlying both of these, perhaps, is simple fear of disobeying. We know that we can get in some kind of trouble if we don't follow orders.

What about obeying the law? Fear, of course, is a paramount reason for doing what government says. But in the case of legal rules and regulations, the fear is reinforced by the belief that somehow the law must be "right" or, at least, inherently worthy of respect. There is, after all, this vast legal edifice: The voting and election; the passage through house and senate; the presidential signature; the codification in the United States Code; judges raised on platforms so that we must look up to them; and courtrooms. And, certainly not least, the physical edifices: the majestic buildings of government designed to inspire, create awe, and perhaps a little bit of intimidation, too. Can this whole process, staffed by intelligent and educated men and women, be wrong?

Suppose, for example, that your local government were to make, after due consideration and debate, and the listening-to of expert witnesses, and the holding of hearings, etc., a law which required every citizen of your city or county to become a Buddhist. Outrageous. Totally hostile to everything this country was created to avoid. What could you do about this law?

Challenge your local government in court, of course. After all, this is an open-and-shut case. You can't lose. But you do lose. Stunned, you go to the state appellate court. You lose again. This can't be happening! Every day that you fail to register as a Buddhist you are being fined $100. You take your case to Federal court and lose. You appeal. No luck.

Finally, you bring your suit to the United States Supreme Court. By this time you are penniless, but, you figure, it will be worth it to have this injustice resolved. But where, you wonder, are your fellow citizens who have complained and griped, but haven't raised a finger to assist you? The supreme court declines to hear your case. Become a Buddhist, or else.

Although this example may seem extreme, it is not necessarily any more so than some real examples of today would seem to the people of yesterday. History is replete with "laws" which were abominable, but supported by the government which made them. Does the fact that the "law" has been tested to the limit and upheld, make the law valid? Does this mean you must obey it?

The earth, and all that is in it, belong to God, and man's law, when in conflict, cannot prevail. This is underscored in the U.S. Constitution which contains a provision (Article IV, Section 2) that any law which is repugnant to the supreme law of the land is null and void from its onset and obliges no one, empowers no one, and need not be obeyed. This was upheld by John Marshall's supreme court during the embryonic stages of our republic in the early 19th century (Marbury v. Madison).

How much more so would a law which is repugnant to God's law be unenforceable? The Constitution does not place any limits on your activities but only on those of government. "That which is not just, is not law," said William Lloyd Garrison.

However, government, with all the big guns, including absolute control of the courts today, does not recognize the invalidity of its actions. In their haste to convert us from a Constitutional Republic under God to a Democracy ruled by man (the majority), they have forgotten the age-old axiom that "there can be no crime without a victim." So when one does ignore the new "law," challenges it, and loses through the long, legal process, he is faced with either submitting and defying God, or resisting and being charged with some form of sedition by man. Upon conviction (almost a foregone conclusion) and sentencing, because his "crimes" have no victim, he becomes a "political prisoner."

The prison population is growing at a rate of 3,000 per week, and currently there are more people being held prisoner in the United States than inhabit thirteen of its states! The Soviet prisons, as reported by the Federal Bureau of Prisons, house 761,000 inmates which happens to be just about half of the number of those held in America. Do we really have that many common law criminals? Of course not, but America now has a new god who has made new laws.

The penitentiary camps and jails in the United States in the 1990's are filled with "political prisoners." Some are there for being found in possession of one ounce of a leafy substance that has been grown on this planet by Mother Nature since the beginning of time; but one that someone in recent years has decided is dangerous and "illegal." Others have been incarcerated for up to two years (for illegal trespassing!) because they have exercised a higher law of protecting life rather than allowing life to be taken by a "legal" abortion.

It is a strange double-standard law that punishes people for causing— accidentally or intentionally, with a gun, knife or automobile—a mother to lose her unborn fetus, but protects those licensed medical practitioners who have taken over 30 million babies through "legalized abortion" since the supreme court ruling of 1972 which made this ungodly act "legal."

"Tax Protestors" go to jail not for cheating, as most Americans have been forced to do (yet they remain semi-free), but for challenging—through supposed Constitutionally protected First and Fifth Amendment petitions for a redress of grievances—an unlawful, confiscatory money and income tax system.

Tupper Saussy of Sewanee, Tennessee, was a successful advertising executive in the 1970s. Prior to that he had been a high school English teacher, a playwright, and a song writer with three Grammy nominations; a "darling" of Nashville society.

Following an aesthetic and intuitive study of the American money and tax system, he stopped filing tax returns in 1977 and began to write about why he and most other Americans were not required to do so. In 1980, the Criminal Investigation Division of the Internal Revenue Service investigated him for the years 1977, 1978 & 1979 but found "no criminal potential." By their own records, he had done nothing unlawful. It could only be his writing, then, that suddenly gave him criminal potential.

Perhaps believing with Heraclitus that "wisdom consists of saying what is true," Saussy faced his fellow men of every kind with the same look of dignified respect and sincerity, without a suggestion of premeditated caution. But he could detect sham quickly, and it was difficult for him to conceal his contempt for falsehood. While courteous, he could not make himself charming to men in whom he detected dishonesty or hypocrisy.

Self-seeking judges, U.S. Attorneys, county prosecutors, tax collectors, and IRS agents felt his silent disaproval, hated him for making them esteem themselves less, and longed for his fall. At the same time, throngs of citizens from every State in the Union, as well as many in elective office, cheered him on and praised him and his research & writings with unabashed superlatives.

In 1984, after years of harassment, he was prosecuted by the Justice Department for three years of willful failure to file (the same years just mentioned) not with benefit of a Grand Jury indictment as the law requires but by "information" from the Internal Revenue Service. Through a strange quirk in the legal system, he was acquitted on the final two years of those charges but convicted for the first one.

After eighteen months of appeals were exhausted, he was ordered to report to the Atlanta Federal Prison Camp "on or before April 10th, 1987." He did so, but, when there was nobody there to receive him, he went his own way, and only a few who knew him before have seen him since. Here is his story as told by one who was with him both before and after U.S. Government Agents tried to murder him in Placerville, California, in June of 1988.

**Tribute to Tupper**
by Robert Nehls


A peaceful man, with a gentle hand
That writes the truth, that's all.
Yes, he tells of lies, and a great disguise
that could cause this nation's fall.

Saying we must see, that our destiny
is here within our hand
If we give our best, we can manifest
what the founding fathers planned.

And because he shows, how injustice grows
like a fungus on a tree
They've gone after him, and the jail has been
where he sits. Is this man free?

And a trial fair is that something rare
for a good man to obtain?
Is it just for those, who will not impose
on the one they wish to reign?

But no matter what, you and I have got
to stand by this justice call
For if we sit still, while they make their kill
soon they may just have us all.

So now let's align, with the one whose spine
stands erect with liberty
And one day will tell, how the tyrants fell
to our freedom's symphony.

# CHAPTER ONE

## YOUTH OF THE HEART

W e often worked a club called The Jolly Coachman in Fort Lauderdale, the first time being way back in 1962. We were The Village Singers then, a trio patterned after the Kingstons and the Limeliters. After the advent of the rock groups of the middle sixties, our act went from near obscurity to complete oblivion.

But I had fallen in love with the beach and the breeze, and, when I finally returned, this time in 1982, I was disappointed to see that what must have been every retiree in the United States had since discovered it, too. Wrinkle City. I was jealous; like my own private property had been invaded by all these *sagatits*. Having spent a few past winters in Australia, I longed for the serenity of the Perth beaches on the Indian Ocean with its authentically filled bikinis.

Nevertheless, neither the crowds nor the commercialized streets and condo-laden beaches could deny me the natural pleasures that had been the original attraction—the sun and the sand and the laid-back lifestyle. I stretched back in my lounge chair at the Miami Fountainbleau and reminisced. There are those who would say that folk music died a natural death, just kind of ran its course and disappeared. But we who were part of it know that it didn't die at all—it was murdered by the Beatles! We were all forced either to conform somewhat, or get out of the business.

One who jumped on the bandwagon was our young friend at the Bayou Room in New Orleans in early 1964. He used to scream and strum an old cheap guitar a la Bob Dylan, maybe slightly better, if that were anything to recommend him. Although he looked a couple of years younger, I suppose he was eighteen years old at the time, because that was the required minimum to be inside a drinking establishment, although that statute was never strictly obeyed, either. He filled in for us between the acts, and Larry Lamarca, the tightfisted owner, gave him only a few beers for his contribution. We, the big shots of the Trio, frankly thought Steve was over-compensated. We liked the kid, but there was no doubt that his music stank.

He used to follow us around like a little brother and would often drop by the apartment on Sunday afternoon to jam a little. "Steve," I would say, "You've got to change your style. Nobody wants to hear that screamin' and hollerin', jerkin' and snatchin' bit. People want to be entertained when they come into a nightclub, not yelled at."

"Oh, man, I'm just doin' my thing," he'd reply. "I can't do what I can't do," and he'd hit a near-chord and start chanting something from "The Masters of War." If we had any influence on Steve's career, it could only have been negative. Sometimes, from the stage, we would even playfully rag him about some particularly atrocious song he had performed earlier and get a laugh from the audience at his expense. But what was only good-natured fun to us had to have been brutal blows to a young fellow chasing a dream and trying to be accepted in the cold world of show business.

At that time one of the partners of the group, Pepper Keenan, and I shared a flat at 314 Exchange Place—more commonly known as "Exchange Alley." It is now an artsy gathering place in the old tradition, which parallels Royal and is across the street on the south side from the old courthouse in the heart of the French Quarter. We didn't know it at the time, but after reading Robert Oswald's book, I learned that ours was the precise third floor apartment occupied by him, his mother, Marguerite, and his younger brother, Lee Harvey, in the late 1940s.

For Pepper and me, the best thing about the location was that it served as an excellent vantage point during the early morning hours for our favorite caper of bombarding the sleeping winos in the doorways below with water-filled milk cartons. It wasn't that we weren't loving and compassionate citizens with concern for the homeless. Meager as it was, this was our contribution towards upgrading the neighborhood.

One Sunday afternoon Steven came over to say goodbye. He had a small grip in one hand, his guitar case in the other, and he was wearing his ever-present blue jean jacket. He had scraped up enough money for a bus ticket to Atlanta, then he was going to hitchhike the rest of the way.

"I'm goin' to New York," he said, "and I'm gonna' make it!" Keenan and I thought he had two chances of "making it—slim and none—but we both gave a little false-hearted encouragement to this blond-haired, freckled-face kid and wished him well. It's people like this who wander into your life and wander out again that you wonder what ever happened to but usually never find out.

It was six years later, 1970, and I had spent a couple of years "Down Under" and was not very up to date on the U.S. music scene yet when I found myself in New Orleans again. I gave my old buddy, Pepper, a call at his insurance office, and after a beer at his favorite watering hole, we went by his apartment for more of the same before going out to eat. As he placed a record on the turntable, he flipped a couple of album covers at me by this new rock group who had made quite a splash at Woodstock the year before. Here was the impish Steve on the cover wearing what must have been the same old, but more faded now, blue jean jacket, along with three other scruffily dressed, long-haired hippies. CROSBY, STILLS, NASH & YOUNG, announced the album cover. Steven Stills had, indeed, "made it."

I still didn't think much of what I heard, but, obviously, a few million others did, and after we overcame our initial touch of jealousy, we both decided that we were proud of him and happy for his success. Pepper reminded me of my wonderful advice to Steve back in '64, and I said, "Yeah, well, so much for my great insight concerning evolving music trends. I think you should sell all your Xerox stock, too!"

It was during this era that Tupper Saussy walked into my life for a brief stay as a temporary roommate in New York City. Not only was he blessed with talent, but he had married well and lived in a small palace in the fashionable Belle Meade section of Nashville. He had songs to publish at the time, and his star was on the rise. I wouldn't see him again until many years later after that star had crashed and burned. It is like that in the world of show business. We meet all kinds of celebrities and interesting characters, sometimes at the most unexpected times.

As a youngster, I knew and cared more about baseball history than I ever did about world history or geometry or spelling or Shakespeare or anything else they ever tried to siphon into me nine months a year. So later, as an adult, whenever I drove highway 49 between Hattiesburg and Biloxi and passed the "Dizzy Dean Museum" sign at Wiggins, Mississippi, I would tell myself that I must stop here the very next trip and take the time to see this. A very hot July afternoon about a year after that last visit with Jerry found me viewing that sign again and finally saying to myself, "I've got some time ... today's the day."

A short jaunt off the exit led me to Dizzy's Shell Station on the left and fifty yards closer set a one-room building with a sign indicating it housed what I was seeking. As I got out into the 100 plus degree heat and near-same humidity and walked to the door, I saw the padlock and didn't bother knocking. Maybe the attendant at the service station could let me in, I thought, as I started towards the gas pumps. He had already seen me and as we strode towards each other I noticed something familiar about the strapping man lumbering across the gravel.

"Hello, Podna', " he bellowed, extending his hand, still ten yards away. "Well, I'll be doggoned," I exclaimed, "I've been wanting to stop here for some time, and if I had known I was going to get to meet the main man, too, I would have done it a long time ago." "Then you prob'ly wouldna' found me, Podna', I'm just fillin' in today. C'mon in. I'll cut on the cooler for us while ya' look around." After a minute of his fumbling for the right key, we were inside, and I was asking him about Pepper Martin, Frankie Frisch and all of the rest of the "Gashouse Gang" from those Cardinal years of the thirties.

Shortly I realized that even though I was a generation younger, he probably hadn't met anyone else since he had moved to south Mississippi with whom he could resurrect some of these old memories. Asking Jerome Hanna Dean a question about himself was akin to asking the time of day and hearing how to build a watch. The Great Man once wrote a discreet autobiography of sorts and merely stated the facts. With remarkable self-restraint he set down these words: "Anybody who's ever had the privilege of seein' me play ball knows that I am the greatest pitcher in the world. And them that ain't been fortunate enough to have a gander at Ol' Diz in action can look at the records." Nope. There was never anything modest about Mr. Dean.

When he was enshrined in the Hall of Fame in Cooperstown, New York, sports columnist Arthur Daley wrote: "The self-confessed Great Man is a welcome addition, though he lowers the humility quotient of the immortals down to virtually nothing."

His wife had erected this shrine to "Ole Diz" after their retirement; having saved a garage full of memorabilia over the years. There were news clippings—framed and in numerous scrapbooks—autographed baseballs, gloves and bats from most of my old heroes of that era and dozens of pictures adorning every wall. He told me that she hadn't used half of what they had and someday they would need to get a larger, more permanent place. I commented that she certainly had made the best of that with which she had to work.

Dizzy had disappeared briefly and returned with a couple of "big orange dranks," as he (and Deacon Andy Griffith) called them, and we sipped and talked as if I had been there in the big leagues with him thirty-five years before. After a half hour or more, I asked if he didn't need to go back to the station and "tend shop."

"Naw," he said, "It's pretty slow today, and most of my customers pump their own gas anyway when nobody's not around and just leave my money on the counter. Do you remember when I broke my toe in the '37 All Star game?..." and we yakked like a couple of old school chums for another hour as we strolled from wall to wall.

Finally, he said he had to close up because it was time for him to go to the golf course to meet his buddies and "take some of their money," his daily avocation after it cooled off each late summer afternoon. "But come back again, Podna', after we get the other stuff up and we'll talk some more," he said. "Bring yore wife or your girlfriend," he paused with perfect comedic timing, giving me a cockeyed glare, "or bofe ub 'em ... and come out to the house for a mint julep. My wife likes to talk baseball, too! This here is me and her and my brother, Paul," he said as he pointed to a framed five by seven near the door. I assured him that I would delight in taking him up on that offer on my very next trip through the area. He assured me that he was serious and we shook hands and departed for our separate destinations.

As I drove south on the four-lane, I found myself wishing that some of my Little League buddies of the fifties—with whom I learned all that Cardinal trivia—could have been there with me. I can still hear Harry Caray, who was only a radio voice to us then, raving about Stan "The Man" Musial's double off the right field wall, or Enos Slaughter going from first to home on a single at Sportsmen's Park in St. Louis. I remember Wally Moon, Eddie Stanky, Red Schiendienst and Harvey Haddix ... and who could ever forget Solly Hemus? It is only since recently turning fifty that I have finally begun to realize that I probably will not someday play centerfield for the St. Louis Cardinals.

I was so glad I had finally stopped. Eighteen months later, not having yet returned but not having forgotten my invitation, either, I picked up the sports page of the Atlanta Constitution and was saddened to learn that "Ole Diz" had had a heart attack in Reno—on the golf course, no less—and had passed away.

I would never have the opportunity to partake of that mint julep and share another reminiscence with one of this century's most colorful characters. He was either 61 or 64 or somewhere in between. Nobody could ascertain his exact age because Dizzy could never remember his birthday and year—or would pretend that he couldn't. During his long career as player and play-by-play sportscaster, whenever he was asked his date of birth, he would always respond with a new and different one. It was part of his charm. A few years after his death, his widow moved the shrine to the capitol city of Jackson and enlarged it with "the rest of the stuff."

When John McKeithen was running for governor of Louisiana in 1964, twice he came into "The Bayou Room," stood in front of the stage with a hundred dollar bill, tore it in half, handed us one half and announced to us that as soon as we sang "Dixie" we could have the other half. That incentive being the equivalent of a night's wages for the whole trio, one can imagine how fast we came up with an on-the-spot arrangement. He promptly turned over the remaining half but asked that we polish up his favorite song because he would be back again.

A few weeks later he repeated his performance but I don't think we had improved ours much because the third time he was there with his entourage the weekend before the election, he ignored us. After allowing ample time and realizing we weren't going to get the third hundred, we gave it to him anyway for free. It's hell to be a prostitute.

And speaking of "The Bayou Room," during Mardi Gras weekend that year we introduced at least a dozen celebs from the audience. Louis Prima's old sax man, Sam Butera, was appearing with his group, The Witnesses, a few blocks down Bourbon Street and would occasionally stop in for a beer, but we could never get him to bring his saxophone with him.

He did appreciate the attention, though, whenever we would make a big deal out of him as we did this Saturday night. A little later, Tiger Jones, our bass-playing tenor, spotted Marty Robbins in the audience and with a little coaxing, got him on stage to say hello.

And then there was Dana Starcher. Straight out of Damon Runyon and looking like a young, but rougher cut, Kirk Douglas, Dana was Lamarca's all-purpose utility man from dark to daylight. He would tend bar when needed, but mostly his time was divided between barking out front to urge the crowd in and bouncing the rowdy ones out, which he enjoyed most.

He was only in his mid-twenties and was much smaller than what one would picture as your typical rough & tumble bouncer. But what he lacked in size he made up for with a fierce, flailing, street-fighting style not unlike that of Roberto Duran a decade later and he delighted in demonstrating it for us on an unruly (and unlucky) patron. Creeping around the nightclub floor with leopard-like stealth, he wore a patch over one eye which women found intriguing and men intimidating.

We never could get the "straight skinny" from Dana on how he had managed to lose that eye—though he did show us the empty hole in his face to prove it was definitely gone. Each time we would ask, he would have a new, more elaborate story:

He had been captured by wild pygmies in New Guinea and tortured; or it accidentally happened at a drunken orgy in Paris when a half dozen women became overly amorous; or he witnessed something one night that was just far too gory to repeat—something his mind just couldn't take—and his eye popped right out of his head.

He was so full of crap and always ready with the new story whenever we were foolish enough to ask. Whenever he finished the new episode of past antics, he would flash that s.e.g. (shit-eating grin) which wordlessly reflected: "You're not dumb enough to believe that, are you?"

If, indeed, it really happened as we suspected, during one of his few losing battles, we were certain that the perpetrator did not live very long to brag about it. I always loved the colorful characters of the netherworld more than the shallow celebs from wherever they came.

Dana had a mythical girl friend, Fonda Peters, who was his "steady" and the only one about whom he ever spoke. Whenever we went out bar hopping in the Quarter after hours, Dana seldom went with us because he was always "going to fondle Fonda." However, he could never bring her in to meet us because, first of all, she was much too classy "a broad" to subject herself to Bourbon Street lowlife and, of course, our style of music was far beneath her, anyway. According to Dana, she was always busy at home listening to her old Caruso collection, teaching her art class, or playing bridge at the Pontchartrain Country Club. We never found out if there really was such a place, but it sure sounded impressive to us.

When we asked how such a classy dame happened to hook up with him, a one-eyed barker from sleazy Bourbon Street, he replied, "She thinks I'm the Chief Brain Surgeon at Tuoro Hospital!" Considering the experience he gained operating on our brains, today he just may be.

When Pepper and I weren't pulling pranks on someone else, we were snaking each other. Around midnight that Mardi Gras Saturday, when the crowd was thinning a bit, I recognized a familiar guy whom I knew to be the former All American fullback of the L.S.U. Tigers. As we were putting our instruments on the rack to take our break, I mentioned to Pepper who it was and that I was going to introduce myself to him. Pepper said, tongue in cheek of course, "You tell him I'm going to get myself a beer, and if he is still around when I get back, I'm going to kick his butt!"

I stepped over to the table and spoke to this rock of a man who was with his wife and another couple, and as he stood up to shake my hand, I noticed Pepper standing beside the stage watching to be sure that I did not follow through with his instructions. But I did. I pointed to Pepper as I spoke ("My friend over there attended Ole Miss, and he said to tell you ... etc.") and we both watched Keenan burlesque with exaggerated, but sincere, panic on his face, his eyes protruding in alarming exophthalmus, as I repeated his false threat to this man-killer who then looked back Pepper's way, sized up the situation for what it truly was, and emoted, "You tell him not to worry, I'll be gone!" Then we all three broke into a belly laugh, Pepper's being the loudest and most relieved. It was Jimmy Taylor of the Green Bay Packers! I don't think even Dana would have stuck around to help Pepper out of that one.

Being a Robert Goulet lookalike, the damned Lothario usually got even with me for that kind of caper by stealing whichever girl I happened to have my eye on at the time. "That's for the Taylor episode," he told me at least five times.

* * *

When my recollections took my memory forward to Boston and 1975, I remembered that my first and closest encounter with someone who had knowledge of corruption and control at the top of government was with Robert Welch, the founder of The John Birch Society.

During a three hour lunch together in Belmont, just he and I, Welch confided, among many other things, that he had the proof that in 1961, then Vice President Lyndon Johnson and Billy Sol Estes (of the infamous grain scam) were running heroin from Red China through Mexico and into the United States at the west Texas border.

What was astonishing then has become ho-hum in the 1990's. But this served to remind me that I had agreed to attend a meeting in a few hours, and I had better snap out of this reminiscent trance, get back to the present and go shower. As the hot sand soothed and tickled my itchy feet during the short stroll back to the room, I hummed and sang to myself an old Irish folk song:

"Oh, the youth of the heart and dew of the morning, wake and they've left you without any warning."

Like Yogi Berra says, it was kinda' deja vu all over again back in Florida now in late 1982. That night, after snapping out of my reminiscent trance, I remembered that I was invited to a meeting by an acquaintance, Gary Beck, who, in his spare time, headed up a group of Constitutional purists in kind of an educational society. They called themselves the Florida Patriots, and I was impressed with both the numbers and the quality of the people at the meeting I attended; both white collar and blue collar, they were a cross-section of middle America.

I don't remember the name of the guest speaker but he gave a most interesting talk about the Federal Reserve system and the difference between lawful money and the "Federal Reserve Notes" that we carry around and use as money today.

After the speech, I visited the literature table and asked the lady attendant which was the best primer on money for one as ignorant as I, and, before she could answer, Gary, who happened to be standing alongside of me, said as he reached for a brightly covered book, *The Miracle on Main Street* by Tupper Saussy."

Never prone to subtleties, I growled, "By whom?"

"Tupper Saussy," he repeated. "Have you ever heard of him?"

"Heard of him?," I said. "I used to *room* with him. Is this what he's up to now? Let me see that."

I knew there couldn't possibly be two people in the world with a name like that, and, sure enough, there was his picture with a short bio on the back cover. He had written songs, television commercials, and advertising, so it shouldn't have surprised me that he would write a book about money, but it did.

"Not only is this the best education on our bogus money," Gary said, "but it is also the easiest to understand, which I guess is what makes it the best. The economists have complicated our understanding of what should be a very simple thing. Mr. Saussy unwinds it with basics. He'll be speaking down here next month. Would you like to come hear him?"

I assured him that I certainly would like to come hear Tupper speak but reminded him that I was booked into Nashville in two weeks and wouldn't return to south Florida for some time. "Maybe I can see him up there," I thought out loud.

I gave them seven bucks and no tax ("After you read the book, you'll know why there is no tax," he told me) for a copy of the book and went back to my hotel room to place a call to Tupper in Sewanee, Tennessee. After his wife summoned him to the phone, we talked awhile about normal things and then I told him of my schedule for Nashville. Unfortunately, he was headed to Puerto Rico for Christmas and wouldn't return until after his Fort Lauderdale meeting in January, by which time I would be out west again. He was pleasantly surprised that I had a copy of his book in my hand, said that he hoped we could get together sometime soon, and was disappointed that we couldn't meet somewhere this trip.

Regrettably, with my hectic schedule, I never got around to reading his book and later misplaced the darned thing. The urgency of getting together again soon faded, as it so often does when the timing is wrong, and another five years would pass before we would—and then it would be in another most unexpected manner.

But there was one thing that stuck with me. When I asked Gary how much the book cost, he said it was "seven ferns." Then, in response to the quizzical look on my face, he went on to remind me of what I had just heard: that we don't have "dollars" per se anymore, and what we actually carry around are dishonored Federal Reserve Notes; FRNs; commonly known amongst the patriot bunch as "ferns."

I have always remembered that and often at the cash register when I am about to pay my bill in a shop or restaurant, I will ask the cashier, "Do you take Federal Reserve Notes?" More often than not the reply will be "No." I then take devilish delight in showing them just exactly what it is that they are refusing to accept. Whatever the varied reaction, it is always good for a laugh.

I made that Nashville Christmas-time gig in 1982 and got back at least once a year for the next four, but I never got a hundred miles down the road to Sewanee, nor ran into Tupper in any of his old Nashville haunts, nor, regretfully, ever called him in his cherished Sewanee to invite him up to the city for an evening. A mutual friend, Dan Hoffman, a radio talk-show host, told me that Tupper was spending so much time with his writing and family life that he seldom took time for nightlife anymore.

It was on the morning of April 12th, 1987 that I was breakfasting at the Ramada Inn and reading the "Nashville Banner" when my eyes caught the headline of the story at the bottom of the front page: "Saussy Defies Court Order—Disappears." The accompanying picture was a 1985 shot of Tupper in handcuffs, with a pencil in his mouth, being led from the Winchester Courthouse by federal agents. The unspoken but glaring message was: "I am still not without my means of communication." The spoken message was from William Waller, his former attorney: "Tupper is the most talented and smartest individual I ever represented. He may be able to find a safe harbor and stay hidden a long time. There are a lot of people out there disenchanted with the tax system."

After eating, I gave Dan a call to see what he knew about it, and we agreed to meet at a coffee shop near the radio station after his three o'clock show. Dan and I had first met when he had done an interview with several entertainers on his radio show a few years before. Today he has a Saturday talk show on a Christian station in Nashville and is an outspoken advocate of Constitutional rights and an avowed enemy of the confiscatory income tax. He is, of course, a great admirer of and sympathizer with Tupper Saussy and of most everything for which he stands, but even Dan was a little confused as to all the "whys" of this current story.

Dan is a big man—6'4" and over 200 pounds.—and he sounds it over the radio air waves. His deep, resonant voice assures the listener that this fatherly man behind the microphone is surely a trustworthy dispenser of the Truth. Being fifty-five now, this made him too young for Korea, and too old to be called up by the time Vietnam became a household word, but his face shows near-nausea when he discusses the 100,000 plus young men who died in those two conflicts "for nothing."

He wonders out loud if it is an ironic coincidence, or a natural evolution of events that William Webster went from Federal Judge to Director of the FBI, and is now head of the CIA In 1990, Dan's own brother would have to go underground for much the same reasons as Tupper, but on the day we met, this, of course, had not yet happened.

"You're not an undercover cop, are you?," Dan said to me, only half kidding.

"Hell no, I'm not a cop!," I said, "I just want to know what's going on here. Something is wrong. The newspapers are making Tupper sound like John Dillinger. This isn't the guy you and I know."

"No, of course it isn't, but you know you can count on the media people making him look like a buffoon. That's part of their jobs." He rocked back in his chair, thought for a moment, and went on, "I don't know why he did it, Pat. He would have had to serve only a year or less. He would make a great interview. I wish he would call me from wherever he is. I'd love to put him on the air live with his answers."

We wondered together what could make a man become so committed to his beliefs that he would forsake his family and comfort. I offered that whatever it is, it must be a touch of the same thing that causes an otherwise normal individual to place his butt on a keg of dynamite and drive a truck into a compound full of a couple hundred sleeping Marines. "Mind you," I said, "I'm not suggesting that Tupper has snapped, though I haven't seen him in a long time, I'm only referring to commitment here, not insanity."

"No, Tupper has not had a mental breakdown, Pat, that I can assure you, and he would never, ever attempt to harm anyone. Whatever his reasoning, I am sure it was cleverly calculated after many prayerful hours."

While we were on the subject of "nuts," Dan fantasized what a benefit to mankind it would have been if that maniac who shot up all the people in the San Diego McDonald's a couple of years earlier had, instead, done his dirty work in the local IRS office. Why kill innocent people when there are so many guilty targets running around?

I chuckled a little unspoken agreement and then, getting serious again, he said, "But you know, Pat, we shouldn't joke about such things because that's the kind of brand that they want to put on all of us. Mark my words, they will attempt to tie Tupper into the Aryan Nation bunch."

"Who is that?"

"A white supremacy group that calls themselves 'Christian,' yet goes around kidnapping bankers and blowing away cops and anybody else who represents establishment."

"A real loving group, huh?"

"Yeah. Non-violent, they ain't. The government loves them though, because they are as valuable, propaganda-wise, as the KKK was to the Civil Rights struggle. They'll have trouble painting Tupper as a violent man, but I guarantee you they will try," Dan said. "After a few cleverly planted stories in the media, they'll have people believing any terrible thing they want them to. Of course, they are programming a jury for the future also; that is, if they let him live long enough to go back to trial."

"Where does this militant bunch hide out?"

"It's not a Dalton Gang scenario where they are all holed up somewhere. It's a mindset. Like Republicans and Democrats, they could be in dribs and drabs anywhere. I've talked to a few who have called into my radio show. In the 'R' rated vernacular of the modern generation, they are red-blooded Americans who are pissed off. But they just don't understand that regardless of how angry we get at government, violent retribution will not work.

" 'He was a member of the Aryan Nation White Supremacy group,' (mocked in a stuffed-shirt portrayal of a news commentator) is a perfect label to give the government goons license to waste anybody. Governments don't *fear* that kind of opposition, they *love* it. It helps them plant more fear in the masses. That's why the first thing a dictator takes over is the communication media. If nobody filed tax returns anymore or used their bogus money, they would lose all control, and their sham system would come tumbling down on top of them."

Before we parted, Dan told me where I could acquire more information by and about Tupper, and then he gave me a copy of *The Miracle on Main Street* and also *Tennessee Waltz*, a recently published hardcover book written by James Earl Ray, the supposed assassin of Martin Luther King, and edited by Tupper Saussy. I had no ax to grind and only wanted another drink to satisfy my salty thirst for this knowledge. Little did I realize that I was off on a roller-coaster ride of adventure, intrigue, education and excitement that few people would ever experience. The ride began when I got back to the motel room after the night's performance and cracked open a beautiful little revelation called *The Miracle on Main Street*.

I had gone straight home that Saturday after closing and by 2:30 a.m. was already thumbing that masterpiece on money. I call it a masterpiece for at least two reasons: First, because of the new education, and I do mean new, found between its covers on only 155 pages for anyone who takes the time to read, and secondly, the simplicity with which the information is provided. And while the education might be considered new, much of the information is 210 years old. Any ninth-grader (well, some ninth-graders today) can read and comprehend this book and certainly should.

Several times while reading, I sat up in bed and whispered (because nobody else was there to hear anyway), "Of course, that's true. Why has no one else ever said these things before? How come I never heard this in school?" I decided that night what a loss it would be if every parent couldn't read this book and have their high school age children read it and then discuss it together at the dinner table. I can't remember ever before lying in bed with a new book and being so captivated that I read until I couldn't keep my eyes open any longer and then leaning over seven hours later to pick it up and finish it before I ever got up. When I fell asleep I couldn't *wait* to wake up so I could read some more. And how come, I was soon wondering, Waldenbooks or B. Dalton or the other popular book stores around the country not only did not sell this book but had never even heard of it? They could sell millions!

I would later learn that I had just answered my own question. Zany, smack-freaked-out Brother Dave Gardner used to say in his night club act when I would see him singing and wise-cracking at Gus Steven's Supper Club on the beach in Biloxi: "Happiness, dear hearts, ain't gettin' what you want. It's wantin' what you get."

I wouldn't see Dan for several days as he was leaving town for a long weekend, but I was off work on Sunday and Monday so I had some time to get into *Tennessee Waltz*, and it had me just as captured as I had been on Saturday. I was now convinced of several new things that just a week before had not even concerned me: (a) Rev. Martin Luther King, Jr. was murdered by someone other than James Earl Ray; (b) Ray has been unlawfully locked in prison and in history as the symbol of that murderer; (c) Americans are unknowingly being locked into a financial prison by perpetrators in high places; and (d) the terms "money," "the deficit," "taxes," "inflation," "revenue," and several others relating to the same subject are all illusory.

Without lawful money, you cannot have the others. How can there be "revenue" in a system that works only with credit? Revenue is as imaginary as our money!

> *None are so hopelessly enslaved as those who falsely believe that they are free.*—Von Goethe

Thomas Jefferson explained way-back-when that people cannot be self governing and free unless public servants are dependent upon being paid with something the people produce. When the people become dependent upon paper their servants print, the roles of master and servant are reversed.

By the time Tuesday night arrived, I was starving for some more information, and I remembered the little, independent bookstore that Dan had mentioned where I could get fed some more.

When I arrived, I asked for everything Tupper Saussy had ever written or edited and was astounded, not only at the immense amount of material I was shown but also with the sheer adoration that was reflected for the man. I asked if they knew him; and they said "no," but they had been to hear him speak and had several of his tapes. When I inquired as to what was available in that department, I was able to pick up at considerable discount a six-tape pack of a meeting of several "hard-money" advocates in Sewanee, Tennessee in 1982. In one of his talks from that seminar, Tupper made several such inflammatory tirades as this one:

> We are here because we want to do something. We want to get something done and we want to do it peacefully and we want to do it within the law. We are tired of complaining, we are tired of sending off telegrams to people to try to change their philosophy towards ours. We have discovered what the solution to the problem is and we have discovered that the solution exists *in the law*. We don't need any Constitutional Amendments; we don't need any new legislation. All we need to do is leave the world of ideas that we have been swirling around in for so long and step into the real world.

> I get my greatest pleasure just being with my wife and family, playing and working with our children, writing an occasional song or piece of theater, making watercolor pictures, being with sympathetic friends, and traveling. I don't get any pleasure whatsoever obeying statutes that don't apply to me. I have discovered, since becoming familiar with the Constitution, that a great many statutes do *not* apply to me, and my obedience to them is entirely optional.

> People who know their rights and privileges under the Constitution of the United States are almost always able to prevent legal tangles by just showing a potential adversary the applicable section of the Supreme Law.

> Like many people in the past couple of decades, I taught myself how to play the guitar. In the same way I am teaching myself the United States Constitution. It's the most exciting course in self-improvement you can take! In the four years that I have been reading this document, I am continually discovering wonderful new authorities I can claim upon life. Probably the most rewarding thing of all, though, is the effect living by the Constitution has upon children!

> As for my own personal beliefs, I am not a gold bug. Though I have been spoken of in the same breath with Howard Ruff and other "gold bugs'" I am not that authoritative on Hazlitt or Von Mises or any of the other so-called conservative economists. I try to avoid economic debate; in fact, I warned against it in my book because I believe the 'debate trap' can get you in a lot of trouble. I have rather inconclusive concepts on money, and I am still learning; just like you are.

I do know that the United States Constitution says that "No state shall make any thing but gold and silver coin a tender in Payment of debts," and I know what led to the creation of that particular law, and I know that those circumstances were identical to the circumstances that we are living in today. And I know that when those words came into effect, beautiful things began to happen to those who were aware of the words and knew what they meant. And I think beautiful things are going to happen to those of us who are aware of those words and what they mean today.

Wow! This is highly treasonable stuff! Here is a man who studies his nation's governing document and advocates the teaching of one's children the same thing. This firebrand could be a very dangerous man! The Swiss philosopher Henri-Frederic Amiel said, "Truth is violated by falsehood, but it is outraged by silence."

So Tupper Saussy discovered a little known truth and trumpeted it to America through his books and from his speaker's platform. Could this really make him such an enemy of the State? I had to know more. It wouldn't take long.

At 9 o'clock on Friday night Dan was seated at the piano bar sipping an orange juice as I took my seat for the second set. I usually do 40-20. Forty minutes on and twenty off, but Durwood McLain, the lounge manager at the Ramada, always let me govern that by the mood and density of the crowd, especially during the early hours. It was early yet, so I did thirty minutes, finished with "A Wonderful Day Like Today," and took a break. Of course, I had an ulterior motive. Nothing else had occupied my mind all week. I wanted to fit more of this puzzle together, and Dan had a lot of the pieces.

After we exchanged pleasantries and found a secluded booth in the coffee shop, I responded to his first query with, "Did I pick up the books! You oughta' see all the crap I got! I've already read both the books, and I got tapes of the 'Seminar on the Mountain,' Tupper's historical stuff about Roger Sherman and George Bancroft, and even a few copies of *The Main Street Journal*. You didn't tell me that he edited a national publication too!"

"Well, there are a lot of things I haven't told you yet, but that came about in 1981 after all the hoopla over MOMS," he said. "He sold over a hundred thousand copies."

"Of the Journal?," I asked.

"No, MOMS."

"What the hell is MOMS?"

"That's what somebody called *The Miracle on Main Street* and the acronym caught on," he said. "We were all encouraging Tupper to start a monthly publication, and who was better to edit it when so many people were having so much success with their POMCs. Do you understand how the Public Office Money Certificate works?"

"Well, kinda'. I know that you give it to 'em in lieu of taxes, but I don't understand all the ramifications. Tell me," I urged.

"Okay, but it's not in *lieu* of anything. Tupper discovered what the law says and we were forcing local governments to obey it. The Public Office Money Certificate looks something like a bank check except that it has no routing numbers on it. It can be used with City, County or State Offices who are required by law to accept *only* something known as 'the money of account of the United States.' When it is filled in for the proper amount of taxes or fines that are due and signed, it becomes the signer's promise to pay in lawful money—the money of account of the United States—if that office will have the right person of authority, which is the Attorney General of the State, tell us exactly what is the *substance* of that money. Otherwise we would be conspiring with government to break the law if we paid our fines or taxes with Fed Notes or in any substance other than what they are required by law to accept." He went on to explain, as Tupper had in his book, that although the government sanctions legal tender, it does so in violation of both the United States Code and the Constitution.

"What about an ordinary check?" I said.

"Well, what about it?" he said, trying to be patient with me. "Isn't that denominated in the same nothing? You cannot *pay* for anything with a *promise* to pay. A debt can only be retired with lawful money. For instance, in a few minutes we will owe this establishment a buck or two for this coffee. Now since I'm broke, we'll let you settle the debt." He smiled. "You reach in your pocket and realize that you don't have any money, neither what you call it or what I call it. In any case, you are financially embarrassed, and, preferring not to wash dishes, you strike a deal with the cashier. You say to her, 'Listen Sugarpie, I am unable to pay for this coffee right now, but I want to give you an IOU' You sign a piece of paper *promising* to pay for the coffee at some later date and she agrees to take it. Have you paid for the coffee?"

"No."

"Of course not, you have only *promised* to pay for it. Now a week or more passes, and you forget to come back in and settle up, so the boss gets tired of looking in the register at the IOU for a dollar and a half, we'll say, and sticks it in his wallet to remind him to collect from you the next time he sees you. Meanwhile, in the barber shop the next day, he had enough money with him to pay for his haircut, but there was a small bottle of aftershave lotion that he wanted to try and it cost a buck and a half. So he says to the barber, 'Here, I'll give you Pat Shannan's note, you know him, he gets his hair cut here all the time, and he will straighten up with you the next time he is in,' and the barber agrees. Has the bottle of after shave been paid for?"

"No."

"Next," he continued, "the barber gives your note to the service station across the street for a tire patch, and they pass it on to the Dairy Dream for a milk shake, and then the Dollar Store gets it for a hairbrush. Has anything been paid for with the note? Of course not," he answered for me.

"Now you could argue that the hair brush was bought with the milk shake, which bought the tire patch, which bought the after shave, which previously paid for our coffee, but there is still *one* payment missing, and the hair brush will never be paid for until you make your note good with some substance, or he finds another sucker to take your note in trade for something of value. A perfect description of a Federal Reserve Note is that it is something that the first person gets for nothing and the last person will get nothing for.

"So the POMC is a very lawful promise to pay the tax or fine in a lawful manner," he proceeded. "We want to pay the tax with whatever substance that the Attorney General determines is the current money of account of the United States. The problem is that not one AG has had the guts to declare it.

The AG of Georgia, Michael Bowers, actually had the audacity to tell a large group of interested citizens congregated in his office that they would have to get a much larger group of people before he would be forced to make that declaration.   In other words, political advancement is much more important to the Attorneys General of the States than is obeying the law. If a servant comes by your farm to pick up ten pounds of produce, don't you think it is within reason to ask him exactly what produce—potatoes, corn, tomatoes, cotton, beans or what—he wants?

"Here's another thought about money creation," he went on:

"Were you to borrow ten thousand for a year, you might pay one thousand in interest. If it were only one thousand you borrowed, then it might be one hundred in interest. In either case, what you "borrow" is only imaginary; just a number added to your account which does not represent anything at all at risk by that bank. Do you think that for writing an extra '0,' the banker is entitled to an extra nine hundred in interest?"  I would have to digest that for awhile, but I thought I understood and shook my head.

"In the first 150 years of our nation, individuals could bring their gold to the government to be minted into coin which meant that the money was brought into existence through labor. A dollar was defined as a measurement of gold or silver. Now all money is created from thin air and *loaned* into existence. Compare this modern money to rain as my friend, Dr. Paul Hein of

St. Louis, does. The rain falls from only one source—the clouds. Once on earth, it ends up in many places: 'on deposit' in lakes and oceans; 'in circulation' in rivers and streams; and eventually it returns, via evaporation, to the sky. There is a balance between the amount leaving the earth via evaporation and the amount returning as rain. Were that not the case, we would end up either flooded or a desert.

Suppose now that the only source of rain, the clouds, were to regard the rain which fell upon the earth as a loan, to be repaid with interest. In other words, more water would have to evaporate than was provided by rainfall. How could earth return to an only source more than it was given? That is the question to ask regarding our money. How can the borrowers of the country return to the banks more than was borrowed? Principal, after all, was borrowed. But principal plus interest must be returned. How can this be done? It can't, except by borrowing the money that must be repaid and that's where your government comes up with another illusory term: 'deficit spending.' Gold and silver coin fall into the category that God ordained 'Just weights and measures' to ensure that God and our brothers would not be cheated."

Even I could understand that one, but, meanwhile, it was getting close to time for my ten o'clock set, and I hoped he could stick around so I could learn some more. Looking at my watch, I said, "Do you want to come back in for another set?"

He pondered that invitation for a moment and then replied, "I can stick around for a little while. I'm enjoying your music and nobody's bothering me about not being a drinker. I'd like to bring some friends out here for dinner before you leave, and we can talk some more. Did Theresa give you any information on Kahl or Kirk?"

I said, "She didn't *give* me anything, I paid for it all, but I don't remember reading about any Kirk or Kahl, who are they?"

"Arthur Kirk was murdered at his home in Nebraska in 1984 by County and State Police because he challenged a mortgage loan with his local bank. After he had been avoiding service on the bank's suit, the authorities deceived his wife into coming into town to the Sheriff's office and kept her there while they lured him into the front yard of his farmhouse and shot him down. The only witnesses were the one's who did the shooting, and the evidence showed that they ate candy bars and drank milk from his refrigerator while he bled to death in the front doorway. The ambulance was there the whole time, but the sheriff denied the medics access to the dying Kirk because he 'did not have the authority to let them inside the gate.' "

I had a few dozen questions about that, but before I embarked, I went ahead and asked, "And who is Kahl?"

"Gordon Kahl. A much decorated World War II fighter pilot who in the seventies began to challenge the right of the government to invade the privacy of one's home without a warrant, among other things. The government had long since labeled him a 'Tax Protestor,' that ever-poisoning label that convinces juries that the accused must be anti-American. Anyway, they attempted to bushwack him near his home in North Dakota late one night on his way in, but they slightly miscalculated.

Gordon's son, Yorie, was driving Gordon's car, and Gordon was in the passenger seat, just the opposite from what the agents anticipated. They even traded hats. At the roadblock, they were ordered out of the car, and a moment after Yorie stepped out in the dark, he was shot down. What would you have done in Gordon's spot? You've just seen your son shot down without provocation. In self-defense, Gordon began shooting back, and, when the smoke cleared, he had killed two agents and wounded a few more. Somehow he escaped, and four months later they hunted him down and shot him in the back of the head as he sat at the dinner table in a farmhouse in the Arkansas Ozarks."

"Dan," I said, completely convinced now that he had seen too many westerns as a child and was experiencing early regression, "This sounds like something out of Jesse James. The U.S. government doesn't hunt down Americans and murder them ... just shoot them from the blind side. This is 1987, c'mon. And how come I never heard of this guy or saw the story in the papers?"

"A cover story *was* in the papers for a day or two, but I tell you what," he said, not willing to belittle my naiveté, "there's an ex-cop right there in Phoenix who has conducted a four-year investigation into the Gordon Kahl murder. I'm not going to take up your short break with what I know about it when you obviously are so doubtful of my sanity anyway. Here's his phone number, if you want the facts, call him when you get home next week," and he scribbled down a name and number out of his address book.

"Look, Dan," I said, "I'm sorry, but this whole thing is coming too fast. I want to know the truth as much as anybody, but you are blowing me away with too much, too soon. But I'll tell you what, I'm gonna' call this cop, and I'm gonna' pick his brain because this danged thing is keeping me awake at night, and a week ago I didn't give a hoot in hell whether a dollar was made of copper or kryptonite. Now you're telling me about all these cloak-and-dagger rubouts and you think that they even wanna' kill Tupper. Just slow down, will you? I can't keep up with all this. And right now I've gotta' go to work. Are you coming in?"

"Yeah," he said, "I'll be along."

A few minutes later from my piano bench, I saw him standing in the doorway, but he must have seen something or someone that he didn't like because I never saw him in the club again that night. The next day I talked to him on the phone and remembered to ask what had happened to him after he said he was coming in. He replied,"I was there for the next forty minutes. I just decided to come through the kitchen and sit in the back and observe." When I challenged that claim, he named several of the songs that I had done during that set and even described an obnoxious old, fat broad who had been making a lot of noise and who had not been there earlier, so he was not kidding.

He was beginning to remind me of a line out of Woody Guthrie's "Pastures of Plenty:" " ... I come with the dust and I go with the wind." I wondered why Dan was so surreptitiously looking over his shoulder.

When I got home that night, I found a crumbled piece of paper in my pants pocket on which he had written the words "Jack McLamb" and a telephone number. I stuck it in the card section of my wallet so I would know where to find it after I returned to Phoenix. It was a good thing I had this new link in the chain. Dan never made it back in before my stint was up at the Ramada.

A week or so after I returned home to Phoenix, I was still being haunted by all this, and I gave a phone call to Jack McLamb. I caught him just as he was leaving to do some errands, and we agreed to meet at his favorite coffee shop on Buckeye Avenue later in the afternoon. I found Jack to be such a warm and friendly person and so eager to discuss the "murders of Gordon Kahl and a fellow lawman from Arkansas, Sheriff Gene Matthews," as he called it, that he didn't even ask me who had sent me until later when we were together and he didn't have to worry about phone taps. When I mentioned Dan Hoffman's name, he smiled and warmed even more.

"Great guy, that Dan. He knows all about this case. He even wrote a book about it. Did he tell you?"

"No, he didn't," I said. "But come to think of it, we were very rushed for time when we were together so he probably just didn't get around to it."

"No, wait a minute, that wasn't Dan, I'm wrong. That was another fellow from Nashville who writes under the name of Capstan Turner. I was still a little skeptical about all this, but I was probably becoming more receptive than I had been in the recent past because everything that Dan had told me about money, taxes, the King murder cover-up, and everything else seemed to ring true. However, I still found it hard to swallow that our government, domestically, hunts down undesirables and eliminates them clandestinely or otherwise.

"It's absolutely true!" said Jack, when I asked him point blank. "It's very possible that the U.S. Marshals and Gordon Kahl were used as pawns in the game in a set-up by federal agencies to discredit activists in the tax resistance movement across the United States. At the time of the murder, there was a tremendous tax prosecution case going on in the State of Texas against a disbarred attorney by the name of Jerome Daly and ten Braniff Airline pilots. The government had spent almost three million bucks trying to convict them, and the trial was getting into the final stages. It was a question of national sensitivity.

All of a sudden, federal officers decided to serve an eighteen month old warrant on Gordon Kahl ... on a Sunday night, at a roadblock, and at gunpoint. It was a tragedy, and I think they were both used to foster discontent against the twenty-five million or more tax resistors in this country."

"Did they have their own marshals shot?" I asked incredulously.

"No, not intentionally, but when you get right down to the bottom line, the agents are as expendable as the citizen, or almost. There were actually two murder scenes:  One in North Dakota in February, and the other in Arkansas. The first one backfired on them, and they lost two agents. Gordon knew he had to go underground after that because they would have taken him out in jail if he had turned himself in."

"Do you really believe that?" I said.

"There certainly was a strong possibility, and it had all the earmarks," he said. "They, obviously, had already tried. The papers would have said the next day that they 'found' him hanging by his belt during the night, and that he had 'suicidal tendencies,' and the night jailer was being punished for not taking the belt away from him, blah, blah, blah, and in a month everybody would have forgotten all about it. Everybody except his family, that is."

Jack McLamb is a retired cop in his mid-forties and, except for the full head of prematurely grey hair, he looks younger. At five foot ten and 200 stocky pounds, he still looks like the football hero that he was in high school, good looking enough to play the part of a private eye in the movies. He had been retired medically from the Phoenix Police force just that month because his superior officers had demoted him back to a foot patrol in the roughest section of south Phoenix, and, subsequently, he had crippled his arm in an arrest of an illegal alien dope smuggler.

Jack had received numerous awards for his work, especially for the time he gave to work with kids, and in 1980, for the second time in only four years on the force, was Phoenix's "Officer of the Year," the most prestigious recognition given to any of their men in blue. The kids had their own name for him: "Officer Friendly." In 1983 he began to publish *Aid & Abet*, a "newsletter for cops," as he referred to it.

He showed me some of the back issues, and I saw it was another newsletter designed to spread truths, this one being guided more towards fellow policemen, explaining to them how the federal government was interfering with local law enforcement to violate the rights of the citizenry and why much of the instruction that the policemen were getting from their higher-ups was Constitutionally wrong. It particularly stressed the necessity of the policemen to protect the rights of the citizens at all costs. To deny the rights of the people now was to destroy the rights of the children of the next generation. He was pointing out to his brother officers that sometimes the law places the whole apparatus of prisons, judges, lawyers, and all gendarmes at the service of the plunderers and treats the victim—when he defends himself—as a criminal.

I could find nothing in *Aid & Abet* to lead me to believe that Officer McLamb was anything but a flag-waving, America-loving patriot who was concerned about the turn that our country was taking and was warning brother officers with the most effective method possible, a newsletter for which they paid ten bucks a year to receive, which was only slightly more than the cost of publication and postage when everything was tallied.

Nevertheless, this was the issue that got McLamb busted from his squad car down to the foot patrol in south Phoenix. He was called in on the carpet and *ordered* to stop distribution of the periodical. When he refused, ("when you tell Officer Joe not to go home and drink a six-pack of beer after work, and when you tell Officer George he can't take his wife to the movies and when you kick Officer Pete out of league softball, *then* you can tell me what to do after hours when I leave here. Meanwhile, butt out!") he got the axe.

When he was fired, he sued the city to get his job back and succeeded, with all back pay several months later. But once back under their thumb as an employee, he had no choice but to do what he was told while on the job, and it was pretty obvious that he was intentionally placed in a dangerous situation by his superiors . . . with them hoping for the worst.

It wasn't the first time. Jack had run for Sheriff of Maricopa County in 1984 and finished second in the Republican Primary, garnering 20% of the vote. Had he won that office, it would have meant that he would have been the "boss" of the current police chief. When he returned to the job following the election, his Chief, Rubin Ortega, removed Officer McLamb from the important job of being the *only* Intelligence Officer of the City's Gang Squad and placed him in the hell hole of the highest crime area of Phoenix, apparently as punishment for attempting to become sheriff.

Jack McLamb was one of the nicest cops I have ever met. He, indeed, is "Officer Friendly." And smart. Not the obstinate, blue collar type who can't even carry on a conversation without peppering it with profanity, but clean-cut and sharp. When he told me of his love for the Lord, I didn't fear his Jesus at all like I did when I heard Swaggart screaming or Bakker crying. As I would later sense in Tupper, he was at peace, vigilant but not fearful.

Jack said that he had the evidence that not only was Gordon Kahl murdered by Federal Agents on June 3rd, 1983 in that little farmhouse near Smithville in northeastern Arkansas, but the Sheriff of that county, Gene Matthews, was shot twice in the back, with one blast from a shotgun and another from a 9 mm pistol and once from the front, by a .223 high- powered rifle. Two witnesses stated that there was a *third* frontal wound from a .38 caliber revolver but a second autopsy must be performed to ascertain that fact. All after Kahl was already dead. Who could have been responsible for that other than the Federal Agents who were on the scene?

As he spoke, I glanced at one of his copies of the news story which headlined the same subject with: "IRS Goon Squads" which went back to the first confrontation in North Dakota, and I scanned the opening paragraph. As Jack talked, I continued listening with one ear and reading with one eye.

> Gordon W. Kahl, a 63-year-old farmer, was driving his family home from a church meeting in Medina, North Dakota, on the evening of February 13, 1983, when he ran into a roadblock. Shots rang out and Kahl saw his son gunned down. He pulled a Mini-14 semi-automatic rifle from his gun rack and a gun battle took place with local and federal officials—a battle that, Tax Patriots say, was fought because the government wanted to silence Kahl's outspoken criticism of the income tax system. When the smoke cleared, Kahl, a decorated WW II veteran, had killed two officers and wounded three others.

"Okay," I said, "this happened in February. How did he happen to end up in Arkansas?"

"No one knows, for sure, what he did for the next several weeks following his flight from North Dakota, not even his wife. He couldn't call her, of course, because they would have nailed him down in no time. We do know that he had been in Arkansas for a large portion of the nearly four months he was hidden, and we know that some of that time was spent in Fort Smith. He was eventually tracked down when an unsympathetic daughter of one of the patriots in Mountain Home called the Feds and told them where to find him."

"So she, unwittingly, I presume, actually set him up for murder," I said.

"Yep. Not only was she a turncoat, but she was a pretty stupid one. She could have gotten fifty, maybe a hundred grand out of them for that information. Instead, because she had a fight with her dad one day and to spite him, she gave them a call in Little Rock, and then it was just a matter of a few recon missions by helicopter before the rest was history."

I read another paragraph:

> Thus began the largest manhunt in Arkansas's history. Kahl went into hiding as 100 heavily armed state and federal agents combed the countryside. On June 3rd, 1983, more than 40 federal agents armed with automatic weapons surrounded Leonard Ginter's farmhouse, here Kahl was purportedly staying. Gordon Kahl was shot at point-blank range in the back of the head. The sheriff who went in with two other officers to get him was shot by one of his own men. The house was then torched and Gordon's body left inside to burn. One deputy later admitted following orders to pour gasoline down the chimney to start the fire. *(Ed. Note: whose orders? His boss was already dead.)* The coroner reported that one of Gordon's hands and both his feet were missing from the body. A few weeks later a New York Times reporter found one of the feet under a refrigerator in the ruins; it had been chopped off.

Jack said, "That part doesn't mention that the forty or more federal agents on the hillside then proceeded to lambaste the building with literally thousands of rounds of high-powered ammunition. I talked to one of the neighbors who was too frightened to come out of his house that evening but said that the barrage went on until well after midnight, before and after the burning.

"But there were many more travesties of justice in that case," he went on, "not the least of which was the conviction of Yorie Kahl, Gordon's 22-year-old son who was driving the car back on February 13th in North Dakota. It was never proven that he ever fired a shot. He was wounded twice as the first target of the agents and yet is currently serving a life sentence in a Federal Pen for murder.

"And poor old Leonard Ginter and his wife, in their seventies, were picked up a few minutes before the melee in June and were handcuffed to sheriff's deputies outside of the house at the time Gordon and the sheriff were shot inside, yet they were charged and tried for murder. That's the kind of enemy we are up against in this country. The legal system is not interested in fairness or justice anymore, just convictions, even if the convicted is knowingly their scapegoat and especially if the person is thought to be challenging some government activity."

Jack told me more of the details of the Arthur Kirk murder in Nebraska, how Kirk had been lured into his yard and blown away by a S.W.A.T. team. His crime? He had challenged the bank's right to lend him its own credit and then demand to be paid back with the fruits of his labor.

Byron Dale is another rancher in South Dakota who happened to discover the law (SDCL 57-A-2-304) that allows for one to pay off his mortgage in goods rather than ferns. When he made the offer to Production Credit

Association in 1983, they refused it and secretly began foreclosure proceedings on his property.

Later, Dale was visited by an army of armed men led by "peace" officers Jerry Baum, Director of the South Dakota Highway Patrol, and Trooper Pat Murphy, a Karate instructor with a black belt in judo. Trooper Murphy later testified in court with the following:

"After arriving at Timber Lake, we reported to the P.C.A. building. Once in the office, I was asked to come into a room with Captain Hammond and Major Zwenke. Zwenke asked me if it would be possible for me to take Byron Dale out. I asked what he meant by 'out,' and he replied, 'With your background in martial arts, you could take out Byron Dale.' "

Trooper Murphy further testified that he had sat in the ranch house with Jerry Baum talking with Dale for about twenty minutes, considering which way to take Byron Dale out. One option he considered was taking Dale's mini-14 rifle, which was nearby, jumping up and striking Dale with it.

A second option was to jump up and, with a roundhouse kick, catch Byron along the side of the head, but he rejected that one "because Byron was always gesturing with his hands as he spoke." Finally when Officer Baum distracted Dale's attention, Murphy picked up a 32 oz. full bottle of catsup and blasted Dale across the forehead, knocking him from his chair, but not unconscious. A scuffle took place before Dale was beaten into submission.

Byron Dale was arrested, tried, convicted and sentenced to the maximum 13 months in jail and a $750 fine for "Obstructing Law Enforcement" and "Resistance to Service of Process." The fact that both Baum and Murphy admitted under oath at the trial that the attack on Dale was unprovoked meant little to the jury after they heard the judge's final instructions to them.[1]

If my mind was bent out of shape before, it was Swiss Cheese now. I needed to sit back in a rocking chair for a few hours and just think, and I told him so. Before we parted he gave me some more printed information about this and other government atrocities and promised to stop in the club some time soon. "I seldom go over to Tempe, and I don't drink. But if I can get a coke, I'd like to come catch your act sometime," he said.

"They'll put you in jail for foolin' with that coke," I punned, "but, sure, you can get coffee or plain orange juice and, as long as you applaud long and loud, you will be very welcome." He smiled as we shook hands, and I thought as I walked to the car that if I don't start filling up those bar seats with some real drinkers, I'm going to be out of a job!

---

[1] *Bashed By The Bankers,* P.O. Box 628, Mandan, N.D., 58554

I went back to the apartment, fixed a pot of coffee, and did exactly what I told him earlier that I felt like doing, except that I don't have a rocker so I flopped down in my favorite recliner under the big lamp and started reading some startling stories that were seldom, or never, seen or heard in the big media. I thought of a man I read about many years ago in school. His name was Philip Nolan, who in this 19th century novel, found himself in court after being wronged by the government. "Damn the United States!" he said. "May I never hear the words 'United States' again!"

"Very well, young man," said the judge, "You shall have your wish. That shall be your sentence." And Philip Nolan was placed on board ship outside of the twelve-mile limit to spend the rest of his life as *A Man Without A Country*. I thought, too, of an old Chinese proverb that says: "It takes little effort to watch a man carry a load."

> *Paper money has had the effect in your state that it will ever have, to ruin commerce, oppress the honest, and open the door to every species of fraud and injustice.*
>
> —President George Washington

# CHAPTER TWO

## AWAKENING

*You have not converted a man because you have silenced him.*

—John Viscount Morley

P hoenix, Arizona is a wonderful place for nine months a year. While most places are miserable from December until March, the Arizona desert is unbearable during the opposite season, mid-June to mid-September. And here I was, of all places, at all times, spending the summer in Phoenix, Arizona. This had become my home in recent years and I had grown to love it.

Another of the fringe benefits of my nomadic work as guitar and piano player (not at the same time) and singer, in addition to meeting all kinds of interesting people, is the constantly changing scenery and climate all over the world. Yet I actually become nostalgic for this place whenever I am away too long ... even in the blistering summer when the thermometer can top 120 degrees.

Paul Hornung once told me he has gone through life on scholarship. So have I, often being paid for what I would have done for nothing as a nightclub entertainer, and I'll bet my next Grammy against his Heisman trophy that his vertebrae and knee joints ache a whole lot more than my fingers and vocal cords.

It was so danged ironic. There I was in Tempe at the Casa Lama Hotel— my favorite club on the circuit—pounding out *That's What Friends Are For* when I looked up and saw him sitting there at the piano bar nursing a white wine. He looked so different, so old, that at first, as he sat there betraying no more emotion than last years bird nest, I thought it was only someone who looked like what might have been his older brother, a reincarnation of the Henry Fonda character from *On Golden Pond*. But as I sang the final lyrics, tickled the last notes, and studied that familiar, briar-eatin' grin, I knew it was my old roommate, Tupper, even before he said, "Hello, Sport!"

We went back to 1964 together, in Greenwich Village, after my trio had split up, and I was struggling with a guitar as a single act for the first time at *The Third Side.* He was supplementing his subsistence playing the piano between acts at the *Village Vanguard* and was spending a couple of weeks hanging around the old Tin Pan Alley attempting to peddle some new songs he had written.

He was a *bona fide* musician while I was little more than your typical folk singer of the 60's—without the hippie getup—still learning all the chords of the guitar. It wasn't as easy as working in a trio where you have two others to help cover up your instrumental mistakes, but I was getting better and ever eager to learn more. When I would strike a cacophony, he would wince in overstated displeasure as though I had driven a spike into his ear. Then he would patiently use the piano to show me how it should sound when it was played correctly. No one better could have come along at that time in my young career. I was a good student who grasped lessons quickly, and he was one fine teacher; four years my senior and forty years my superior.

We had mutual friends who had thrown us together as roommates out of our financial necessity, and it was a timely bonanza for me. I had a bigger place than I needed with an extra bedroom, and he needed an inexpensive place for two weeks. I was lucky enough to be renting the downstairs of a widow's large home which contained a grand piano, of all things. She loved our music—especially Tupper's long-hair stuff—and was happy for us to play it anytime except late at night, which suited our schedule just fine because we were seldom there at night anyway, except when it was time to crash.

I would marvel at the élan of his nimble fingers to caress a Bach or attack a Jerry Lee Lewis. He was only the second person I had ever met with absolutely perfect pitch. This is one who can hear a note and tell you what it is; hear a song and know all the chord changes. These gifted people are in perfect concert with the keyboard, and it is an auricular pleasure to watch one work out; to dictate to the instrument what "we" are going to do next.

He had taught me a lot during our short tenure together, and, although I had thought of him often over the years, I had only seen him once since that summer of `64, maybe ten years later. Still later I had called to congratulate him on what was his third Grammy nomination, but except for an occasional telephone conversation like the one from Florida five years earlier when I had bought his book, we really had been out of touch for most of twenty plus years.

Now here I was sitting in *his* chair doing *his* thing and he was sitting at the other end of the piano applauding me. What a switch!

"You son of a gun," I barked as I stood up to go towards him. He came off his stool and met me half way up the piano, shook my hand, and as we embraced he whispered in my ear, "Don't call me by name. Just call me 'Jim,' and I'll explain later."

Of course, I knew what that was all about and played it cool. The past April when the "escape" stories hit and I was in Nashville, I had tried to call his wife in Sewanee without success but finally caught up with her at her parents' home in Puerto Rico. She was petrified to talk on the phone and could only tell me that she did not know anything of her husband's whereabouts. She was certain she was being followed and was very close-mouthed about the whole situation, out of fear of eavesdroppers. As Dan had predicted, the media had made the subsequent stories very anti-Saussy, but I knew there was something fishy about this whole thing and relished the thought of hearing it from the horse's mouth.

We chatted briefly, and, after I sang a couple more tunes, he came back to the bench and asked if we could get together later for a chat. Currently he was with some people for dinner in the other room and he had just strolled out to say hello after he had seen my name on the hotel's lobby marquee. I suspected that that wasn't the whole story. This was a little too coincidental, and I surmised that he must have talked to Dan to learn where I was. I suggested that since we both were tied up for now, we should meet the next day for lunch.

He said, "Where?"

"What about right here?," I said, "I'm always up at the crack of noon and can meet you at one o'clock after the rush, and we can put it on my tab."

"That decides it then!  See you at one," he said and disappeared into the crowd as I replied, "Okay, *Jim!*"

I wanted to tell everybody at the piano bar that that was the fellow who wrote and arranged the music for Anita Bryant's orange juice commercials that they had all seen on network television for years, but thought better of it and went back to work on the current business of keeping people around long enough for one more drink.

Juan Lombardo, the owner of the Casa Loma and my good friend, would appreciate it. I appreciated him, too. This had become my "home club" in the last decade, and I spent more than a third of my time here, year-round. His wife and family treated me like family. One winter, I even played on the church softball team with his two teenage sons. Juan had told me once that I was "Vice President in charge of entertainment" and that I should run it as if it were my own club. That meant longer breaks sometimes and shorter ones when necessary, but he and I had never had a problem. I liked the arrangement and cherished his friendship. There are not very many people in the world that I can call in the middle of the night and ask for a thousand dollars and get it with no questions asked, but Juan is one of them.

As I pedalled along, an old protest song came to mind which Phil Ochs had given me in 1963. I closed the set with ...

Show me the prison, show me the jail.

Show me the prisoner whose life has gone stale.

And I'll show you, young man, with so many reasons why,

There but for fortune, go you and I.

* * *

He was already seated in the restaurant wing when I arrived back at the Casa Loma promptly at 12:59 p.m.

"We strive to be punctual," I announced as I approached the table and brought him out of his concentration from back of his newspaper.

"Yeah, I just got here myself five minutes ago and grabbed the first booth that opened up."

"By the way, Jim," I asked, extending my hand, "What is your last name?"

"Gordon," he said. "James Gordon."

"Okay, Jim Gordon," I said, "it's nice to meet you."

We yakked discursively over coffee for thirty minutes about old times and friends before we got around to ordering. I had to tell him about all the joints I had been working in over the last two and a half decades, and when he showed particular interest in my two years spent in Australia and my recent trips back, I knew where the conversation was leading and said, "Okay, enough about me, what about you? Did *you* see that picture of *me* in the paper last week? Just kidding. What about you? I presume you are still on the lam."

"Well, yeah," he said, "but that's no real problem because the Lord Jesus Christ stands between me and those who would harm me." Although I tried to mask my reaction, I couldn't have been more stunned if he had lit up a cigarette, which he always abhorred. Was this the same guy I used to know? I bit my tongue for the time being.

He proceeded to tell me the whole story: His years in Nashville advertising prior to his in-depth study of the money issue; the uncovering of the conspiracy between powerful men in the US government and the international bankers who founded the Federal Reserve system in 1913; his writing of his first book, *The Miracle on Main Street*, in 1980 of which I was aware, and the harassment by government agents that followed, of which I was not; the assault and battery of his wife and children by the FBI behind the scenes at the Federal Court in Tennessee.

He told me of his later collaboration in the authorized autobiography of James Earl Ray, the accused assassin of Martin Luther King, who now appears to have been railroaded by the FBI, and his publishing of Ray's book,

*Tennessee Waltz*, in 1987. (Ray had called from prison in 1986 and told him, "You are the only one I can trust to print it as I told it."). He continued, telling me of his acquittal for two years but conviction for one year (all by the same jury, strangely) of Willful Failure to File, his one year sentence and finally his "willful failure" to serve the time out of fear of being murdered which led to his disappearance two months ago on April 10th, 1987.

This whole scenario was boggling my mind; straining my credulity. It was like talking to Philip Agee about his CIA revelations of the 60's. This sort of thing doesn't happen in America. The U.S. government men are the good guys. The cops are there to "Protect and Serve" us. We are supposed to be the freeest people on earth with the Constitutionally protected right to petition for "redress of grievances." This was a story that one would expect to come out of Russia or Red China, not America.

"C'mon Jim," I said, proud of myself for maintaining the name discretion on the first try although I would slip later, "Aren't you coloring this whole story with just a little bit of bias? You don't quite sound like the flag-waving American I used to know."

I remembered the pride in his country he would espouse when discussing his trips to European countries in the fifties and sixties. "Hey man, you don't understand yet. You will after you spend some time reading the historical truth that is no longer taught in the public schools. But understand this now: I love my country now more than when you knew me. It's the Mafioso tactics of a criminal government that I fear! They have destroyed my family, stolen my property, and driven me into seclusion out of fear for my life. Patriotism is not loving your government. A patriot is one who loves his country and *watches* his government. We don't have many of them today."

I still had my doubts about the severity of his problem—that he might be running around with a target on his back—but there was no doubt that he surely had a problem. There must be federal arrest warrants on file in every state computer in the nation by now, and, if everything he said was true, then he was damned if he did and damned if he didn't. I wondered how he intended to rectify this situation.

If he turned himself in, which, I could tell, was out of the question at this point, he would probably face an extra five years for "escape." If he continued as he was, well, then what prevented this from being a life sentence? I found myself wondering if my friend had blown a gasket. They say that people can exhibit completely rational behavior and still be nutty as a fruitcake. But what contradicted this theory was the didactic manner in which he presented his case. It reminded me of how he had taught me the finer points of music nearly a quarter century before. Most of us who have ever screamed out, metaphorically speaking, "I gotta' be me," have been ostracized to some degree in one way or another. No man is a prophet in his own home town.

It is a curious fact that within every human being—whether prince or pauper, philosopher or truck driver—there lies a mysterious ingredient which he neither understands nor controls. It may lie dormant for so long as to be almost forgotten; it may be so repressed that the man never realizes it is alive.

But one night while he is alone in the desert under a full moon and starry sky; or one day as he stands with bowed head and dampened eyes staring into an open grave and tossing a rose onto a cold metal casket; or there comes an hour when he clings with desperate instinct to the rain-sprinkled rail of a storm-tossed boat, and suddenly out of the forgotten depths of his being, this mysterious something leaps forth. It overreaches habit; it pushes aside reason, and with a voice that will not be denied, it cries out its queries for truth and its prayer for guidance. For some, it is a career-change or marriage decision. For Tupper, it was in deciding to defy, and perhaps even single-handedly slay, the oppressive dragon.

A little knowledge is a dangerous thing, but it sure beats a blank stare for starting a conversation. What was his motivation, I wanted to know? Why had he not served his time? He would have been placed in one of those luxury white collar "Holiday Inns" with all of the amenities of home for only ten months or so.

"Because after learning what they had done to Mr. Ray, I began to fear for my life," he said. "No government likes a writer who tells the unfettered truth. *Miracle on Main Street* told the truth about how people's money problems could be solved and called for the individual's repudiation of Federal Reserve money. Within three months, people were in court, challenging the government and arguing the money issue. In April, I was invited to speak to a large group of tax protestants in Pontiac, Michigan. I returned home on a Sunday evening, and, at eight o'clock the next morning, two IRS agents from the Criminal Investigation Division were at my front door with guns wanting to talk about my income taxes. If they would do this after a simple little essay on money, what would they do after *Tennessee Waltz*, which demonstrates that the government killed King and framed Ray?"

"You tell me."

"All right. Before I got involved with working with James, my only experience with prisoners having no rights had been in the Hamilton County Jail in Chattanooga and the Atlanta Federal Prison Camp. In the camp, I learned that there was a little cemetery behind the penitentiary and from time to time you could see, usually around midnight, small processions—burial processions—consisting of several guards with flashlights following a slow moving truck to a freshly dug grave. 'Convicts die in this place,' one inmate told me, 'who nobody remembers what they were in here for.'

"But with James, I learned how the Alke-Bulans, an obscure terrorist group with orders coming from high outside, can force compliance from prison officials in standing aside while a troublesome individual is dispatched with butcher knives. The willingness of the officials to help set up the circumstances making James's assassination possible just chilled me to the bone.

"All James wanted to do was facilitate the Truth. That's all I wanted. I had the truth on two very important issues: the non-resident alien issue, and that political assassinations were engineered by political developers which included Time-Life, Inc., and high government agencies, federal and state. The Justice Department, which not only prosecuted me but also operated the environment I was destined to occupy for the year starting last April 10th, was being run by people very close to the murder of Martin Luther King. Which would be more expedient for them? To let me continue teaching that U.S. citizens whose sole income is derived from sources within the United States are not required to participate in the income tax unless they want to, and that Time-Life conspires with the Executive Department of the United States of America to kill national leaders in the name of political development ... or simply to kill me, either through an AIDS injection or some trumped-up 'fight' I might have initiated with another inmate?

"What *really* got me to thinking very dynamically about this was Jim Garrison's reaction to my *Politics of Witchcraft*, the epilogue I wrote for *Tennessee Waltz*. In a letter, Garrison warned me that the federal government tries to destroy 'courageous individuals' who dare to tell the truth, and who should know better than he? He even suggested that reprisals could be expected: 'I'm not telling you how to run your business,' he wrote me, 'but if I were you, I'd get Ray's book distributed as early and as widely as possible.' I slept on that warning for a few days, and then decided it was probably not a good idea to entrust my life to those people. I have no doubt that the decision was prompted by the Holy Spirit."

Harold Weisberg wrote an epic book in 1971 named *Frame-Up*, the product of a relentless investigation covering more than twenty-four months. Weisberg not only addresses himself to the circumstances surrounding Martin Luther King's death but to the unsavory underside of a judicial process that, in this case, worked in such a way that it brought about a result tantamount to frame-up.

With devastating impact Weisberg showed that all the active participants in the legal process—the bench, the defense attorneys, the prosecution, the justice department, the FBI—failed to uphold the standards of impartial justice and, in fact, in specific instances that he documents, acted with clear disregard for the truth and the discovery of the facts behind the King assassination.

The hapless James Earl Ray realized all this too late and was snookered out of his day in court. Fifteen lonesome years—during which he narrowly survived a vicious knife attack—would pass behind bars before he would be able to tell his story. He wanted to be certain that it would be repeated in print exactly as he told it. Tupper Saussy became his trusted friend.

* * *

Before I realized it, four o'clock had passed, and I had some errands to run before the stores closed. A night owl schedule requires one to plan a little more precisely than most to adhere to society's norm. The 24-hour supermarkets are nice but the banks and dry cleaners haven't stretched to my nocturnal habits yet.

Since I had no way of reaching him, he promised to call or come by the club in a few nights. My brain would be spinning with a thousand new questions by then, and as many new ones were provoked as old ones answered as I read old news clippings of what happened in the Winchester, Tennessee Federal Courthouse on January 24, 1985.

Federal judges are not referees today but rather part of the prosecution when a private citizen goes up against the wrath of the government, I was beginning to learn. Tupper, following various motions and pretrial proceedings prior to this "trial," was denied probable cause evidence, counsel of his choice (then later, any attorney at all), his star witness, his documentary defense—all without any accuser. What was his crime? Who had been harmed?

When he appeared in court, Saussy pointed out all of the above to Federal Judge Tom Hull, denied any jurisdiction had been established, and attempted to leave. Before he could take ten steps, Judge Hull ordered the federal marshals to arrest him.

Mrs. Saussy, sitting nearby, arose and took her husband's arm, and their two small boys grabbed their father's legs as the four of them were dragged from the courtroom. During the melee, Frederique Saussy received an abdominal blow which was serious enough to cause internal bleeding, and required hospitalization later in the day. The one hundred or more witnesses, who had come from as far away as Texas and Colorado for the trial, were horrified at what they had seen in an American courtroom.

During the following two hours, Mr. and Mrs. Saussy and the boys were held incommunicado—Tupper in a cell, the others in a backroom of the courthouse. Initially, Judge Hull told the courtroom that there would be a "thirty minute recess" while the prosecutors could research the law and determine whether or not any jurisdiction had been established.

Approximately one hour later, a federal marshall, who refused to give his name or show any identification, informed the angry but non-violent crowd of citizens that there would be no more trial today, but that the court would reconvene the next day. Meanwhile, Mr. Saussy would be incarcerated in Chattanooga. The summation of the proceedings was simply: "We do not know if we have the jurisdiction to put you in jail or not, but until we find out, we are going to put you in jail."

In American jurisprudence, an accused has the right to be confronted by his accuser. The accuser makes himself known by affidavit, swearing under oath or affirmation before an impartial judge or an investigative grand jury body, to certain circumstances which would cause an impartial judge or a grand jury to believe that a crime had possibly (or probably) been committed by a certain individual.

This is the only lawful process that can be used to bring a criminal defendant under the jurisdiction of the court (Amendment IV, U.S. Constitution) *unless* the accused waives this process by voluntarily submitting himself to the jurisdiction of the court. Even further, there are imbedded in this process certain guidelines and criteria which must be met to make the process lawful; i.e., the information (or indictment) may not be proceeded upon by implication but must contain the specific charges based known facts related by the accuser.

The government had charged Tupper Saussy with Willful Failure to File an Income Tax Return. In order to lawfully invoke the jurisdiction of the court to adjudicate this allegation, it was (is) necessary to have an accuser come forward and swear before a competent judicial officer (or Grand Jury) that the person so accused did, in fact, fail to file an income tax return.

This never occurred in Tupper's case, either in presentment of the original information or the superseding indictment. *There was no accuser*. And how could there be? What person is going to come forward and swear, under oath, that Tupper did not, in fact file an income tax return? There is a great difference between saying, "I saw him do something wrong," and "I saw him not file ... " Could it be possible that he *did* file his "required" returns and someone in the processing office threw them away? Current news stories pertaining to the IRS show that it wouldn't be the first time some bonehead pushed the wrong button.

Tupper was jailed by Judge Hull for exercising his right to depart the presence of the Court when that Court, in actuality, had no lawful jurisdiction over his person. He was sentenced, in absentia, to 90 days in jail for this "contempt." His sentence was later commuted to time served and he was released. This process occurred under charges brought by an *information*.

At the hearing to commute the contempt sentence, Judge Hull ordered Tupper to appear in Chattanooga on April 1st. In the meantime, the government took their case before the grand jury and obtained a rubber stamp indictment on March 22, 1985. The information and the indictment both contained the same charges.

The indictment automatically, by operation of law, supersedes all preceding processes in the matter prosecuted. That is the reason the new arraignment was necessary, but the two cannot stand together. The superior process of the indictment supersedes the inferior informational process. Tupper was ordered, under the inferior process, to appear in Chattanooga on April 1st. This order became void by the subsequent grand jury process.

*Chattanooga Times* reporter Dick Kopper wrote, "Assistant U.S. Attorney John Littleton said last week the indictment was obtained only 'out of an abundance of caution and solicitude for Mr. Saussy.' "

Cabdriver Amos Bruce of St. Louis, who knows more law than most lawyers, said that the backroom gossip among the prosecutors probably went more like this: "Hey fellows, this guy's got something with this probable cause crap. Maybe if we took it before the grand jury, since we could get a ham sandwich indicted before them, he might forget this probable cause stuff. Maybe he won't be aware of the fact that no accuser was presented to the grand jury because we can keep those proceedings secret. Maybe, in this manner, we can get him to 'voluntarily' submit himself to the jurisdiction of the court."

The ramifications of these proceedings were awesome. Under the common law, judges have absolute immunity for acts committed by them while acting within the scope of their lawful jurisdiction; but let the judge step outside his lawful jurisdiction and he sheds the mantle of immunity (Pulliam v. Allen 104 S. Ct. 1970).

If Saussy had been successful in his allegations, that is, that the court had no jurisdiction over his person, and the court was obliged to dismiss the charges against him, the Judge and the U.S. Magistrate both would have become subject to criminal prosecution for his unlawful incarceration.

Personally knowing him as I do, I doubt that he would have considered such action; he's not vindictive. It was apparent from his stance that he was merely trying to obtain a fair trial from the courts, a foregone impossibility when those charges are income tax related. The government has too much to lose in affording a defendant a fair trial in a so-called "tax protest" case.

Instead, all of the above was ignored and he went to trial; and on May 30th of that year, the jury returned with a verdict of "Guilty" for Count One (1977), but "Not Guilty" for the other two counts (1978 & 1979). It was then that the long appeal process began and was eventually denied all the way to the top. Tupper had realized too late that he was trying to argue with Caesar in Caesar's court.

*This is a staggering thought. We are completely dependent on the Commercial Banks. Someone has to borrow every dollar we have in circulation, cash or credit. If the Banks create ample synthetic money, we are prosperous; if not, we starve. We are absolutely without a permanent money system.*

—Robert K. Hemphill, Federal Reserve Bank Of Atlanta

*And all that live Godly in Christ Jesus shall suffer persecution*
— 3:12 of Paul's Second Letter to Timothy.

Perhaps the truth manifested in the above Scripture is more obvious today because of the *political*, rather than religious persecution of Christians. Regardless of the source—Paul didn't say whence it would come—the persecution of Christians has never been more harsh in this nation's history; or so cleverly concealed. Certainly the source would ultimately have to be Satan. But, I wondered, could this be the reason that so many hate groups want to blame the Jews for all the nation's problems?

There is certainly an interesting anomaly here. Many, maybe even most, of the Congressmen, governors, federal agents, politicians, and bureaucrats in general attend "the church of their choice" regularly, and some even have the courage to profess their Christian convictions publicly. Those aren't Jewish cops beating defenseless men and women on the sidewalks in front of abortion clinics. Nor are they all Jewish judges passing out those jail sentences to fellow Christians who are obeying a higher law. What about these church-going attorneys who collect large fees and then sell out their clients by advising them to plea-bargain? Do these people profess the same Lord but worship a different one? And if government people are sincere in their Christian beliefs, why are they obeying Caesar? I was confused. But, of course, Satan is the author of confusion.

\* \* \*

A housewife in Lawrenceville, Georgia answered her doorbell one morning with, "Who is it?"

"Federal Agents," came back the voice from the outer side.

"Do you have a warrant?"

"Yes, we have a warrant."

"Move over to the window and show it to me."

Instead, Bridgit Hall narrowly missed injury as the double doors splintered apart in the center and a battering ram came blasting through her foyer. Suddenly the sanctity of her home was disrupted by the presence of upwards of a dozen armed men and one woman wearing bullet-proof vests and carrying fully automatic weapons.

When her husband, Harry, heard the commotion and came bounding down the stairs with shaving soap all over his face and clad only in his pajama bottoms, he was grabbed and slam dunked into a straightback chair from the dining set, had a .357 magnum pistol placed against his temple, and was warned: "Don't move or I'll blow your fuckin'[1] head off!" This was the scene that greeted their five and nine-year-old daughters as they crept downstairs cowering behind their father.

Harry and Bridgit Hall home-school their children because they disapprove of much of the curricula taught at both public and private schools. This alone is enough to make them enemies of the State, but Harry is also a financial advisor who helps people establish perfectly legal off-shore trusts—the same tax avoidance protection used by members of Congress and the nation's super wealthy, but such a thing is anathema to the establishment when found in the hands of the little people.

Harry was never charged with any crime; but his records were confiscated, and several of his clients were later harassed with IRS audits. None of the clients was found to have done anything criminal nor were they assessed with any penalties or back taxes. The goal of the whole mission was obvious: Attack with such force to ensure that even honest people will fear to do what is honest.

The Hall children were so terrified by the eight hour visit from these "mean and evil" strangers that they could not sleep another night in that house.

---

[1] The author is baffled by the meaning of the adjective used in this context and can only conclude that it is a *non sequitur*. We have suspected for a long time that its derivation must be "fecund" which means" fertile" ("fecundate" is to fertilize; evolving to fecking, etc.), productive, or fruitful (which also suggests a likely nexus to the socially acceptable birds and bees but this has never been confirmed to us by any expert in Latin and/or English history. One, a cosmopolitan linguist and gourmet chef by the name of V. Russell Burnham of San Francisco, disagreed and offered that the word was older than the French language, from which "fecund" comes, and said flatly that it was his belief that the word was onomatopoeic, maybe even older than English. Regardless, with the proclivity of moviemakers and street imbeciles alike to use this word—as a noun, verb, adjective or adverb—to describe almost anything today, it is impossible to define. The author repeats it here only because Mr. Hall later stated, "That's precisely what the son of a bitch said."

Two weeks later, Harry and Bridgit packed up their things and left—not only Georgia, but the United States of America.

\* \* \*

A woman in Fairbanks, Alaska locks herself in her car on a downtown street when IRS agents attempt to confiscate it. After a too embarrassing public confrontation, they smash the window and drag Mona Oliver out through the broken glass and across a sidewalk before towing the vehicle away. The Volkswagen is sold for $500 at public auction where the IRS photographs sympathizers in the crowd and records their license numbers.

\* \* \*

Dwight Snyder supports his family as a self-employed cabinetmaker. He lives near Oakland, Maryland, a sleepy hamlet surrounded by rolling hills and tidy Amish farm settlements.

Snyder is a member of Dunkard Brethren Church, a fundamentalist group that, like his Amish neighbors, hews to ideals of pacifism, hard work, family values, and plain living. They frown on television, movies, alcohol, tobacco, and similar worldly diversions. We're plain, honest people, said Snyder, the father of three children. "I ain't never had a traffic ticket."

In 1980, Snyder was beginning his day's labors in the workshop next to his house when a procession of unmarked cars, police vehicles, three wreckers, and an interstate moving van halted outside his home. About forty U.S. Marshals, state patrolmen, IRS Revenue Officers and Special Agents— brandishing automatic weapons, shotguns and handguns—surrounded his property and took up positions near the house, the workshop, and along the highway.

It seems that the government claimed that Snyder owed $73,000, and the negotiations had been calm, courteous, and civil until Dwight filed a "Fifth Amendment" return—one that denies answering the questions pertaining to income and/or signing the return "under penalty of perjury" because the Fifth Amendment to the Constitution protects one from being a witness against himself. It made sense to me. To give sworn information on a government form could be construed as nothing less. But to the agency desiring that information it was construed as nothing less than defiance. It was a stand that reeked of tax protestation.

All of his vehicles, machinery, tools, and stock were seized—from a pick-up truck and tractor down to towel holders, soap dishes and toothbrush holders and even a half-empty box of staples. Although Snyder's neighbors rallied to the rescue and had him back to near normalcy in home and business in a week, Snyder's wife spent a month in a mental hospital because of the trauma.

All of this was done without a search warrant, as it is in nearly all IRS seizures. Because Snyder had committed no crime—the IRS would not accuse him of a crime because this would have given Snyder the opportunity to have a trial by jury—a search warrant could not be issued. The IRS, however, gets around this obstacle by a technicality called a "Writ of Entry." This statute—another of the many obviously unconstitutional ones that allow the IRS to operate under "color of law," such as Section 6331 of the IRS Code—permits the IRS to seize, by force, without due process of law.

The IRS seized thousands of dollars worth of the Snyder's property—as it has from thousands of other citizens—and sold it at public auction.

* * *

As Congressman George Hansen says in his book, *To Harass Our People*:

> The most disgusting part of the whole thing is that no creditor—not the federal government, not the state, no private citizen, no foreign government, literally no one—is empowered by law to take another's property without due process of law, except the IRS. It would take the declaration of martial law by the President to authorize any other federal agency to seize private property without a court order. Law-breaking government at all levels jails ministers and church members, makes fugitives of women and children, rigs juries, conducts illegal wire taps, and spends millions to send innocent citizens to jail.

* * *

In Louisville, Nebraska, Pastor Everett Sileven spends more than two months in jail for refusing to obey Caesar when he is ordered to close his Christian school at Faith Baptist Church. Eighteen ministers from all over the country who have gathered there in peaceful protest are bodily thrown into the street, and the church is padlocked.

* * *

Franklin Sanders of Memphis, Tennessee writes a monthly newsletter on the scholarly level of Saussy's *Main Street Journal*. He also, in recent years, has headed up the R. L. Dabney Memorial Warehouse Exchange, a private association of members similar to the N.C.B.A in Denver that the Feds like to call a "secret bank." In this case "secret" means "not a part of the Federal Reserve System, and they did not ask us permission before they set it up."

Must society really be protected from such "conspirators?" Apparently so.

At seven o'clock one morning recently, a large contingent of SWAT team members from IRS/CID and Tennessee Department of Revenue in black ninja suits burst into Sander's home and arrested his wife and him and held his seven children captive for eleven hours. His computers and private papers were taken (who knows what else?) and he was placed under $100,000 bond and spent four days in jail before it could finally be raised. (Murderers get $10,000 bail.)

Who is this dangerous person, and what terrible thing had he done? Let's hear it from Franklin Sanders:

I was the first journalist to expose the IRS secret Five Year Plan to construct a computer dossier on every American citizen. I have warned that the government and the IRS are trying to destroy our personal and financial privacy. I have warned about the danger of a 'surveillance state.'

"I wrote a novel, *Heiland*, that projected where these trends could end if they are not stopped. Almost everything I warned is now happening.

"This is a political charge. In America, the government is afraid to put dissident writers up against the wall and shoot them, so the IRS brings tax charges. The purpose of this prosecution is to shut me up; to make me stop writing my financial newsletter.

"Over the past four and a half years the IRS has secretly investigated me, harassed my wife and me, ruined my business, and financially endangered the lives of my wife and seven children. All my warnings of the past ten years are now coming true. All this proves that I was correct.

"There never has been any 'secret' bank. Everything I have done has been done in the light and open for all to see. There is no 'secret' about anything I have done. I thank God for the opportunity to face my *secret* accusers in court. The evidence will show that there is no truth in any of these charges."

I had no doubts about the validity of that last statement. He may have the evidence, but will the courts ever let him show it? The big question is: What remnants of the Sander's business, family, financial stability, and sanity will be left when the attack is finally proven to be groundless? The enemy has paid character assassins. Their apparent *modus operandi* in this case, as the others, will be three-tiered:

1. Destroy the dissident's credibility. Interrogation of neighbors with some cleverly planted innuendo about the "criminal activity" of the dissident is the common starting place. One of their best lies has become, in recent years, "...suspected of drug activity," because, like "..suspected of child abuse" or "...has homosexual tendencies," such a rumor is impossible to defend.

2. Destroy the dissident financially. $100,000 bonds are only the beginning. Next come the gigantic legal fees which usually result in a courtroom loss which then incarcerates the dissident after his family is destitute.

3. Destroy the dissident. This drastic method need only be resorted to when the unusual situation arises that the first two are unsuccessful; e.g. the cases of Gordon Kahl or Arthur Kirk. The dissident must then be forced into a confrontation where he can be coerced into armed retaliation; and/or where he can be killed without witnesses other than the government attackers.

\* \* \*

By increasing the brutality of "treatment," the public expectance of such treatment will be assisted, and the protest of the individual to whom the treatment is given is impossible because immediately after the treatment, he is incapable. The family of the individual under such treatment is suspect for having had in its midst, already, an insane person. The family's protest should be discredited. The more violent the treatment, the more command value the government will accumulate.

The society should be worked up to the level where every recalcitrant young man can be brought into court and assigned to a governmental operative, be given electric shocks, and reduced to unimaginative docility for the remainder of his days.

Basically, Man is an animal. He is an animal which has been given a civilized veneer. Man is a collective animal who enjoys State protection from the threat of environment. Those who so group and control him must then have in their possession specialized techniques to direct the vagaries and energies of the animal Man toward greater efficiency in the accomplishment of the goals of the State.[2]

At the time Jack and I were talking in June of 1987, former congressman, George Hansen of Idaho was serving an unspecified term in jail as a political prisoner. Congressman Hansen was singled out for prosecution by the Justice Department for failing to report one of his wife's financial dealings. This came after he had reported the activity to the House Ethics Committee, consulted two lawyers and was told that he need not report the information.

Further, over 100 members of Congress testified that they had no intention of creating a criminal penalty for violation of the act. Over 200 Congressmen

---

[2] *The Soviet Art of Brainwashing*—Noontide Press, P.O. Box 1248, Torrance, CA 90505

were allowed to amend their financial disclosures after Mr. Hansen's indictment. Of course, none of these 200 had spoken out publicly or written a book *(To Harass Our People*—1980) about the financial, emotional, and physical abuse of citizens by the IRS as had George Hansen.

So Big George was prosecuted and convicted (of course) and served six months in federal prison before being paroled in December of 1986. He sold his house and car in order to meet a fine of $40,000. He refused to agree to parole conditions which forbade his travel and applied for a waiver since he earned, as he still does, much of his living as a lecturer.

On April 15th the following year, a significant date referred to by patriots as April Fools Day (the day that 100 million fools voluntarily step forward and file their annual confession sheets), George was at the Omaha, Nebraska airport awaiting a flight back to Washington, D.C. He had spoken that day for Dr. Sileven's group at Faith Baptist Church. Three federal marshals arrested him without a warrant and placed him in handcuffs, body chains, and leg irons for supposed parole violations. He was taken to the local jail for one day after which the officers rented a Lear Jet and whisked him away in the middle of the night to the same place for which he was headed when he went to the airport. It was not reported whether or not he was able to obtain a refund for his air ticket.

Obviously, this overkill was not necessary with a prisoner who had such a history of preaching non-violent protestation except for, once again, the psychological impact this kidnapping would have on the nation's public and, especially, anyone else foolish enough to challenge the King.

Hansen was then taken to the Alexandria, Virginia city jail under the false name of "Frederick Smith" to prevent his family, his attorney, and the press from knowing his whereabouts. He was forced to wear the same Omaha jail overalls for ten smelly days, and it was only after the press tracked him down that he was allowed to make any phone calls. He would eventually be incarcerated for a total of ten months.

Even liberal syndicated columnist, Jack Anderson, was outraged at this treatment of a political conservative. He said, in part, "If a public figure who commands the attention of the press can be bullied by the authorities, what happens to the ordinary individual who enters the system without cachet?" Well, the previous vignettes should help answer that for you, Jack, and if not, just keep reading. Because "When plunder becomes a way of life for a group of men living together in society, they create for themselves in the course of time a legal system that authorizes it and a moral code that glorifies it." (Frederick Bastiat—from his book called *Economic Sophisms*.

All of this is not to say that good and peaceful men cannot sometimes be driven to violence. Minnesota farmer Donald McGrath did not believe he owed the IRS $39.65, and he wrote and told them so. When they failed to respond, he pretty much forgot about it until they took it from his bank account after McGrath had put his bank on notice not to cooperate with them without a court order.

Instead, "They turned my money over to the IRS and sent me the cancelled check they had forged on my account," said McGrath, a crop duster and farmer who then acted as his own attorney and filed a claim against the bank in district court. In the meantime, he refused to continue payments on a $3,000 combine which he had financed at that bank until the court rendered a decision on his suit. On July 28, 1980, an order was issued by the local court to seize McGrath's combine for non-payment.

McGrath, 51, with his wife and son in the car, took out after the sheriff's vehicles to intercept them and ended up in an armed confrontation on the highway near Grand Forks. Deputy Sheriff Shroeder hit McGrath in the head with a blast from his shotgun (he said that McGrath had fired first) which proved to be fatal a week later.

McGrath's wife and son were arrested and charged with attempted murder. Why? Any smart cop can tell you. If these two in the McGrath car were not felons, the sheriff's deputy who opened fire on the car would be open to a charge of felonious assault or attempted murder. At minimum, if they were not criminals, the sheriff's men would be guilty of criminal negligence in handling the matter. There would be a similar replay in North Dakota with Gordon Kahl's wife and son three years later.

* * *

Eldon Warman was an American Airlines pilot for nineteen years when his year of 1984 became a personal horror story rivaling George Orwell's *1984*. In 1983, the IRS, without Mr. Warman's consent or knowledge, changed his 1981 return to reflect an additional tax of over $105,000 after his having already paid a tax of some $8,000 when he had filed, in his words, "... a timely, honestly, and correctly prepared return." His protest letters fell on deaf ears, including a letter to the Secretary of Treasury asking for help.

When the IRS "letters of extortion" became more frequent and demanding in the spring of 1984, Mr. Warman issued a strongly worded caveat warning his adversaries of the ramifications should they illegally trespass on his property in Benicia, California without a warrant or attempt to confiscate any of his belongings without due process of law.

A short time later, in Eldon Warman's own words, "The IRS then sent a couple of their goons to my home and proceeded to fabricate a scene that *did not* happen. Then they began to trump up charges against me for 'threatening officers or employees of the United States in carrying out the tax code' and had the F.A.A. withdraw my medical certificate, whereupon American Airlines suspended me from employment with them as a Boeing 767 Captain. The following year I was terminated permanently by them for being charged with a crime and refusing to obey orders. I felt I could not attend the firing hearing in San Francisco because the Federal Magistrate had issued an arrest warrant for me."

But by this time, Mr. Warman had little else to lose by defying an arrest warrant. By the end of 1984, in addition to losing his $10,000 monthly income, his home in which he had an equity of $30,000 was confiscated. He also lost a $36,000 mobile home property in Ukiah, California; $20,000 equity in a vacation home near Reno, Nevada; $25,000 was lost by the forced sale of three motor vehicles and a power boat; $25,000 more was taken with a second mortgage he held in Vallejo, California; $24,000 was taken from his pension fund and vacation pay at American Airlines; $15,000 more from his household furnishings; and $27,000 equity in his private plane, a Beech Bonanza—all by the IRS and without benefit of due process. A bureaucrat decided that this was the amount that was due and they went after it. If this isn't enough to drive a sane man to the brink of destruction, the last chapter of that year surely is:

In a three-page letter to the Secretary of the Treasury, dated January of 1986, Warman reiterated all of the above and went on to say, "On December 12, 1984, my wife of 22 years took her own life by self-inflicted hanging, using an electrical extension cord. She had no previous history of depression or mental illness. The direct and only causes were the continued actions by the IRS against me. With this, and upon seeing that the legal proceedings against me were a farce being run by the IRS agents in the courtroom, I decided to take my two children and the few possessions I had left and take refuge in Canada, at least until I got my children somewhat re-established, which they are now."

His closing paragraph pointed out that the previous actions by the several government agencies had given him good reason to die and demanded that someone address this situation and offer some reasonable restitution; and if he were ignored at this final level as he had been in the past, he would "borrow a Boeing 747 and, using the skills I have learned over the past 25 years, pay a visit to Congress or one of the other offending federal institutions, at 550 miles per hour, assuming that I might make a deep and lasting impression on you *bastards*."

Despite the imprecation, Eldon has not (yet) brought himself to that end although, he did receive a visit from the Royal Canadian Mounted Police after they were contacted by the American Secret Service concerning this threat. After hearing Warman's whole story and seeing a copy of the whole letter, the two investigating Canadian officers said, "Why don't we just tell them to go to hell!" He has heard no more since.

However, knowing what I now know about the way such dissidents are handled by our government, I decided to give Mr. Warman a phone call at the number on the paperwork I had received to be sure that he was still alive. I found him without much trouble and at this moment, in April of 1990, can report that he is not only alive and well but still angry as a mother porcupine flushed from her nest.

I said, "Were you serious about taking that trip to D.C.?"

"As serious as a heart attack," he said. "But right now I just want them to leave me alone. If they leave me alone, they have nothing to fear. You see, Pat, I beat cancer in 1981, and I'm not sure how much longer that will stay in remission. But I know that if they attempt to come get me, it would be a death sentence too, with a dose of AIDS or some other chemical injection at their nuthouse in Springfield. With either death sentence, what do I have to lose? I still have my uniform in storage and wearing that, I can walk into any airport on the continent of North America and be in the cockpit of a plane in fifteen minutes and, I might add, it would be a completely rational and premeditated act."

I believed him. He didn't appear nuts to me; not ranting and raving; just stating the cold, hard facts. He has had his life destroyed, been deracinated, apparently without just cause, is mad as hell, and is not going to take it anymore. After wishing him well and hanging up the phone, I thought: *I hope no damn fool U.S. Agent goes after him like they did Kahl.*

I have read much literature that talks about the persecution of Christians and the threat of persecution to come. The persecution talked about always turns out to be physical. But what about spiritual persecution? In today's society, are not nominal Christians really afraid of physical persecution? When the supreme court rules that the laws of God must bend to the rules of man, as they did with their 9-0 decision against the Amish who were challenging the Social Security system, do not "Christians" and humanists alike agree that "this is Caesar's law and we must obey it?"

Freedom evidently exists only as long as you do not threaten the government's money, tax, and control system with your ideas. It is very interesting to note that in all these cases, historically as well as currently, the primary reason for targeting has been *opposition to government policy.* I now knew that not only was Tupper not insane, he was probably correct. His was not an isolated case, and, because he had gone beyond the first two tiers, he very well could be the next target.

In 1975, after that lunch with Robert Welch in Massachusetts, I had read a book he gave me called *None Dare Call It Conspiracy* about the "unseen hand" that controls this nation, found it to be interesting reading, but had thought little more about it. It had been but one byte in my brain's computer until now. But everything new I was uncovering reminded me a little of something I had heard before. I wanted to find that book by Gary Allen and read it again. Maybe our government *is* a wolf in sheep's clothing. These revelations were getting curiouser and curiouser.

> *Thus our national circulating medium is now at the mercy of loan transactions of banks—which lend, not money, but promises to supply money they do not possess.*
>
> —Professor Irving Fisher

*Thou shall not have in thy bag divers weights, a great and a small. Thou shall not have in thy house divers measures, A great and small. But thou shalt have a perfect and just weight, A perfect and just measure shalt thou have; that thy days may be lengthened In the land which the lord, thy god, giveth thee.*

— Deut. 25:13-15

Tupper Saussy is just one more of many people who have something in common with Charles Lindbergh, Sr., Abraham Lincoln, Andrew Jackson, Samuel Adams, and other heroes of American history not covered in this text such as Judge Roger Sherman and Thomas Jefferson at the founding, George Bancroft in the 19th century, and Congressman Louis McFadden of Texas in the 20th. What did they have in common? Their revulsion for schemes to cheat people out of their money and property.

I am not a history teacher, but then the history teachers I had, undoubtedly through ignorance alone rather than contrived deception, did not do a very good job of teaching me the *true* history of the American monetary system. So, bear with me for a few pages while I tell you what they should have told me!

I found myself racing through the early history of libertarianism as I continued to uncover these government offenses. My condensed study of recent history made me realize that we have become, during the lifetimes of many living people, a nation subservient to a government that was reducing people to serfdom. Their tool was a *power* that robbed from the poor and gave to the rich and left the diametrically opposite impression. I found some very interesting facts of history that were never taught to me, or anyone else, in public school.

Abraham Lincoln, one of the heroes of American history and always one of mine, was also actually one of the early villains. Maybe, it could be argued, the end justified his means. In 1863 his beloved United States of America was in shambles. Robert E. Lee had been kicking hell out of the Union troops at two out of three confrontations. Morale was down, and there was little chance of raising it when there was no money available to pay the current army, let alone the new conscriptees coming in. There were no more lawful ways to tax the people; he had already found out that the American people will not finance wars. So President Lincoln had a brainstorm and created our first unconstitutional money—"Lincoln Greenbacks"—to finance the "War of Northern Aggression," as modern-day southern sympathizers refer to it with tongue in cheek. (We prefer a new term which we will coin here: "The War of Federal Aggression."

The Civil War was just another battle in that 200 year war as, we now believe, the attack from a federal level upon state's rights has been ever-increasing since our government's inception in 1789.

Lincoln was forced to this decision after he invited the International Banksters (jargon that should need no explaining as we continue) to come to the White House to arrange a loan. Their terms, which included twenty-eight percent interest, so infuriated Lincoln that he sent them packing with some choice, curt words, and instead directed the Bureau of Printing and Engraving to create out of thin air 150 million paper bucks that were absolutely as unconstitutional and bogus as any that any counterfeiter before or since has ever created. A quarter billion more were foisted upon the American people through payment to the Union soldiers during the next two years before the practice was stopped.

There is one rectifying fact, however, that one should consider before cursing the memory of ol' Abe: His ultimate goal was to save the Union, and there was no other way to do it. If he couldn't pay the soldiers, the war and the union would be lost. Had he succumbed to the seductive desires of the banksters, the amount of interest due them from the government coffers on just the first loan of 150 million would have exceeded eleven billion by the time Franklin Roosevelt, the consummate father of legal tender in this country, took office in 1933. "Lincoln Greenbacks" were terminated before the war ended with 400 million "dollars" in circulation. Their value today only slightly exceeds that of "Confederate Money" hoarded by collectors.

Did Lincoln plot with the banksters? Did he tell them first that he needed an ultra-high interest rate to justify his unconstitutional legal tender acts? Or did the Banksters really want the legal tender acts and, for that reason, stood firmly on their twenty-eight percent demands?

These are questions that may never be answered, barring some turncoat Rothschild exposing the family archives, which is very, very doubtful, even if those records exist. However, the last question appears to have been plainly answered by history.

For all of his heartaches, Lincoln had uncovered another. There are those war history buffs who maintain that his murder was carried out because he had cut out the banksters. They would maintain that the American Civil War was planned in London in 1857; that certain banksters made an agreement that the Paris branch of the Rothschild group would support and finance the South and the British branch of the same faction would support and finance the North. Otto von Bismarck, first Chancellor of the German Empire he founded, confirmed the facts in a letter to a fellow German, Conrad Siem.

His statement was published in *La Ville France*, page 216 in March of 1921. He said, in part "...Lincoln never suspected these underground machinations. He was against slavery. When he had affairs in his hands, he perceived that these sinister financiers of Europe wished to make him the executor of their designs. They made the rupture between the North and South imminent. The masters of finance in Europe made the rupture to exploit. Lincoln's personality surprised them. His being a candidate had not troubled them; they thought to easily dupe the woodcutter. But Lincoln read their plots and understood that the South was not the worst foe, but the financiers."

Some very convincing circumstantial evidence shows that it was very likely Lincoln's entanglement with the money powers that led to his early demise. John Wilkes Booth had just returned from a clandestine meeting with the Banksters in Montreal prior to the assassination. They may have even very cleverly planned Booth's escape as there is some confusing evidence surrounding the body.[1] of the man (later buried under the name of "J.W. Booth) shot by Boston Corbett in the burning barn two weeks after the Presidential assassination.

Regardless, Bismarck said later, "The death of Lincoln was a disaster for Christendom. There was no man in the United States who could wear his boots. The money powers went anew to grab the riches of the world. I fear that foreign bankers with their craftiness and tortuous tricks will entirely control the exuberant riches of America and use it to systematically corrupt modern

---

[1] For instance, John Wilkes Booth had obviously broken his left leg when he jumped to the stage at Ford's Theatre. This was witnessed by hundreds in the theatre audience who watched him limp across the stage to the rear curtain in route to the back door. The body of the man found in the barn after the fire two weeks later had been treated for a broken right fibula. This was not the only physical discrepancy at the autopsy. One story, circulated much later, had Booth living until 1904 where he was finally murdered in Oklahoma by members of the "Knights of the Golden Circle,"a forerunner of the Ku Klux Klan, because Booth, by that time, was a garrulous drunkard who was talking too much about his true past and was revealing secret plans of the Knights, of which he was a member. This faction had supposedly recovered hundreds of millions in Confederate gold and actually believed "the South shall rise again" until it was finally disbanded in 1916.

civilization. They will not hesitate to plunge the whole of Christendom into wars and chaos in order that the earth should become their inheritance."

The next Federal shot fired at the States was in 1894, but it missed. It was the first attempt to foist a federal income tax on the people.[2] After great debate, it was passed by Congress and then shot down by the Supreme Court the following year because the U.S. Constitution forbade a direct tax on the people without apportionment. (It still does.)

The first decade of the twentieth century saw the "Panic of 1907," which now appears to have been rigged by Paul Warburg and the House of Rothschild, to display the need for a central bank. The second plank of the Communist Manifesto cries for a need of a "Heavy progressive or graduated income tax." The fifth denotes the necessity of a "Centralization of credit in the hands of the State by the means of a national bank with State capital and an exclusive monopoly." Neither of these was ever necessary in a free society where men exchanged with each other in a barter system of gold and silver, but they go hand in hand for financial control of the masses in a paper money and credit system.

The year 1913, which surely must be the darkest of our nation's history, saw them both passed as law as well as the Seventeenth Amendment which took away the power of state legislatures to appoint their U.S. senators, and with it went the power of the States to keep a thumb on Congress. The income tax, sold to our grandparents as one that would "soak the rich," actually became a Constitutional Amendment—the Sixteenth—although now it appears that it was never lawfully ratified.[3]

Nevertheless, it is more than coincidence that these three "laws" were passed by the same people in the same year. The big foot was finally in the door. Congressman Charles Lindbergh of Minnesota, father of the famous aviator, said to his peers on the floor of Congress concerning the Federal Reserve Act:

---

[2] Actually, the second. There was a temporary tax on income, also authored by Lincoln, foisted on the people in the northern states to help finance the Union Army. It was terminated in 1866.

[3] All forty eight State Legislatures suspended their rules for the ratification of the 16th Amendment. For documentation on this subject, one should see *The Law That Never Was* put together through extensive research by M.J. Beckman of Montana and Bill Benson of Illinois, both of whom have been under constant harassment by the federal government. Benson recently served time in a federal penitentiary as another political prisoner. His case was overturned by the Appellate Court.

This Act establishes the most gigantic trust on earth. When the President signs this bill, the invisible government by the monetary powers will be legalized. The people may not know it immediately, but the day of reckoning is only a few years removed. The people must make a declaration of independence to relieve themselves from the monetary power. Wall Streeters could not cheat us if you Senators and Representatives did not make a humbug of Congress. The worst legislative crime of the ages is perpetrated by this banking and currency bill.

By this time Lindbergh had found secret collusion between Southern and English bankers prior to the "War of Federal Aggression," citing proofs in his book, *Banking and Currency and the Money Trust*. This included the text of the 1862 "Hazard Circular" which revealed how labor would henceforth be controlled by the amount of currency the bankers permitted in the market, since chattel slavery would be abolished by the war.

Over and over, the plans of the manipulators had to be revised because of exposure by Congressman Lindbergh. He had become such a thorn in their sides that he was offered a two million dollar bribe—an astronomical sum of lawful money—to stop the circulation of his book, according to *The Lindberghs*, by Lynn and Dora Haines (Vanguard Press, 1931).

That day of reckoning is, apparently, here. The suppression of the problem by the oppression of the people through restriction of consumption is only a temporary stop gap that cannot possibly put the brakes on the all-encompassing problem of the (pending) complete destruction of our monetary system. With only a cursory examination, one can discover that in the history of the world, no paper money scheme has ever survived. Are we really stupid enough to believe that this one will?! Only the most obtusely imperceptive would. Those who do not learn from history are doomed to repeat it.

This nation was founded on the principles of the Bible. The Declaration of Independence of 1776 threw off the shackles of King George III, and the Constitution of 1789 spelled out rights on which government could not impinge. Here is the great difference between our Constitution and those of other nations: The others are written by the government, and the people are told what they can do. Ours was written by "We the People" and it dictates what the government can do and no more.

The rights of the people were so spelled out that the Ninth and Tenth Amendments even went on to say to government, in so many words, that "... if we forgot anything, you can't do that either!" It was signed "... on the Seventeenth Day of September *in the year of our Lord.* I supply that piece of information for those today who would deny that Jesus Christ was ever the acknowledged King of America. Is there any other Lord from whose birth the very essence of time is measured?

Where are the Paul Reveres, Samuel Adamses and Charles Lindberghs today, and what are there names now? I will tell you: They are the ones who have refused to accept the new, progressive state of affairs. They ask disturbing questions such as, "Since the government is the people, where does it get the money to give the loafers all these benefits?" They insist on upholding the rights of man, including property rights. They deny that government can plan the people's lives better than the people themselves.

They believe that the government should not create "money" out of nothing or spend more than it takes in, and they dispute the ability of the bureaucracy to override the limits of the Constitution. They believe that no action should be a crime unless it has a victim, and their Christian heroes are not Billy Graham, Robert Schuller and Charles Stanley who rake in millions from their television ministries while ignoring abortion clinics in their own neighborhoods, but rather the likes of Pastors Bob McCurry of Georgia, John Lewis of Virginia, and Greg Dixon of Indiana who deny the right of the government to even register their churches because to do so would place that government, instead of Jesus Christ, as the head of that church.

They believe you should wear a seat belt if you deem it necessary, and they reserve the right of anyone to engage in any field or profession without the permission of the government. They do not apply for business licenses, driver's licenses, or any other licenses in order to do what is already lawful. They have rescinded their Social Security numbers and resigned from all government benefits. They do not believe in robbing from the rich and giving to the poor, and certainly not in robbing the poor to give to the rich.

Clearly they are dangerous radicals who cannot be tolerated if the existing order is to be preserved.

I knew the name of one of them today. He was the old musician, songwriter, playwright, adman, and friend of mine, Tupper Saussy. For his part, he insisted only on government holding to its oath. "The covenant between us is broken," he had said, "and there is lawlessness. One's only alternative is to claim Jesus Christ or move to another nation."

Born in Savannah, Georgia in 1936, Frederick Tupper Saussy was the first eldest son in four generations not to become a professional lawyer. His forebears emigrated from France to Georgia in the early 19th century "not because of any 'American Dream,' " he explains, "but because the people of the United States had just created the world's finest Constitution. The French know quality."

Thus, through osmosis or acculturation, he had acquired a reverence for the law. He graduated from the University of the South in Sewanee, Tennessee in 1958 with a B.A. in English and taught school in Nashville before becoming an advertising executive. However, his real love was music, and his greatest satisfaction came from his natural creativity—composing songs and writing plays—and his efforts earned him three Grammy nominations in 1968.

He wrote "To Watch A Beautiful Sunrise," a comedy in two acts published by Samuel French & Co. in New York and personally opened and ran the Appletree Dinner Theatre in Tennessee in 1977. After marrying Frederique Blanco in 1973, their son Pierre Phillipe was born in 1974 and son Laurent in 1978.

It was at the Appletree Dinner Theatre in 1978 that Tupper began to draw the attention of the government. The first dart he threw at Caesar was the writing and producing of a satirical barb, *The Gimmies*, which poked absurd fun at the IRS. Shortly thereafter, he began to hear the proverbial knocks on his door at home and at the theatre. Undercover agents testified later that they illegally spied on him and took license plate numbers of patrons at his dinner theatre.

For six years, Tupper successfully warded off the numerous civil attacks by the IRS and frustrated his adversaries by cleverly divesting himself of ownership of all property and bank accounts. In 1984 it began to get ugly. Criminal charges were filed against Frederick Tupper Saussy for "Willful Failure to File" income tax returns for the years 1977, 1978, and 1979.

One of the basics of courtroom procedure is the right of the defendant to challenge jurisdiction at any time, at which time jurisdiction must be proven by the prosecution. After discovering this tidbit of legal information, this man, who could now play the Constitution almost as sweetly as the piano, coupled it with something even more basic that is found in the Fifth Amendment to our great document:

"No person shall be held to answer for a capital, or otherwise infamous crime, unless on a presentment or indictment of a grand jury."

His defense would be simple: This court had not the jurisdiction for a prosecution of F.T. Saussy because the charges had been brought by "information" from the IRS to the Federal Prosecutor. There had been no charges even *presented* to a Grand Jury for consideration of whether or not to indict.

On January 24, 1985, the whole Saussy family, Tupper, Freddy and the two boys, ages seven and eleven, walked into the Federal Courthouse in Winchester, Tennessee for the hearing previously mentioned. Unbeknownst to the court authorities, someone had placed a small recorder in a picnic basket containing the defense documents.

Tupper, never one to shun the spotlight, then proceeded to politely but firmly explain the law to the judge, prosecutor, and courtroom audience of nearly 100 who had jam-packed every seat. The whole scene was over in two minutes, climaxing with Tupper's final statement of: "...and therefore, there being no jurisdiction properly established in this case, I am leaving," whereupon he took his wife under one arm, his two boys under the other and began to march up the courtroom aisle towards the door.

"Arrest that man!" cried the judge.

To the horror of all who witnessed it, officers and agents grabbed the family and dragged them screaming across the courtroom floor to an interrogation room in the back of the building. The boys were cut and scratched, and Frederique received a blow to the abdomen that caused internal hemorrhaging for which she had to be hospitalized. The judge did not release any of them for over two hours at which time Tupper was taken to the county lockup in Chattanooga and his family went to the hospital.

Witnesses in the courtroom described the scene as akin to something they had read out of Alexander Solzhenitsyn and most surmised that the delay in releasing the family was tied to the long, private meeting held by the judge and prosecutors in trying to decide how to cover up their procedural mistakes. A dozen F.B.I. agents held the irate crowd at bay in the lobby after the judge had ordered the courtroom cleared.

Tupper served 50 days in the Atlanta Federal Prison Camp for contempt of court. How challenging jurisdiction can be construed as contempt of court is known only to Judge Tom Hull of Greenville, Tennessee and the federal judiciary. Those present assumed it must mean doing anything the judge does not like. Following Tupper's release, the U.S. Attorney presented a Grand Jury Indictment to the Federal Court and virtually confessed to "political persecution" by telling newspaper reporters, "Now, Mr. Saussy has his Grand Jury Indictment." In other words, *Mr. Saussy has been right all this time, and now we have corrected our error after holding him in jail for fifty days while we got it corrected!*

On May 30th of that year, Tupper Saussy was found innocent by a jury of the two counts against him for 1978 and 1979 but guilty of "Willful Failure To File" for the year 1977. The jury's reasoning being that he had acted "willfully" the first year because he had done it on his own without professional advice. He had contacted attorney Donald McPherson of Phoenix, Arizona, before not filing the following years. McPherson had told him that he knew of no laws requiring him to file a 1040 form that did not also require the waiving of his rights under the Constitution by doing so.

Tupper appealed his conviction mainly on the grounds that the Statute of Limitations had expired on the 1977 conviction prior to the grand jury indictment, which was a fact. It is common knowledge among criminals that if the man had robbed a bank, he could even have stepped forward and bragged about it on the radio after expiration of the time limitation without fear of prosecution. However, at least when it comes to tax "crimes" in this country, we seem to be a nation of men and not laws. The Statute of Limitations was ignored, and Tupper's conviction was upheld by the Appellate Court. He was sentenced to one year in jail and ordered to surrender his body at the Atlanta Federal Prison Camp on or before April 10, 1987.

Being a word mechanic, he followed his orders to the letter. The order did not instruct him to seek out and surrender himself to any individual. Quite plainly, the order was to surrender to the institution; and at 4:38 p.m. on April 9, 1987, along with a friend armed with a video camera, Tupper arrived at the Atlanta prison camp, as his papers decreed, and surrendered himself "openly and notoriously to the institution."

The institution did not respond. He stood in front of the prison gates holding the front page of that day's newspaper, and while being filmed, again and repeatedly with a straight face, surrendered himself, but the institution said nothing. He then announced that he was leaving.

He did leave and went straight to the post office and mailed the film to Alicia Ames, a Chattanooga television reporter. When the judge who had sentenced him, Tom Hull in Greenville, Tennessee, saw it on the evening news, he hit the ceiling and promptly turned the case over to another judge who, reportedly, issued an arrest warrant. Two months later the fugitive was in Phoenix and found me at the Casa Loma in Tempe.

While this action by the convicted may sound absurd to the layman, most lawyers would recognize it as "strict construction" of the law. Black's Law Dictionary calls it: "a close or rigid reading and interpretation of a law."

It is said that criminal statutes must be strictly construed. And while it goes on to say that the "Rule of Strict Construction" has no definite or precise meaning, it points out that "the criminal statute will not be enlarged by implication or intendment beyond fair meaning of language used, or what their terms reasonably justify and will not be held to include offenses and persons other than those which are clearly described and provided for, although the court in interpreting and employing particular statutes may think the legislature should have made them more comprehensive." Tupper, arguably, had obeyed his court order.

The best illustration for "Strict Construction" that I have been able to uncover in my short tenure as a researcher comes from the old English Common Law, whence the rule comes. In 1213 the English Parliament enacted a statute that said, word for word: "Any man who shall steal horses shall be hanged by the neck until dead." So when a man who had stolen a horse was brought to the magistrate by the constable, the magistrate said that he could not be tried. Because there were witnesses and the man had been caught red-handed, the constable asked, "Why not?" The magistrate pointed out that under the statute, there was no law against stealing a horse, but only against stealing horses. Strict Construction of the law.

*Give me the control of a nation's money supply; then I will not care who makes its laws.*

—Meyer Rothschild, 19th Century
—Anselm Rothschild, 20th Century

*The rung of a ladder was never meant to rest upon, but only to hold a man's foot long enough to enable him to put the other somewhat higher.*

—Thomas Huxley

It had been two weeks since I had seen him. I wished I had a way to make contact, but he was keeping that on a "need to know" basis, and I really was not among the needy. He knew where to reach me when it was necessary. When June ended without another appearance from him, I began to suspect that he might come in the following Friday which was July 3rd and, I remembered, his 51st birthday. I figured he would be feeling a little nostalgic and looking for a friendly face with whom to celebrate a little. I was right.

When I walked into the club at 7:45, he was already there perched at the piano bar and, I knew, itching to be sitting on the 88 side. He didn't see me slip up behind him.

"Happy Birthday, Jim!," I whispered right behind his ear, "You sure look old for only *sixty*-one!"

I had caught him unaware, and he was momentarily speechless, most uncharacteristic for him. That I had remembered his birthday puzzled him, and then, too, I could see the wheels grinding as he attempted to discern whether or not I was joshing about his age. He stood up and sputtered for a moment as if trying to decide whether to thank me or retaliate first, he decided on the latter: "C'mon, you know I don't look a day over forty-one, even in this get-up.

I just grinned, "Oh, of course not!"

"How did you know it was my birthday today?"

"Don't you remember that big blast we had in New York in '64?" I reminded him. "After we returned from the World's Fair with your friend, Basil. It was a combination celebration for you and Uncle Sam, and I've always remembered that your birthday was the day before his."

My songwriting, folksinging friends, Tom Paxton and Phil Ochs, who would later reach heights in the industry, were there at that party along with a whole host of entertainers from Greenwich Village. The house, for a few hours that night until our landlady got home, had looked like a hippy commune.

"What a memory," he said, "but let me tell you that now I know my birthday is actually the day after the signing of the Declaration of Independence, instead of the day before."

I said, "Do you mean that your birthday is actually July 5th?"

"Nope," he replied with cocksureness, "Mine is today. Uncle Sam's was yesterday. The Declaration was actually resolved on the *second* of July, 1776."

I had never heard that before and made a mental note to ask for some "whys" later, but my experience the last several weeks had already taught me not to bet against him. I knew that he had to have some feasible explanation that would prove him right, and I had to get set up to entertain, so I just said, "Ooookay."

I never remembered to ask him about it, but a year or so later when I saw a television rerun of the movie version of Sherman Edwards's Broadway play *1776*, it was confirmed. The Declaration was actually signed on July 2nd, 1776[1]

After singing a couple of opening numbers, I realized that there were not very many people in the club yet, and I decided it was time to spring a little surprise on Jim without checking with him. So I just said, "Ladies and gentlemen, there is an old friend of mine here tonight who can play this big ol' box a lot better than I can, and I'm going to give you a little treat. So please give him your undivided attention ... today's his birthday ... his fortieth, I think ... so please welcome, Jim Gordon!!"

I jumped off the piano bench to make it available to him before he could object, and I think at the same time he quickly calculated that this shouldn't provide very much risk to his security and obliged. He really was being more careful than necessary in my opinion, and I really believed that with his current look as compared with recent pictures, he could get along anywhere as unnoticed as Whistler's Father. Even, maybe, in the Federal Courthouse.

---

[1] Everyone present in Congress that day, July 2nd, assumed that, henceforth, it would be known as Independence Day. 'I believe that it will be celebrated by succeeding generations as the great Anniversary Festival,' wrote John Adams to his wife Abigail. (*The Road to Independence* by Thomas Fleming.)

He took to it like a duck to water, and I could tell he had been practicing some place recently. He played some pop, carefully avoiding the hits that he had written, then some long-hair classics—including a piece of absolute musical genius he referred to as "Caribbean Bach"and—twenty minutes later—finished by playing, while I led the singing of, George M. Cohan's "Yankee Doodle Dandy," and we made an on-the-spot change of the lyrics to ... "born on the *third* of July." The crowd loved it and so did I. He had done half of my work for me in the first set. I wound it up with a couple of more, and we ambled back to our favorite booth in the coffee shop.

"I'm movin' on," were his first words after we were alone.

"Whadda' you mean, you just got here. I need you to help out again later."

"No, forget that. That's my last public appearance for awhile. But what I mean is, I am blowing town this weekend."

"Why?"

"Because I'm about to wear out my welcome where I am, and it continues to be that way wherever I go. I spent the first month with some great people in Atlanta. Then some other friends arranged for me to go to Haiti, but the plans fell through at the last minute. I flew with a friend in his private plane to Dallas where I spent another week before coming out here. I have been shuttled from one home to another for a few nights each, and, most recently, I have been with just the most generous guy you ever wanna' meet. Charlie owns a printing business out on the south side. I've been with him for the last week while his wife is out town, but she is returning Sunday; and we are certain that she won't be comfortable with me there, so we agreed that it would be better for all if I pulled a disappearing act."

"Well, you're pretty good at that," I cracked.

"I have got to get to some place more permanent," he went on, ignoring my levity. "It places too much of a hardship on friends to ask them to put me up anymore; even those who can afford it financially cannot afford the risk. I have been asking too much of people. Charlie has made some phone calls and arranged for another private plane to take me up north where I can privately purchase an old Dodge motor home that has all the comforts of home. It will be a perfect place for me to live on a more permanent basis. Maybe Freddy and the boys can come out when I get more settled."

"What are you going to buy it with?" I queried. "I thought you were broke."

"No, I'm not broke, just badly bent. I didn't come away with exactly nothing. I've got my computer from which I can earn a living, and I do have some gold and silver that I have earned as a word processor and editor over the years, and this person is willing to trade for lawful money instead of Fed notes."

"Where will you park it?"

"There's a couple in Placerville, California who has a few acres of ground, and they know only that "Jim Gordon," who is down on his luck, will be parking there for awhile. They have an organization called Management of Business Associates—MBA—that I may be able to help out in without jeopardizing them. They can use me as an independent contractor and not have to be concerned with social security numbers as they would if I were an employee. I understand that they are writing a new business manual and can use my talents in completing it. Maybe it will work out for awhile until the Lord directs me elsewhere.

"All who have helped me up until now have placed themselves at risk because they knew very well who I was. This, I think, will be a better way to live and operate. I hope so. I don't like putting people in a position of having to risk their own hides in order to protect mine. This way there won't be any pressure on anyone, and I can still cover my own backside."

"What's your E.T.D.?"

"A twin engine plane will take me out of a private airstrip at eight o'clock tomorrow morning, and we'll be in Sacramento before noon. If everything goes to schedule, I should have my motor home business all transacted and be parked in Placerville before dark. I didn't want to leave the area without telling you adios."

"Do you need a co-pilot? I've got a multi-engine ticket. If I can get back here before work time, I'll be happy to go along and help out."

His face lit up in surprise. "You've got a pilot's license? You didn't tell me that! How long have you been flying?"

"Oh," I replied, "about ten years. I had a Cessna 310 for a couple of years, but I didn't fly it enough to really justify the costs. It was an expensive toy, so I leased it out to a charter company for a couple of more years, flew it when it was available, and then sold it. I've got around 600 hours but don't fly more than 20 a year now. Sometimes I go out to the airport, especially when I'm in a new town, shoot a hundred bucks, rent a plane, and just fly around the area for a couple of hours. It's a great way to kill an afternoon."

"Do you want to fly with us tomorrow?"

"Sure, I'd love it, as long as the plane is coming straight back. I don't need to leave Juan here with no entertainment on a Saturday night and on a holiday weekend to boot."

Those plans for me to go along were scratched when Jim made a call and learned that the pilot had already made plans to stop in Las Vegas on the turnaround and spend Saturday night with some other friends. But we talked some more during that break and Jim stuck around for another. It was then that I related to him the high-speed education I had acquired during the last couple of weeks and my hunger to know more.

He advised me to keep on reading; that they were uncovering more and more truths all the time; that there was a great patriot attorney in Phoenix who is a West Point graduate, Vietnam veteran, and a true believer in the cause whom I should meet sometime.

"He appeared as an 'expert witness' at my trial two years ago," he said, "and helped me immensely. The fact that I had consulted him after my first year of non-filing and he had advised me that, indeed, there is no law on the books that required one to file a 1040 form for income taxes, was the overriding reason that the jury had to acquit me for the last two counts. Because I had not talked to him, or any lawyer, before dropping out the first year, they determined that I was "willful" on the first count. Isn't that ridiculous? Talk to one of their boys first and it's okay. But don't get clearance and you're in trouble!

Anyway, you would enjoy meeting Mac McPherson and he's a good man to know. I would introduce you except that he doesn't know I'm here, and I don't need to involve him right now. After I'm gone, you might give him a call and invite him out for a drink. Tell him you're an old friend of mine and even that I was here, if you like, but don't tell him where I've gone.

You know that it goes without saying, but I'd better say it anyway, that you should tell *no one*, not even Freddy, of my whereabouts. Phones are tapped everywhere they think I might call, and if you talk to anybody, the information will eventually get back to the wrong people. I've only told you because I know I can trust you and, from time to time, I may need a window to the outside world, and I imagine it should always be safe to call you at whatever club you are working. Can I count on you to relay some messages for me?"

"Sure. Wherever I am," I said, "I almost always go on break on the half hour or slightly later, so a call at ten minutes before the hour will usually be perfect."

"You think I haven't noticed that?" he said.

I assured him that there was nothing to worry about; that my lips were sealed, and if they hung me by my toes and beat me with wet noodles, I would spit in their faces. With his caveat in mind, and knowing that the rumor mills were always grinding in a case like this, I decided that disinformation would be better than no information at all. Since he was on the west coast, I would place him in the east. New York would be a good place for him to hide. Dan had told me that the Binghamton area was a hot bed for "patriots," and I decided that's where he would choose to lay low, with plenty of sympathetic allies. The first time the question came up, much later, I was ready with my cover story.

I asked his permission to turn on my tape recorder so I might save as much of this detail as possible. It was the same procedure I have used for years in plagiarizing songs from other entertainers. Reluctantly, he agreed. I think he knew how thirsty for truth he had made me and that it was only general information that I wanted to record. I again assured him that we would not let the conversation drift to anything about his current situation while the recorder was on. Then I asked him about James Earl Ray.

"James contacted me after he became educated on the workings of the establishment's media. Time-Life, in particular, had published prosecution-oriented distortions a few days prior to each of his new trial hearings. Since we both lived in Tennessee at the time—I by choice—he had seen many stories in the Nashville papers and on TV about this renegade editor in Sewanee who wasn't afraid to attack lies.

In 1986, after he read the misleading stories about my federal prosecution and probably viewed me as some sort of confederate, he decided I would be just the editor to help him publish his autobiography because he felt he just couldn't trust any of the government controlled corporations. At first, I didn't want anything to do with publishing the memoirs of an assassin, but he would call me everyday and I was floored when I learned his side of that story."

"Do you think Ray was King's assassin?"

"I doubt that anyone who reads his autobiography could reach that conclusion. James never rants and raves about his innocence. He simply demands probable cause. None of the documents brought before the Tennessee criminal court contain the least shred of probable cause. He says that the FBI possesses documents that would exonerate him, but those have been sealed away until the year 2018. I have a copy of the Archivist's letter to that effect.

"The draft of his book was very rough. Editors who contribute as much as I did usually claim 'as told to' status. But I thought it should be James's book. It was his life, after all. So I downplayed my involvement. The book came out just after I went into seclusion, and now I hear that James has found some errors. I can't get involved without blowing my cover, but I am blessed to have a brother who, though he has no publishing experience, can step in and fix everything to James's satisfaction. There will be a second edition soon.

"You know it saddens me to see Americans rallying for political prisoners when the one most affecting our liberties is in our own backyard. James Earl Ray is the Sacco and Vanzetti of our age. The government officers who wanted King killed, went down their list of guys nobody cared about and selected James. Everyone figures that since James Earl Ray pled guilty, he must be guilty. Ray was a petty crook—no getting around that—and he freely admits it. But petty crooks can be redeemed. I detest the unlawful deprivation of anyone's freedom."

"What was unlawful about the treatment he received?"

"The man was tortured. The government knew that he was not the assassin but that confession was imperative, even if they had to beat it out of him. He was placed in a windowless room with bright lights in his face and denied not only counsel, but *sleep for days at a time*, and for eight months!

There is some pretty strong proof that the FBI knew all the time James was not the killer but a cleverly established patsy. If you believe James is innocent, you have brought yourself to the threshold of one of the most important decisions of your life. Because, you see, if James and his extensive documentation are telling the truth, it must follow that his accusers with their stifled evidence in obstruction of justice are *not* telling the truth. His accusers are, to put it in the simplest terms available, liars, and the Good Book warns us that 'If a ruler hearken to lies, all his servants are wicked' (Proverbs 29:12).

"Lying is deadly and highly contagious. The man who receives his information from a liar will spew out lies when he passes the information on. When you have liars trained in the demonic arts controlling the highest seats of governmental authority, you will have liars controlling the information channels. When their lies fill the printed pages, loudspeakers, and TV screens, you will have liars administering the work places, market places, schools, churches, and homes. Without realizing it, your nation becomes possessed by demons. Your nation practices the politics of witchcraft.

"A liar's fortunes are very cleverly established on his pretenses of virtue, otherwise well-meaning people would have nothing to do with him. He will not think twice about murdering to protect his good reputation, just as a woman cursed with a fetus from a lie-marriage will murder the baby to keep demands on her time and finances at a minimum.

"In a lying society, murder is an acceptable alternative to radically changing one's views. In lying societies, the virtues are brutishness, deceit, sodomy, theft, debt, suicide, art. He who is most menacing and monstrous is most popular. The most powerful liar rules. The Oscars and Emmys and political elections go to the best impersonators while the Grammys and centerfolds go to the best seducers."

I stared silently spellbound, and his words kept flowing.

"Though powerful in appearance, liars are in reality extremely fragile. There is no protection for a liar except darkness or the mercy of a more powerful liar. This is why lying societies crave dimness of room and of mind. It is why they seek bondage to human, rather than Godly, authority. Other humans can be deceived; God cannot. Now the bondage won't always manifest itself through the familiar symbols of slavery. Not all American lie-families keep on hand whips and chains like those found in eminently respectable CIA agent Clay Shaw's home by investigators searching out Shaw's supervisory involvement in President Kennedy's assassination.

"In demonic political systems, the bondage is assumed through adhesion contracts extended by liars to lie-believers. Nearly every American is bound by such a contract. The most prevalent one is the process by which citizens periodically give power of attorney to liars through voter registration. A registered voter is subject to every regulation passed by his representative, regardless of how tyrannical or insane.

"When founding father Elbridge Gerry condemned 'the fury of excess democracy,' not one framer of the Constitution took issue with him. They all knew that 'democracy' was government by mob, by demons, by wicked servants, and this is why they put the U.S. Senate beyond the reach of the people. National senators were elected only by state legislators until May 31, 1913, when the 17th Amendment opened the Senate to the fury of democracy.

1913 was also the year the Federal Reserve was created by Congress to burden the people with usury and debt. It was the year, too, of the creation of what has become the Internal Revenue Service."

"That was the 16th Amendment," I interjected to show him that I had done *some* homework, "but what is this I read about it not ever being lawfully passed or ratified or something?"

"This is exactly what I am saying!" he exclaimed. "Whether it ever was lawfully ratified or not—and now I don't believe that it was—what difference does it make if they have caused everyone to *believe* that it was? 'If a ruler hearken to lies, all his servants are wicked.' We live in a deceitful society. The beneficiaries of the greatest political experiment in the history of the world sold themselves down the river in the 1930's. The spirit of free enterprise was dimmed by a contrived Federal Reserve catastrophe which sent millions of Americans praying to Washington, D.C. for salvation. They got the best a democracy could come up with, the ancient 'devils pact:' 'We will protect you socially in exchange for a lifetime of tribute.'

"What was not revealed was that the security depended upon a uniform social bondage, and he who attempted to revolt, reform or break free would be condemned. All claims to Constitutional rights were waived upon signing the contract. That contract might also be the social security application, an IRS 1040 form, or even a driver's license. Each, as well as many others, causes a person to relinquish a right in order to receive a government privilege. As the signpost at the gate of hell says, 'Abandon all hope ye who enter here.'

"Giving power to a liar by contract is suicidal. When you later come to your senses and point out his fraud, he exercises the power you gave him and declares your complaint 'frivolous.' After all, you authorized him to change the rules according to his changing needs. 'Substantial penalty for early withdrawal,' when uttered by a liar, means 'slight forfeiture' in one generation, 'shot on sight' in the next.

"That reminds me of another familiar contract holding millions of Americans in further bondage: the standard bank loan. The lender gives 'value received' in exchange for units of the borrower's labor. The contract seems perfectly fair until it's discovered that the 'value' received determines the worth of the units of the borrower's value. That 'value' is regulatable and changeable up and down by the party issuing —the Federal Reserve system. This is why the bottom falls out of the grain market just as it looks like the farmers will pay off their loans.

"This is why the FDIC—owned also by the Federal Reserve—closes a bank because of 'risky loan portfolio,' then calls in the outstanding loans, taking possession of the collateralized property when the borrower can't pay. Every victim of usury knows that the financial rope thrown by a liar to pull you up an escarpment becomes elastic as you near the top. But it only stands to reason: What lender in his right mind wants a borrower liberated from debt bondage?"

The word "listen" contains the same letters as the word "silent," and I continued with both.

"Lying is so much a part of the utter fabric of American life that whole generations are now addicted to lies. The same schools that stimulate children to sexual awareness before puberty and offer suicide as a viable alternative to a miserable life and teach that the State is sovereign ... these same schools train pupils to believe that Lee Oswald murdered John Kennedy with three shots from behind. This, despite the fact that in March of 1979, the House Select Committee on Assassinations quietly and reluctantly found that acoustical evidence and witnesses proved a *fourth* shot had been fired from the front of the President.

Jim Garrison, the New Orleans District Attorney, said, 'The last word on the U.S. government's adjusted posture seems to be that Lee Harvey Oswald killed President Kennedy with three shots from the back and one shot from the front.' That same school teaches the children that Sirhan Sirhan and only Sirhan Sirhan killed Senator Robert Kennedy at the Ambassador Hotel in Los Angeles with an eight-shot Iver Johnson .22 pistol although *eleven* bullet holes were found in the room and in Kennedy's body.

"Both of these conclusions are proven lies, but imagine the person who sits back and accepts such a conclusion, and you have a lie-believing citizen of a nation that practices classical witchcraft."

Here was a subject with which I was very familiar, and I had reams of information by a dozen or more authors saved over the years. I knew that it was an impossibility for Oswald to have acted alone and very probable that he had not even fired a shot. The accepted conclusions on Sirhan—and Ray, I was now finding out—were just as ridiculous. I nodded with an affirmative smile, hating the fact that I was about to have to get back to work for half an hour.

"The consciences of the people are seared with the lies of who killed the Kennedy brothers and Dr. King, and the liars and lie-believers who make and enforce law in the United States today are giving succor, privilege, amnesty, haven, and nobility to the real killers."

"Listen," I interrupted, turning off the recorder, "Please don't confuse this with disinterest. I am fascinated with all of this, but I have got to tend to business for 30 or 40 minutes. C'mon, I'll buy you a birthday drink. I don't want you to get away or forget where we were."

He sipped a glass of white wine while I tickled the eighty-eight and sang along. I couldn't have told you an hour later what numbers I did that set. My mind was on neither lyrics nor music. I could think of nothing else but getting back to the coffee shop to listen to and tape more of this diatribe. No one in four years of college ever got the education I was getting in one night!

* * *

"Do you remember the telegram we reprinted in *Tennessee Waltz*," he began as soon as we got seated again, "the one from the CIA ordering the 'removal' of Patrice Lumumba in the Congo?"

I did and said so.

"That is called 'political development' at the higher levels," he went on. In the October, 1977 issue of *Rolling Stone* magazine, Carl Bernstein of

Watergate fame, cited official CIA documents reflecting that over the past 25 years more than 400 of America's leading communications resources, including NBC, CBS, ABC, Associated Press, United Press International, Copley News Service, Hearst newspapers, Time, Inc., The New York Times, and Newsweek had received payments, mainly in cash from CIA officials, in exchange for publishing material designed to keep certain operations covert— hidden—from the people. Operations like the King assassination.

I wonder how many decisions in our lives, just yours and mine, have been based on the disinformation broadcast from these sources.

"If you wonder how Dr. King's murder might have assisted political development, recall how the unpopular, dictatorial Civil Rights Bill of 1968 had lost most of its steam in the House of Representatives in March of 1968. Representatives are closer to the people than Senators, and the people, black and white, clearly didn't want this legislation. Suddenly, King is shot. Six days later the bill sweeps through the House 249 to 171. Time magazine noted, "King's death immediately realigned forces on both sides."

A professor, Richard Fagen, said something like: 'Individuals, groups, organizations, and the mass media are all linked together and all interact in the political process ... the deaths of kings occasion a great deal of communication.'

"And do you recall," he said, "that virtually none of the dailies, weeklies, or electronic media ever questioned the propriety of the FBI's involvement in a state murder case. And worse than an absence of debate, there was a discouragement of debate, and what about the destruction and suppression of evidence liberating to James Earl Ray and incriminating of other parties?

"The Civil Rights Act had little to do with racial dignity. Knowledgeable black leaders saw through it. 'This is a hoax on the black people,' snarled Roy Innis, associate director of the Council on Racial Equality. What did the act do? It transformed a sack of potatoes into a federal puree. Federal credit would increase exponentially, sucking millions into usurious witchcraft contracts.

The most insidious result, of course, would be the literal handcuffing of local police to the federal police, which is seen today in the American flag arm patches worn by local law enforcement officers, signalling the formation of a national police force more respectful of appointed professionals in Washington than elected representatives from the neighborhood."

Shades of Jack McLamb, I thought. "Reflect on American life since the murder of Dr. King; the increased controls and loss of individual freedom, the proportionate increase in depression and suicide. How many millions of babies have been sacrificed to the gods of time and money since the warlocks took King? Why are things better only in the pictures and fictions projected in magazines and TV, in the lives of celebrities and rulers? Have the political developers paid the communications media to be Weavers of the Spell who, like Donahue, recruit you into witchcraft by offering you the choice of agreeing with a transvestite or a child molester?"

"What about AIDS? I asked.

His face rose into a sly smile, and he came back with, "What made you ask about that?"

"Your mention of talk shows reminded me that there are those who have some pretty convincing proof that fluoride is a deadly poison placed in the water by design to keep nonproductive people from living too long, and the same faction is very suspect of this whole AIDS thing. Do you think it's a hoax?"

He said, "I'm smiling at your question because I have been a dedicated AIDS stalker for more than four years. I've clipped news articles from all over, spent many, many hours watching celebrities and media hosts interact with AIDS information, spent as many hours consulting with medical doctors, chiropractors, naturopaths, and natural hygienists,and have just written an article on the subject. I've studied extensively the research compiled by Fry and his associates at the College of Life Sciences in Austin, Texas, and quote liberally from their published findings. It just doesn't mesh with what the establishment is saying.

"Of course, Pat, you know that I am not a doctor, medical reporter or even one with any kind of medical background. I'm just a semi-retired, technical professional who has reached a point in his life when he can look around and see what's going on. What's going on is a grand design to destroy first your mind, then your life. The design is AIDS, and it's working far better than the designers ever imagined. Now don't take this to mean that evil conspirators are manufacturing a virus to eat up the world. The deadliness of the AIDS panic is not biological at all. It is a spiritual disease caused by false information.

"The CDC—federal Center for Disease Control—just reported on the front page of nearly every paper in the country that ninety-five percent of the American people *know* that AIDS is a sexually transmitted disease. Considering that a mere seven years ago nobody had ever heard of a deadly and incurable disease called AIDS, this is quite an accomplishment in mass education. Could it have happened without stars and socialites for educators, the nation's communications media for a classroom, and the entire medical establishment as curriculum author? Highly doubtful.

"The CDC were careful not to say 'believe.' They said 'know,' which implies 'certainty.' Up to now, no one has disputed CDC's statement that ninety-five percent of the people are *certain* that AIDS is a disease, that is transmittable and is transmitted through sex. C'mon now, do ninety-five percent of us really know that AIDS is sexually transmitted? Or have we been told enough times in enough media impressions by enough stars and socialites to *think* we know?

"This concerns me, for when a whole population is certain of a subject, it is ready to enact laws on that subject and to be bound by those laws. Do ninety-five percent of us really know enough about AIDS at all to permit ourselves to be bound by AIDS-related legislation? Look at the way the people have allowed their rights to be violated by the drug-control hysteria. Now the government is confiscating million dollar yachts because one of the crew members had one ounce of pot on board, and the owner of the boat wasn't even present at the party!

"We are risking plenty on this so-called 'knowledge.' AIDS laws will give government officials the right to take you into custody without traditional due process safeguards, put you in—worse than jail—hospitals with barred windows, drug you, perhaps even execute you for the sake of 'public health.' This is not a possibility in an Orwellian future. It's already happening.

"Now, I also have some proof that the whole AIDS hysteria lies somewhere between 'grossly overrated' and 'complete hoax.' Take the case of my friend, Robert _____ , who four years ago was diagnosed by a company doctor as AIDS-positive. *(Editors note: Here we maintain Robert's privacy for obvious reasons.)*

"This meant at the time, according to accepted scientific evidence as to how AIDS is contracted, that Robert must either be or have been a homosexual, a philanderer, a Haitian, a needle-using drug addict, or the recipient of a blood transfusion. None of the above applied to him.

"He and his wife lived rather pleasantly isolated lives. Their friends were not wife-swappers, and they were not the type to cheat on one another. Yet there Robert was, caught in the jaws of 'sexually transmitted' killer disease. The diagnosis hit his marriage with the force of a bomb. Many were the nights that his wife cried herself to sleep.

"Robert sensed that it was not his illness that was causing the anguish but rather the ideas associated with it in the newspapers, magazines, and on TV These ideas seemed to be the raw materials his own mind was using to formulate his death. They were urging him to drastic thoughts.

"That's when it hit me that AIDS might be a spiritual disease grounded in social attitudes; a disease that could be regulated up or down by whoever had access to the organs that generated public opinion. It was through Robert's affliction that I began seeing with increasing clarity that AIDS was a means of using health to manipulate thought and behavior.

"Robert perceived the company's laying him off with a generous severance as a blessing because it relieved him of the supervision of the company doctor. He prayed for life. Not long after, Hereward Carrington's book on fasting was loaned to him by a vegetarian friend. Carrington claims that fasting is the solution to all diseases.

"Robert's 20-day distilled water fast is not the subject of my article, but the fact that his body was healed of what was universally subscribed to as a horrifying and incurable disease was my inspiration for writing it."

I was astonished. "Do you mean that, in just 20 days, he was completely recovered?"

"That is exactly what I mean. I saw him in both conditions. A simple fast caused the disappearance within 20 days of most of Robert's AIDS symptoms. And today, more than three years later, he is in robust health, enjoying plenty of exercise and superior nutrition. We have encouraged him to write a book and appear on talk shows to spread the truth about AIDS, but the psychological scars have not completely healed yet... so great is the social stigma of the mere *name* of this disease!

"Why hasn't he done it?"

"He doesn't want to give medical professionals the opportunity to declare that his AIDS only 'appears' to have healed; that it will 'surely' return in a year or two or ten or twenty. This is the horror of AIDS: that once it has been associated with you, it lingers like a curse, subject only to the infallible judgment of what I call medical politicians. This is their stock answer every time someone reduces or eliminates cancer lesions in some part of their body with Laetrile in the famous Ernesto Contreras Clinic in Tijuana. 'Oh you probably never really had cancer but something else,' says the same doctor who diagnosed the cancer in the first place.

"If you will view AIDS through the information I'm offering you—and I'll give you a copy of the whole article—as opposed to what the experts are telling you on the big international media, you will begin seeing a pattern here of a government using a fatly rewarded elite class of licensed political developers, including the medical politicians, the merchant bankers, and the press, to control with terror the lives and thoughts and property of all who trust them."

The conversation hit a lull as he paused to arrange his thoughts, and I decided to fill the void with a question that I had been wanting to ask him since we got together that first time for lunch more than two weeks before. "You know, Jim," I said, "I never knew you to be a religious man in the old days. Has all your research and study into government offenses been the primary impetus that moved you to the study of the Bible?"

"Precisely," he replied. "American Constitutional history began with the people's turning back to God, renouncing and declaring themselves independent of the politics of witchcraft administered by demon liars. It's all there in the Declaration of Independence. Moreover, they knew that human effort alone wasn't sufficient to escape the 'protection' of such brutal masters as parliament and the crown. So they humbly appealed, right there in their declaration, to heaven's providence for support in this dangerous revolutionary undertaking. History proves the appeal worked. "But since you mention it, let's not call my faith 'religious' without defining it. Organized religion is about the greatest enemy Christianity has ever had. I believe in religion, the religion of Paul, the only true religion. There are lots of false religions which only give the word 'religion' an ugly appearance, just as so many false christians have made the word 'Christian' ugly. I can read the Truth for myself. You should too.

"Take it from one who appeals to heaven all the time; it still works, and it's the *only* way to liberate yourself from the liars of this world. My daily prayer is for divine protection as I carry out the heavenly mandate to resist the devil and his lies. If resisting the devil does not cause him to flee from me, then the Bible is a lie and nothing makes sense, and we might as well forget it. But my finding is that the Bible and God's promises are truthful and that truth dynamically asserted *does* send liars away and clear the air. I can say to you from experience: Appeal to heaven for protection, and your resistance will be perfect."

I would have many occasions during the next year to reflect upon that last statement. Meanwhile, I had to get back to work again.

*The real truth of the matter is, as you and I know, that a financial element in the larger centers has owned the Government ever since the days of Andrew Jackson.*

—President Franklin D. Roosevelt

*Give me the control of a nation's money supply And I care not who makes its laws.*

—Meyer Rothschild, International Banker

Beyond the desert horizon the July sun had heaved up like a captive balloon, and the heat was unbearable—even at 7:30 in the morning. Only south Florida or the Panama Canal zone could be worse this time of year. The desert gets a reprieve only because of its low humidity. The temperature was already in the high nineties, would be 110 by early afternoon; and this Saturday morn, on the way to the country airstrip on the southwest side of Phoenix, was like driving through a giant sauna room. We were halfway there before the feeble and struggling air conditioner began to give us some relief.

"It'll be a pleasure to get up north," he said.

"Yeah, I know what you mean," I sleepily replied and facetiously added, "With my luck my agent will book me into Calgary and Anchorage for the winter and Miami and Lauderdale next summer, instead of vice versa."

As we pulled off the pavement and made the turn onto the dirt road, I could see the windsock dangling on the pole a mile away. As we approached, I got a stomach thrill of nostalgia at the second we eyed the beautiful white with blue trim, twin-engined Beech Baron idling at the end of the grass strip, which was more sand than grass. We pulled right up to the fuselage and were stifled by the breath of hot air and exhaust fumes that blasted forward as we stepped out into the desert sun. The pilot was already in the left seat, anxious to get going. With his shielding dark glasses, he appeared as a clandestine character out of a Bogart movie. There appeared to be no one else aboard.

"Thanks for interrupting your short sleep to give me a lift out here," Jim said.

"Glad to do it, Jimmy. "I'll get a nap this afternoon for a couple of hours, and I won't even know the difference tonight." This computer overload my brain has been experiencing the last few hours and weeks may keep me awake, though. How do you suggest I counteract that?"

He smiled confidently. "You will find that your new knowledge is a blessing, not a curse. Just don't trust anything government officials or their accomplices in the corporate press tell you," he said, "... at least not without your personal investigation or confidence that the reporter is committed to truth. I hope you will study the Holy Bible... not as a scholar, but as a child .

"Regardless of your religious conviction, you have to agree that Truth is the light that sends liars fleeing in every direction, and if you become committed to Paul's message, you'll never be deceived by false religions. If you live truthfully, you'll demand Truth from those you depend on for your information and guidance. If they don't give it to you, just resist them out of your life. Let your commitment to Truth be so great that any punishment you might receive for adhering to it will give you pleasure."

With that, he shook my hand, slung his solitary suitcase into the back, jumped into the right front seat next to the pilot and slammed the door. With a "thumbs up," they began to creepily roar away. I returned the signal as I slowly retreated from the backwash towards the car. After a half minute of engine revving and final gauge-checking at the west end, they went roaring down the strip, were airborne in another few seconds, and, with the sunlight glistening off the wings, disappeared straight into the sun. He had seemed to be excited and happy while the feelings I harbored were bittersweet—maybe like watching your mother-in-law go off a cliff in your new Porsche.

He had been set free by God, but, in order to exercise that freedom, he would have to live indefinitely as a captive in his own land; yet he was the most roseate individual I had ever known. I was happy that he was continuing to elude those mendacious government weasels but wondered how long that could go on. Would they really try to kill such a peaceful man if they could find him?

Nearly nine months would pass before I would see him again, and a couple more after that before I would learn the answer to that question. It was July 4th, 1987, and Jim had been on the run for a few days less than three months. As I took the half hour drive back to my apartment, this all served to remind me of "The Fugitive," a hit television show of the sixties which starred David Jansen as a doctor falsely accused and convicted of killing his wife, but who escaped on his way to the deathhouse. It was a serial—running for several seasons—roughly based on the true story of Dr. Sam Sheppard of Cleveland, Ohio who was convicted of killing his wife; first by the newspapers before he ever went to trial, and then by a biased jury later when he did.

After F. Lee Bailey took hold of the case in the early sixties, but after Dr. Sheppard had served nine years, it became pretty obvious to the appellate courts that he would never have been convicted by an unbiased jury had they been able to get the facts, and he was released. More legal lies exposed. I was familiar with the Sheppard case and was disgusted and outraged when I had read of the intentional deception that supposedly honorable people in the media as well as lawyers and even the judge had used to prejudice the jury and the public.

But now that Tupper had been freed by God, when would he ever be set free by man? Would he have to run from job to job for nine years or more too, before anyone would hear the truth. He hadn't even been accused of a common law crime. He had not harmed anyone. But then Jesus Christ never broke any laws either but was persecuted and finally crucified for breaking tradition. What was the difference here? The Bible says there can be no crime if there is no victim. Who is the victim—and what is the crime—when a citizen says he can no longer abide by a tyrant's dictate?

"Let your commitment to Truth be so great that any punishment you might receive for adhering to it will bring you pleasure," kept ringing in my ears. I decided that that would be my watchword, and, when I got home, I lettered it in large print filling a single sheet of stationery and stuck it under the frame of my bedroom mirror. I didn't fully understand everything my friend said, but I knew that he was fully convinced that he was living in Truth. And I knew that anything to which this obviously sane and articulate man could be this committed surely demanded some more attention from me to be certain that he was right... or wrong. I wanted his same plerophory and read in bed for an hour or more that day before falling back to sleep.

When I awoke with a new thirst for knowledge and realized that I had no more new material on the subject, I decided that the next best place to go was to the local attorney that Jim had told me about, Don McPherson. I would have to wait until Monday since all I had was an office phone number, and his home number was probably unlisted anyway. Meanwhile, I knew where I could find the oldest source of law in the world, and it would be a whole lot more informative than talking to a lawyer ... and a whole lot cheaper, too.

When I did call, McPherson was out of town for the next several days or weeks trying a case, but his receptionist was kind enough to invite me by to pick up some free literature which proved to be valuable. Unfortunately, by the time he returned, I was already working a new club in Denver, and it would be two and a half years before we would meet.

One of the turning points on Tupper's Street of Knowledge had been the Holy Bible, and, as I dusted mine off, I realized how long it had been since I had cracked the covers. I grew up in the church, and while I didn't bother to attend anymore—I am usually still asleep on Sunday morning—I still considered myself to be a Christian. Doesn't everybody? I mean, if someone had asked me, I wouldn't have hesitated to say it. I surely wasn't a Hindu or a Buddhist. I went to Sunday School as a child in the Protestant church so I must be a Christian.

Muhammad Ali was the only Muslim I had ever knowingly met, and I figured that conversion of his was just a slick maneuver to stay out of Vietnam. However, I did empathize with his stand against the hypocrisy of his being able to go to Rome in 1960 and win a gold medal for the United States yet not being able to come home and order a meal in a Louisville restaurant while wearing that medal. In his 18-year-old anger he had run from that restaurant and flung his Olympic medal from a nearby bridge into the Ohio river. He blamed all of America's problems on the white race and joined a sect that would exclude all except blacks. Yet when this WASP met him in 1986, he was as cordial as one could be.

Today, after my study of American history, I would like to tell him what a huge mistake he made by denouncing his original name of "Cassius Marcellus Clay" as a "slave name." It is a matter of fact that the original Cassius Marcellus Clay, on whose farm in Kentucky Ali's great-grandparents did live and work as slaves, was actually one of the most hated Abolitionists of his time and a Senator from Kentucky who argued, screamed, and fought to "set these people free." Did the same people who deceived Cassius on his history also deceive Muhammad into a new religion?

But so much for that. We live in a world of deception from morning till night every day of our lives. From the coy high school cheerleader with the kleenex stuffed in her bra to the blowhard politician making campaign promises that he knows are impossible to keep, the whole realm of our existence is permeated with lies. Pretension is a way of life. Hypocrisy has longed seemed to me to be a more grievous human fault than the so-called seven deadly sins.

Hypocrisy is more detestable than pride, anger, envy, gluttony, avarice, sloth, and lust, all of which are more natural and can be more easily condoned. Man is the only hypocritical animal (unless we include the ants) who is deranged enough to make mass warfare on his own kind. He talks one way and acts another, and we can see him at it all over the world ... especially with government spokesmen. Will we ever, as a people, rise above our own hypocrisy and say to these blatherskites, "Get out of my life, you liar," instead of standing in hopeful, silent reverence of every piece of gobbledygook they utter?

But then....

We are born into a world of deception and are at the total mercy of a control system that is so absolute that most people never suspect the deception, let alone inquire into it. In fact, people are so conditioned to a spiritual, economic, and political system that they are horrified when they are confronted with information that does not conform to their pre- conditioning. Most just immediately discredit it and the person presenting the new information. This is known as the Theory of Cognitive Dissonance, which holds that the mind involuntarily rejects any information *not* in line with previous thinking. Very, very seldom do we meet an inquiring person such as Tupper Saussy. Only a few come along each generation.

## SOCIAL INSECURITY

In 1937, after we were deceived into the Social Security contract, there were 40 people working to support one retiree with a smidgeon of one percent being withheld. The American people strode to it like cows to the feed trough. Now, by accepting the government's figures (with sixteen percent being withheld from each, including the employer's contribution), we learn that it takes two workers to support one, except that there is no Social Security fund anyway.

If this piece of information challenges your credulity, write, as I did, to the Social Security Administration in Washington D.C. and request a written tabulation of the total monies now built up in your account after "X" amount of years of working. Their response is guaranteed not only to change your thinking but your mood that day.

In the real world there are no individual Social Security accounts. Why should they bother with that when there is no money in existence? The numbers are extracted from the worker's paycheck and employer's bank account but are then flushed down the federal sewer. The "payments" are created out of thin air in the form of a government check. This "inflation" is created one year through beeps on a bank computer and is vacuumed up the next with something called "income tax," by which time another mess has been made which requires more vacuuming. We have been pre-conditioned to believe that it is "patriotic" to volunteer into this servitude with our painstaking endeavor each April in order to "support the country."

In fact, the Income Tax funds nothing. By going back to your past cancelled checks to the IRS, you will see that each was endorsed over to the Federal Reserve Bank. Agreed, your consumption was restricted because you had less with which to get along that year (some of the excess credit and paper in circulation was reduced), but your "money" funded nothing, unless you consider the bureaucracy that survived another year through the deception, imagination, and trust.

In "Willful Failure to File" and "Tax Evasion" cases (26 USC 7201/ 7203), juries are deceived by the prosecutors into believing that "because this terrible, unpatriotic person did not pay his fair share, you will have to pay more." Utter subterfuge. In truth, no one pays anything. The government creates the credit each year via the Fed, and vacuums it up via the IRS.

## LITTLE BITTY PEOPLE

During the late evening hours of July 2, 1947, Rancher Mac Brasell, who lived on a piece of land about 75 miles northwest of Roswell, New Mexico, heard a thundering clapping of noise outside his small ranch home a shortways in the distance. He wrote it off as simply thunder at the time from a passing storm. However, the following morning he was riding his horse along his border fence line when he came along a ridge and spotted something he couldn't believe. Spread out over an area of about a quarter of a mile, was what appeared to be the debris from some sort of flying craft.

Air Force Major Jesse Marcell was dispatched to the crash site to investigate the debris. Under orders from General Roger Ramey, Marcell never spoke about what he saw until nearly thirty years later. "I was amazed at what I saw," said Marcell in 1976. "The amount of wreckage scattered over the area, it took me awhile to realize that there was something strange about it. What it was I didn't know; I still don't know!"

After inspecting the incredibly odd material that had fallen from the sky, Major Jesse Marcell loaded up his car and a van full of the stuff and brought it back to his home in town. He and his twelve-year-old son began piecing together the debris on their kitchen floor. The material was like nothing they had ever seen. There was writing on the inner surface of the I-beam struts that consisted of geometric designs and figures that were from a strange language. The military moved in on Marcell's house a few hours later and confiscated the debris.

The following day, Air Force News Officer Walter Haas's press release saying that an UFO disc had been recovered was altered by General Ramey to say that it was actually recovered from a fallen weather balloon. Marcell was ordered to appear with the debris for photographers to confirm that story but the remains that Marcell appeared with were not authentic. The actual debris had been replaced with that of a weather balloon. Marcell was ordered not to make the switch known.

Bob Shurkey was an assistant Flight Safety Officer at Roswell Air Force Base when the debris was loaded for transfer. He remembered seeing pieces of material that looked like sheets of aluminum.

What was more astounding to him, however, was a conversation this military officer had with his friend, the town's mortician. The mortician reportedly received an emergency request from the military at Roswell the night of the crash. They wanted to know how many "child size" caskets they had on hand ... three feet, four feet ... and three or four were sent out. Shurkey said that immediately following the crash, everyone involved was transferred out of Roswell to the Philippines and elsewhere.

To this day, the government refuses to comment on the Roswell crash and the allegations that what they recovered might have been a UFO with bodies. Whatever happened at Roswell, what are the reasons that the government must take over forty years to prepare people to hear the truth? Are they really afraid we cannot handle it emotionally if there are little green men running loose? C'mon. Orson Welles inoculated us against that hysteria in 1938. Personally, if and when they show up, I would like to meet and talk to one of the little rascals. Maybe I could get him to take me back with him to visit for a few light years.

Meanwhile, while we are waiting, let's think about the previous story and a similar, more current one for a moment. Do you believe that man has walked on the moon? I did, as I sat spellbound in Biloxi, Mississippi that historic Sunday night in July of 1969. And if Neil Armstrong had done it on his own like Charles Lindbergh, Jr. did his thing in his own craft—with or without the help of General Motors, for instance—there could be no doubt. But can we really *know* it is so? Only government has told us so, and they have proven to be notorious liars.

There would be tremendous propaganda advantages for the United States, however, if the world could be made to believe that NASA made those outer space journeys; not to mention the taxes that could be extracted from people by inventing such a reasonable excuse. Understand, we are not saying that Armstrong and a half dozen others following him did not walk on the moon. We are asking you:

*How do you know that they did?*

## MURDER VIA "SUICIDE"

In 1962, we were told that Marilyn Monroe committed suicide (which she had apparently attempted several times before, the media made sure we knew), and, for twenty years or, more everyone believed it. It was a "fact." We could ask anyone. Much in the same manner that the magazines, books, movies, and daily news media hyped into the next generation that Lee Harvey Oswald was "... the lone, crazed assassin who shot President Kennedy," the Monroe demise was always "certain" to have been a suicide.

Now it is a known fact that she was murdered. Reams have been written in the last decade by knowledgeable people (such as her ex-husband and a Los Angeles private detective) proving the evidence of her murder was covered up by police and even the autopsy doctor. For some time her house had been wired for eavesdropping. She had had a sexual liaison with at least two of the Kennedy brothers, the President and the Attorney-General, and was planning to call a news conference on the Monday following her death to expose this information to the public.

An additional soupçon is the farrago of witnesses who placed Bobby Kennedy at Marilyn Monroe's house at 5:00 p.m. on the day of her death. A later investigation of telephone company records revealed that there were eight phone calls from Marilyn's house to the Attorney General's office in Washington during the last six weeks of her life. Of course, she may have been returning the attorney general's calls because he had solicited her advice on how to best handle the integration of the University of Mississippi with the arrival of James Meredith the next month. Also, she may have had prior knowledge of the Cuban missiles and was phoning to warn the Kennedys in an attempt to avert what became the "October Crisis." Or maybe she was really calling for Ethel and kept dialing the office number by mistake.

## OIL FLEECE

In 1974, when gasoline was 40 cents a gallon, we were told that the Arabs were holding us hostage and the price of oil and gas was about to triple. Sure enough, in 1975 gasoline was over a buck a gallon and the profits of Exxon, et al, began to triple every quarter what they had been in the previous year. Were the Arabs really the bad guys?

## WATERGATE AND IRANGATE

'Nuff said.

## GOVERNMENT DIRTY WORK

There is a former FBI informer and admitted CIA hired killer by the name of Jules "Ricco" Kimble in the El Reno (Oklahoma) Federal Penitentiary (double life sentence for underworld murder) who has confessed to being part of the conspiracy to murder President Kennedy. In an exclusive interview with the BBC, he also admitted doing dirty work for the government in the Ku Klux Klan, participating in the Bay of Pigs fiasco, and even flying into Charley Brown airport in Atlanta to pick up James Earl Ray and fly him to Montreal in 1967. It was his CIA contact that provided Ray with the alternate ID he needed to travel internationally after the King murder. Judge Jim

Garrison, the former New Orleans D.A. who did such extensive investigative work on the first Kennedy murder, says that every single piece of information that Kimble gave them turned out to be true. This, of course, has to mean that everything (of importance) that the government has told us about the King/Kennedy murders is false. Kimble did not, however, implicate Ray in the actual shooting of King.

## MURDER VIA PATSY

The world will never know the full story of the high level plot and coverup of the murder of John F. Kennedy; not even in the year 2039 when the records are supposed to be unsealed. But if you will look very closely at a super-slowed-down version of the "Zapruder Film," the only movies taken of the actual assassination in Dallas that day, you will see some very interesting antics performed by William Greer, the driver of Kennedy's limousine; some things that happened too fast to be noticed even by local businessman Abraham Zapruder as he shot the film or by any of the hundreds of horror-stricken witnesses, all of whom were focused on the exploding head of the President right before their eyes![1]

During the mini-moments after Kennedy clutches his throat but before he is obviously hit from the front the last time, driver Bill Greer turns around and points something directly over the seat at the President; something that reflects the sun. The car is precisely in front of the camera at that second in a proximity that was never equalled in the rest of the film, before or after the fatal shot. Following the explosion of Kennedy's head, this glistening instrument in Greer's hand immediately pulls back and seems to disappear into the inside pocket of his coat as he floor-boards the Lincoln towards Parkland Hospital.

The autopsy doctors reported that the fatal shot hit Kennedy in the left temple. The Warren Report says that Oswald did it from the School Book Depository which was at Kennedy's right rear. Skeptics, like New Orleans District Attorney Jim Garrison et. al., say that it came from the "grassy knoll" which was at the limousine's right front. Either position would have had an

---

[1] We have been told over and over by the news media through the years that the Zapruder film was the only film of the actual murder. Not true. The House Assassinations Committee in 1978 heard testimony from a woman named Beverly Oliver who had stood across the street from Zapruder and had seen (through her Super-8 lensfinder as she filmed) the rifleman shooting from the grassy knoll. The FBI confiscated her film the next day with the promise to return it after it was copied. She is still waiting and has been told that the Agent, whose calling card from that day is still in her possession, is dead.

impossible target to Kennedy's left temple unless his head were turned, and it was not. The 8mm movies show him looking straight ahead at Texas Governor John Connally in the right center seat in front of him. This position, however, does make a diametrically perfect focal point of the left temple for the driver.

Another interesting scene to ponder is the reaction of Mr. and Mrs. Connally who were already cognizant of the fact that shots were being fired—the Governor had previously been hit—but were still sitting upright. At the moment of the fatal shot, both the Connallys hit the deck as though a bomb has just gone off inside the car.

Because I own a bootleg copy of the Zapruder film, edited in normal, slow, and super-slow motion with stop-action, I have watched this scene literally hundreds of times with dozens of friends and acquaintances over the years. No one can see this action take place at normal speed, but it is obvious in super-slow motion. Many believe that it could be movies of the actual final shot that finishes President Kennedy. None casts it aside as unimportant.

Most see it as inconclusive, but something that should have been investigated. The fact that it never was; that it was never even mentioned by any writer inside or outside of government or the Warren Commission leads any student of the case to believe that there was, more likely than not, something to it.

Jim Garrison, now a Louisiana Appellate Judge, who has written two books on the subject, says: "Precisely how many shots were fired, from precisely where and by whom are questions that remain unanswered. But one thing I am quite sure of is that Lee Harvey Oswald did not fire at anyone on November 22nd, 1963. His negative nitrate test, his abysmal marksmanship record in the marines, his generally unaggressive personality, the poor quality of the Mannlicher/Carcano rifle he allegedly bought through the mail and used, and the lack of any evidence in the Tippet murder all confirm that he killed no one; that he was merely, as he claimed, 'a patsy.' "

## MURDER VIA ENDORSEMENT

In December of 1941, we were told that the Japanese surreptitiously "and without warning" bombed Pearl Harbor. Now it appears that the real "Day of Infamy" was that November election day thirteen months earlier when Americans re-elected Franklin Roosevelt[2] to be President. Pearl Harbor was a

---

[2] "And while I am talking to you, fathers and mothers, I give you one more assurance. I have said this before but I shall say it again and again. "Your boys are not going to be sent into any foreign wars."

— (Fireside Chat, 10/30/40)

setup. Authors John Toland and Joseph Lieb and others have much documented evidence that Roosevelt, Cordell Hull (Secretary of State at the time), and several of the Pentagon Brass had broken the code of Japanese Intelligence (at least a week before). They knew precisely when the attack was on the way but kept quiet about it. In order for the U.S. to enter the war, the American people would first have to be rallied by the provocation of an outrageous attack. Secretary of War Henry Stimson recorded in his diary: "The question was how we could maneuver them (the Japanese) into firing the first shot without too much danger to ourselves."

Culpability for the disaster was admitted in 1944 when Army Chief of Staff George Marshall implored Thomas Dewey, F.D.R.'s election opponent, not to mention in campaign debate what he knew. Jonathan Daniels, F.D.R.'s administrative assistant, later said, "The blow was heavier than he (Roosevelt) had hoped it would necessarily be ... But the risks paid off; even the loss was worth the price." We wonder if the parents and wives of the more than 2,400 Americans who died that day would agree.

## KAL 007, THE MASS "MURDER" THAT NEVER HAPPENED?

On August 31st, 1983, over the northern Pacific or Bering Sea, maybe in the immediate proximity of Sakhalin Island and maybe not, Korean Airlines Flight 007 was bushwhacked by Russian fighter jets, hit twice with rocket blasts and, reportedly, crashed with no survivors. Americans were incensed.

Georgia five-term Congressman Dr. Larry P. McDonald, arch-conservative, scion of the John Birch Society, and Purveyor of Truth was on that plane. Later evidence showed little likelihood (Japanese radar had initially confirmed that the aircraft had landed) that such a crash landing in the water could have taken place, but every theory as to what actually did happen was based on little more than speculation—until now.

The Toronto *Saturday Sun* on October 19, 1991 carried a story written by William Stevenson in which it was stated: "Western Intelligence Agencies are now studying evidence from other sources that Flight 007 made a soft landing in shallow waters and all 269 persons on board were not killed."

Avraham Shifrin is Executive Director of the Jerusalem-based Research Centre for Prisons, Psychprisons, and Forced Labor Concentration Camps of the USSR. He is considered to be the top authority in the world on Soviet Prisons. He should be. He spent ten years in Soviet camps and another four in exile before he was allowed to return to his home in Israel.

In July, Shifrin issued the press release which later spawned the blurb in the Toronto newspaper. His press release received little attention from the national media in spite of the fact that it mentioned Congressman McDonald and several other identified 007 passengers being sighted in actual places. The Centre's press release outlined and detailed many astounding, documented facts, such as:

After descending from 35,000 feet to 16,000, the plane's captain requested and got permission to *reduce his speed of descent* from 4,750 FPM to 1,875 FPM and continued to descend gradually for another eight minutes.

At one point during those eight minutes the plane, which was heading *away from* Saklahin at the moment of attack, made a 180 degree turn and started moving *toward* Sakhalin looking for a spot to make a forced landing.

The Boeing 747 landed on water to the north of Moneron, not far from Port Nevelsk. The water is shallow, the plane did not sink, and the people began to disembark on the emergency floats. All experts agree that, in the case of uncontrolled plummeting, a Boeing 747 could be seen on radar screens for only two minutes, while in fact 007 was seen for at least twelve minutes. The normal descent procedure from an altitude of 35,000 feet for such a plane takes about 15 minutes.

The pilots of 007, having a radio connection with Japan for nearly an hour after the attack, never transmitted the "Mayday" emergency message, which would be logical and quite normal to expect of the pilot whose plane is out of control and cartwheeling toward the sea. Instead, he reported the decompression and their intention to reach a certain altitude—which would be absolutely senseless in the case of a plane uncontrollably plummeting from the skies.

Fifty minutes after the attack, an officer-on duty at the Japanese Narita airfield heard on the radiophone the voice of KAL 007 Captain Chon Biun In reporting a safe emergency landing. This was confirmed in the USSR by Soviet correspondent Sergei Agafonov who had been shown a tape of this radio transmission by a reporter of the Japanese "Asakhi" TV in Moscow.

This was reported in the USA by investigator John Kappel. It was finally confirmed by the Soviet central newspaper *Izvestia* along with the fact that the plane had made an emergency landing between Moneron and Sakhalin.

Tommy Toles, Congressman McDonald's press aide, received a call a few hours after the attack from S.K. Luh, manager of the Korean Airlines office in Los Angeles, informing him: "I have just received information from our office in Seoul that the U.S. Embassy in Korea has informed the Korean government, Minister of Foreign Affairs ... that the plane has landed in Sakhalin."

This landing was confirmed by FAA. representative Dennis Wilhelm in Tokyo who was advised by his Japanese counterpart, Mr. Takano, that "Japanese self-defense force confirms that the Mokaido radar followed Air Korea to a landing in Soviet territory on the island of Sakhalinska ... and it is confirmed by the manifest that Congressman McDonald is on board."

The Soviet coast guard under command of KGB General Romanenko alerted all its vessels along the coastal line as soon as it received information that a plane had been shot down. Therefore, the Soviet patrol boats approached the plane almost immediately upon its water landing and received on board all the plane people. By order of General Romanenko, all the passengers and crew were transported to a coast guard base. The passengers luggage was unloaded, also, and transported to the coast guard base, further indicating a relatively safe landing.

General Romanenko reported on the incident and his consequent actions to the Far-Eastern District Army commander General Tretyak, and the latter transferred it further to Andropov that Flight 007 had not crashed. As a result, General Romanenko received Marshal Ogarkov's order to tow the plane from the shoal to deeper waters and sink it. It was also ordered that the passengers be transferred to a KGB guarded camp on the mainland (Soviet Gavan), while Congressman McDonald was to be sent, strictly guarded and incognito, to Moscow, along with the plane's pilots.

General Romanenko was ordered to keep a strict secret whatever concerns the fate of the plane and its passengers and to insist that the plane had crashed into the sea killing all on board. At the same time the Soviet Union released an official TASS statement "confirming" the crash of the plane and the deaths of everybody on board.

It is interesting to note that sometime after McDonald and the other passengers disappeared into the bowels of the Soviet gulag, General Romanenko himself disappeared, too. His name has been erased from the KGB computers and such a man seems to have never existed at all. Avraham Shifrin's Centre investigation, yet incomplete, has brought them to the tracks of the kidnapped people.

They have learned that Dr. McDonald has gone through a number of prisons in Moscow, among them the Central Lubyanka, Lefortovo, a "special dacha" of the KGB in a suburb of Moscow. His present location may be known by the group, but the unconfirmed information available at the moment cannot be disclosed for obvious reasons. They know some of the camps where the plane people were held and, very likely, are held now. Shifrin's investigation shows that the children from the plane were separated from their parents and safely hidden in the orphan houses of one of the Soviet Middle Asian republics.

The technical members of the interministerial commission were surprised that the divers who were sent to recover the "black box" (the recorder which tells investigators the whole mechanical story of any plane crash) were not asked to look for corpses. They were surprised a lot more when the divers came back flabbergasted by the fact that there were neither corpses nor luggage on the plane. There were no life-saving vests on board and all of the seatbelts were unfastened, unambiguously confirming that the passengers safely left the plane after the water-landing. This officially registered fact of absence of both corpses and luggage on the plane can serve as objective proof that, by orders of the highest Soviet leadership, the passengers and crew of KAL 007 were kidnapped.

Perhaps the most shocking and disgusting information in this report is not all of the above plus much more, but the fact that Avraham Shifrin and his Research Centre transferred the results of their investigation to the United States Senate over one year ago, and no real action aimed at saving the people has been seen so far. He says that their data have been checked there and found to be "trustworthy and conclusive." Does the U.S. Senate and House of Representatives not even *care* that one of its members has been kidnapped and is still being held in a Soviet prison? Ho-hum.

## CIRCUMVENTION VIA SOPHISTRY

Every lie that we are told by government is designed to deceive the people into some new program that is for the "good of the people" while, in fact, it is for the advancement of governmental power and the destruction of God-given laws of freedom. Every Constitutional amendment since the first ten (The Bill of Rights) is indicative of that fact.[3]

But, by far, the biggest lie of all—maybe the biggest lie in the history of the world and undoubtedly the biggest coverup of the twentieth century—has

---

[3] Yes, ladies, even the Nineteenth, which gave you the privilege of visiting the ballot box. Whenever the above statement is made, the most controversial argument becomes the Nineteenth Amendment. We are not arguing against your right to vote or anything else except the above premise. Women's Suffrage helped create divisiveness in the family and contributed another giant step towards democracy. Don't forget that by being registered to vote, you have contracted away your "power of attorney" to whomever is elected; that they may vote for whatever they can be coerced into by a force that is stronger than fear of impeachment or losing the next election. Interviews with experts in subsequent chapters provide more information on the subject.

been the sham perpetrated on a naive public by the Federal Reserve System. Merrill Jenkins called it: *Money—The Greatest Hoax on Earth.*

It wasn't that we didn't have warning. We have been warned since God laid out His laws to Moses three thousand years ago. Godly men and reprobates alike have recognized the evils of paper representing money before the founding of our nation and since. Daniel Webster—and I am not sure which category he falls into—said: "Of all the contrivances for the cheating the working classes of mankind, perhaps none is so effectual as that which deludes them with paper money."

Almost every lie that government promulgates today revolves, in some way, around the bigger hoax of phony money. When it is tackled head-on, the attack is ignored and not responded to. When response is forced, as when it has been carried all the way to the supreme court, the court has refused to rule on it. It is the one lie that supports all the others and the one lie that must be continued to be covered up by government at all costs.

Truth creates so many problems for them, it is no wonder that government representatives don't use it much. As we said earlier, the people could not be so deceived were it not for the complete control of everything—particularly the Congress, media and the churches—that such a scheme affords. From the reading that was picked up in Phoenix and Nashville, I was learning how it is worked on us.

The Constitution, in Article I, Section 10 says that no State shall make any thing except gold and silver and coin and tender in payment of debts. The Coinage Act of 1792 defines a "dollar" as a measurement of gold or silver. The United States Code (12 USC 152) tells us that "The terms 'lawful money' and 'lawful money of the United States' shall be construed to mean gold and silver coin of the United States." These are not the only laws that bind us to Truth in money, but even if they were, it would be enough because these have never been amended or repealed. These are still law.

However, since June 24, 1968, the last day that the government honored its obligation of redeemability, the people have been hoodwinked into exchanging their labor and services for imaginary payment. This leads us to tell you:

## A SCENARIO FAMILIAR TO ANY FARMER

Sixty-six year old Farmer Brown of Tifton, Georgia lumbers into the First National Bank of Tifton to borrow some "money" in 1988. Shylock Smith, highly respected citizen, former Masonic Lodge High Panjandrum and current president of the bank for the last 20 years since his daddy died, invites Mr. Brown into his office for a cup of coffee and a chat. They went to school together 50 years ago and have been friends ever since. In fact, Farmer Brown has been doing business with this bank ever since he can remember and his daddy before him. Nearly every year since he started farming, Mr. Brown has traipsed into this office around February 1st to discuss a "furnish,".some financing to get through until the harvest at which time it can be paid off, hopefully, if not in full, then maybe he will be able to pay some of the principle and all of the interest.

"Well, how much ya' gonna' need this year, Brownie," queries Mr. Smith, after they say their howdies.

" 'bout a half million, it looks like," he replies.

"Whatta' ya' got for collateral?"

"You know what I got for collateral, Shylock ... same danged thing you been gittin' ever' year ... my house, my farm and my equipment."

"Okay, I guess there's no need to send my appraiser out there, we know your place is worth over $750,000. Gimme back your land and equipment titles and sign here."

*A false balance is abomination to the lord but a just weight is his delight.*
—Proverbs 11:1

Now Farmer Brown walks out with a half million "dollars," not tangibly held in his hand, but credited to his bank account and has become the world's most recent victim of Fractional Reserve Banking. Since there are no dollars of gold or silver in the bank, only imaginary "dollars" can be deposited. So with the pressing of a few computer buttons followed by the sound of "beep, beep, beep," Farmer Brown has had $500,000 deposited to his account. He knows that he has it. Shylock Smith told him so and gave him a deposit slip (more paper) to prove it.

Farmer Brown has pledged his life's wealth but the bank has pledged nothing. The bank has nothing, absolutely *nothing*, to lose when Farmer Brown has a crop failure. They haven't lent any substance for which they traded their own labor. They simply created "money" out of thin air... within the four walls of their own building! If Farmer Brown had considered what the bank had to gain by his success in the fields this year compared to what they had to gain by his *failure,* he would have run from his "friend," Shylock Smith, like a scared rabbit.

Instead, he is now being charged fifteen percent annual interest (more or less) on something that was ninety-five percent *nonexistent* just five minutes ago.

*The rich ruleth over the poor, and the borrower is servant to the lender.*
—Proverbs 22:7

*He shall lend to thee, and thou shalt not lend to him; and he shall be the head and thou shall be the tail.*

—Deuteronomy 28:44

(Part of the curse that God promised His people for disobedience)

*Inflation is nothing accepted for something.*

— Merrill Jenkins, 1971

So what has just happened in that little bank in Tifton, Georgia? The credit supply has just been increased by a half a million "dollars." No silver or gold was mined; no oil was drilled; no crops were grown. Just Presto! and it appeared. With dozens of similar transactions transpiring in thousands of banks across the United States weekly, the banks are inflating the economy multiple-times faster than the Federal Reserve could ever hope to by just printing paper bucks. So the cost of goods and services gradually increases as more and more credit is chasing the same amount (or less) of production.

The slickest trick in the whole chimera is the continuance of *creeping* inflation without *explosive* inflation. This provides for the annual defalcation of property without exposure of the banking scheme. Will it be any surprise to Shylock Smith to see Farmer Brown shuffling into his office next year or the next, hat in hand, looking for some financing? The scene looks and sounds like this:

"Hello Shylock."

"Hi ya' Brownie! It's great to see you again!" (You bet it is. It is time to pay the piper.)

"Shylock, You know I didn't do too good last year, like everybody else, and I need some money to plant a crop. I got just a little to get started with, but you know that the cost of seed is up, fertilizer's up, labor's up, poison's up, fuel's up, and I need to increase that loan." (Of course, Shylock Smith is aware of all this; it is part of the master plan.)

"What else have ya' got for collateral, Brownie?"

"Nuthin,' you already got it all."

After a minute or two of histrionic shuffling and reading of papers, Shylock Smith says, "Well, Brownie, you know that you haven't reduced that principle a bit since you initiated this loan. All you've done is pay the interest. You know, we've got our banking regulations that I just can't fudge on in this day and time, you know, with the, uh, economy being so fragile and all, so, uh, if you can't make some other arrangements, I guess we're just going to have to foreclose. I am sorry."

So Farmer Brown ambles out of the office and out of the bank with his tail tucked between his legs and he swears under his breath. "Damn, if daddy were alive today, he'd kill me. I blew the family farm."

No, he didn't blow it at all. *It was stolen from him.* Just as surely as if the Mafia had come with guns and kicked him off the place. The bank loaned him thin air, thereby having nothing at risk, charged him extortionary rates of interest from the first day (fifteen percent interest on a $500,000 loan from which only $25,000 or five percent was the bank's obligation to the Federal Reserve, yields $75,000 interest the first year), purposely inflated the economy with the cooperation of the bank's partners in crime nationwide, then confiscated the only real property that was at risk in the deal when the "borrower" finally couldn't pay.

When one has *unlimited* funding at his finger tips, what prevents him from manipulating the whole economy? What prevents the Chairman of the Fed from creating credit with which to sell the market short to pull down the price of corn, wheat, or pork bellies? Why would he want to do that? To prevent the farmer from making enough profit to pay off his loan. What prevents this from happening when so much power is at the fingertips of a few? Nothing. It happens several times every year.

Why is this not generally known? Because complete control of an economy also provides complete control of the media which means complete control of the public's knowledge. What do you really know about the activities of our government except what you see and hear on your television or read in your daily newspaper?

Why do all of our politicians chirp about our "great democracy" when our Constitution guarantees to every State in the union "a *republican* form of government?" We are not arguing semantics here. Nor are we speaking ofj political parties. James Madison wrote in Federalist Paper #10 that "A democracy will be as short in its life as it is violent in its death." And ... "Democracies have ever been found to be incompatible with personal security or the rights of property." This is no semantical debate.

Each reminds me of two big jungle cats. One, the Republic, is a lion with that majestic bearing, the leonine mane of hair; truly the king of the beasts. The other, the Democracy, is a fierce, raging tiger that will turn on man whenever it gets hungry. I'll wager that a few million witnesses around the world who have been raked by this irony, as well as the founders of our nation—could they speak—would not dispute my metaphor.

Our founders knew the evils of a democracy and carefully took the steps to avoid it. What happens if your majority are tax consumers? If you have a tax consuming majority, what will stop them from taxing the minorities to buy goodies for themselves? When the majority taxes the minority, how long will the minority continue to produce taxable goods and services?

A Constitutional Republic, such as the United States of America, is set up with rule by law. The majority rule ends at the ballot box where we elect our representatives to oversee that Republic and law. Each takes an oath to "uphold and defend the Constitution of the United States." When that republic evolves into a democracy, such as in the United States today, fifty-one percent can be brainwashed into overriding that supreme law and force the other forty-nine percent to do whatever. It then is no longer rule by law (God) but rule by man.

Here is how the *Soldier's Training Manual* issued by the War Department in 1928 correctly defined *democracy* and *republic*:

## DEMOCRACY

A government of the masses. Authority is derived through mass meeting or any other form of direct expression. Results in Mobocracy. Attitude toward property is communistic—negating property rights. Attitude towards law is that the will of the majority shall regulate, whether it is based on deliberation or governed by passion, prejudice, and impulse, without restraint or regard to consequences. Results in demagogism, license, agitation, discontent, anarchy.

## REPUBLIC

Authority is derived through the election by the people of public officials best fitted to represent them. Attitude towards property is respect for laws and individual rights, and a sensible economic procedure. Attitude towards law is the administration of justice in accord with fixed principles and established evidence, with a strict regard to consequences. A greater number of citizens and extent of territory may be brought within its compass. Avoids the dangerous extreme of either tyranny or mobocracy. Results in statesmanship, liberty, reason, justice, contentment and progress.

Now isn't it strange that by 1952, the new issue of the *Soldier's Training Manual* began the same subject by saying: "Since the United States is a democracy...?"

Have you ever found yourself praising our great "democracy?" If so, you were parroting another portion of that great deception which was planted firmly in your mind by the educational system and news media. Please don't allow this to make you feel stupid. You are human. If you hear something often enough from others and repeat it over and over yourself without being challenged, you become 100% certain, without a doubt, that what you are saying is true and begin to speak it more confidently and emphatically as your conviction grows, although you have never bothered to check the facts.

The bastardization of our system by the word "democracy" is only one example of the verbicide committed by spokesmen of government. Ask the IRS to define the word "dollar" for you and prepare yourself for two things: A good laugh; closely followed by a telephone call inviting you in for a tax audit.

James Thurber said, "Let us not look back in anger, nor forward in fear; but around in awareness."

> *The issue that has swept down the centuries and must be fought sooner or later is The People vs. The Banks.*
>
> —Lord Ashton, Lord Chief Justice Of Great Britain

> *But, if you wish to remain the slaves of Banks and pay the cost of your own slavery, let them continue to create deposits.*
>
> —Sir Josiah Stamp

# CHAPTER SEVEN

## NINETEEN EIGHTY FOUR

*Men never do evil so completely and cheerfully as when they do it from religious conviction.*

—Blaise Pascal

S omeone—a teacher, a scoutmaster or maybe it was in Sunday School—told me a long time ago that whatever you accept as your source of Truth will be your god. The King James version of the Holy Bible has always been my source although, like I said, I got so blasted smart in my adult years that I didn't get around to referring to it very much anymore. It had taken a swift verbal kick from my old friend to make me hunger again. I had known for a long time, like everybody else who was over forty, that something was wrong in the great United States of America, but I had never thought that solutions could lie farther away than the U.S. Constitution.

I was some right ... but more wrong. I found that the basis of the U.S. Constitution went right back through old English law, the rights guaranteed by the Magna Carta in 1215, and all the way back to the Old Testament laws laid down by God Almighty Himself in the Books of Exodus, Leviticus, Numbers and Deuteronomy. Our nation's law wasn't 200 years old but more like 3,000.

I was coming to find out that there is a great deal about this country and how it came to be that I didn't know. You see, history hasn't changed, but somewhere along the way the real story was put on the shelf as we passed down America's history through the years. And, at least in most of our schools and textbooks, we've left out God—the very author of history. If it were not for manuscripts by men like Christopher Columbus and George Washington, it might be impossible to learn the true story. Gary Demar and Ralph Barker of *American Vision* in Atlanta[1] supplied me with these little known truths about our nation's founding:

These words are from Columbus's book entitled The Book of Prophecies:

It was the Lord who put into my mind—I could feel His hand upon me—the fact that it would be possible to sail from here to the Indies. All who heard of my project rejected it with laughter, ridiculing me. There is no question that the inspiration was from the Holy Spirit because He comforted me with rays

---

[1] *American Vision*, P.O. Box 720515, Atlanta, Georgia 30328

of marvelous illumination from the Holy Scriptures. For the execution of the journey to the Indies, I did not make use of intelligence, mathematics or maps. It is simply the fulfillment of what Isaiah had prophesied. No one should fear to undertake any task in the name of our Saviour if it is just and if the intention is purely for His holy service.

It appears that Christopher Columbus, whose very name meant *The Christbearer,* could see something that his companions could not. He showed faith where his critics showed fear. When Columbus finally found land, it was a small island in the Bahamas. Imagine the relief of his crew, several of whom had been close to mutiny, as they set foot on dry land again for the first time in seventy days. Do you know what Columbus did as soon as they had landed? (If your education stopped with public school or university, I don't know how you could.) First, he christened the island San Salvador which means Holy Saviour. Then, he led his men in prayer.

Columbus and his men discovered quite a few islands and when he finally returned home, they were met with a hero's welcome. The entire city of Barcelona turned out while the grateful King Ferdinand and Queen Isabella dispatched a special mounted escort and color guard to guide Columbus to their palace. The city had been decorated in festive colors for the occasion.

The records tell us that when Columbus entered the court of the king and queen, he brought with him tales and proof of lands abundant with spices and gold and dark-skinned natives who were peaceful and friendly and receptive to the Gospel.

When King Ferdinand and Queen Isabella heard these things, they were exceptionally grateful. Grateful enough to thank the One who had opened this door for them. With tears in their eyes, they joined in a song thanking God for the success of the voyage:

We praise thee, O God. We acknowledge thee to be the Lord. All the earth
doth worship thee, the Father everlasting. To thee, all the angels cry aloud,
the heavens and all the powers therein.

I found myself suffering from intermittent flashes of doubt as I tried to imagine the king and queen of one of the mightiest nations of their time, unashamedly and publicly praising God Almighty, and thanking Him for His blessing. It is difficult to visualize such a sincere public display by national leaders in any country today.

About the same time America was being discovered, a priest in Germany named Martin Luther was challenging some of the practices of the church of Rome, and there were other reformers like John Calvin in Switzerland. Starting in 1517, this wave of reformation swept across Europe, eventually reaching the shores of England. In 1534, King Henry VIII broke away from the church in Rome. At that time England and Spain were the two major powers, and their rivalry broke into open warfare in 1588.

In May of that year, the King of Spain sent his entire armada, 130 ships in all, to conquer England. Now the English didn't have much of a fighting force in those days but they did have a powerful ally: a God who answers prayer. The people of England knew the situation would be hopeless if the Spanish landed. They just didn't have the weapons or the army to fight them. So they began praying to God for help and here is what happened:

The Spanish decided to blow the sixty-seven English ships out of the water rather than land their troops. But just about the time the Spanish ships lowered their sails and began to blast away, a gale arose and blew the Armada dangerously close to the shore of Holland. This broke up their formation and allowed the smaller, more maneuverable English to move in and set fire to many Spanish vessels. Battered by the Atlantic waves and English shot, the Armada was defeated. England was saved! Coincidence? Maybe, but read on.

Holland's government acknowledged God's intervention by striking a coin which said, "Man proposeth; God disposeth—1588." On one side of the coin is a sinking ship, and the other side shows four men on their knees praying.

Only a short time later there were a number of Englishmen who disagreed with some of the practices of the Church of England. And by now with all the countries adopting their own official religions, there wasn't any place for them to go, except to the new world—America.

Two groups of Christians in England, the Pilgrims and the Puritans, had the same vision in mind for America: to form a nation where the government would be established according to the Scriptures. They had studied the Bible diligently to find the principles they needed to govern a society. The Pilgrims temporarily took refuge in Holland to escape the persecution they were receiving in England because of their faith. During the next twelve years there, they endured many hardships which prepared them for their trip to come.

In September of 1620, 102 hearty souls set sail for America. The Pilgrims were armed with a working knowledge of how to apply God's principles to all situations, including civil government, and they also had experience in persevering under tough conditions. When they left, they fully intended to land in what was then northern Virginia.

When unusual wind and weather conditions caused the *Mayflower* to land several hundred miles north of the area specified in their original charter, those aboard were forced to draw up their own governing charter: the *Mayflower Compact*. The importance of this *Mayflower Compact* is that it allowed the Pilgrims to establish a civil government which was based on the laws of God. William Bradford, the Governor of their new colony, told us in his diary why they came. "A great hope and inward zeal they had of laying some good foundation or at least to make some way thereunto for the propagating and the advancing the gospel of the Kingdom of Christ in those remote parts of the world. Yea, though they should be but even as stepping stones unto others for the performing of so great a work."

The *Mayflower Compact* said, in part: "Having undertaken, for the glory of God, an advancement of the Christian faith and the honor of our King and country, a voyage to plant the first colony in the northern parts of Virginia, do by these presents solemnly and mutually in the presence of God and one another, covenant and combine ourselves together in a civil body politic ..."

Interesting. For the glory of God, an advancement of the Christian faith. It was obvious that the Pilgrims were here to spread the Gospel.

But then they were just one small settlement out of many that would spring up in America. What about the others? Did any denounce Christianity and run Judaism, Hinduism, or Humanism up the flagpole? Hardly. Let's see what the first Charter of Virginia says:

> We, greatly commending and graciously accepting of their desires for the furtherance of so noble a work, which may by the providence of Almighty God hereafter tend to the glory of his divine majesty in propagating a Christian religion to such people as yet live in darkness and miserable ignorance of the true knowledge and worship of God ...

And in Connecticut in 1639:

> ... on the river of Connecticut and the lands thereunto adjoining. And well knowing where a people are gathered together, the Word of God requires that to maintain the peace and union of such a people, there should be an orderly and decent government established according to God.

> —Fundamental Orders of Connecticut

On May 19, 1643, several of the colonies decided to get together and draw up a document they called "The New England Confederation." It is interesting to see what they all had in common:

"Whereas we all came into these parts of America with one and the same end and aim, namely, to advance the Kingdom of our Lord Jesus Christ and to enjoy the liberties of the Gospel in purity with peace."

> These liberties they were seeking did not come all at once. In fact, during the first two years of the Plymouth Colony the Pilgrims almost starved. In case you are one who has been advocating communism, you should know that it has already been tested in this country, and we are happy to inform you that it failed. The Pilgrims' financial backers in England had insisted that they farm in a communal way. Instead of having private plots of land, the colonists worked together and shared the produce. The Pilgrims believed this system was unbiblical,but they tried hard to make it work because they still felt obligated to follow their original agreement with their financial backers.

However, facing their third year of starvation, the elders of Plymouth demanded that the colony embark on a Biblically based free enterprise system in order to prevent their total destruction. This made all hands very industrious. There was much more corn planted than otherwise would have been by any means the governor or any other would use. The women went willingly into the fields and took their little ones with them to help with the planting. Their obedience to God's principles of individual initiative and private property resulted in God's blessings. Their example led William Bradford to write: "As one small candle may light a thousand, so the light kindled here has shone unto many... Yea, in some sort to our whole nation ..." That light did keep shining, and the nation kept growing and prospering.

By 1732, the year of George Washington's birth, America was made up of thirteen colonies. Up until this time, God had blessed the colonies beyond measure. Then, like a slowly dying fire, the Spiritual light began to dim. By the mid-1700's, what had been a blazing light had become only a faint glow. It took the breath of God's spirit to revive our national faith, and that revival was called "The Great Awakening."

"The Great Awakening" created a sense of national unity. This unity helped foster resistance against the expanding power of the British Parliament. By the time a national crisis came, the colonists were ready. That time of crisis came in April of 1775 when the Revolutionary War began. Over a year of fighting followed before the colonies could agree to break their ties with Britain. And then, finally, Independence Day of 1776.

> We hold these truths to be self-evident that all men are created equal; that they are endowed by their Creator with certain inalienable rights; that among these are life, liberty and the pursuit of happiness. That to secure these rights...

Please notice the acknowledgement by the founders that each of us was endowed by our Creator with certain inalienable rights. Our forefathers understood that it was God, not man, who was responsible for supplying them with rights, and they believed enough in those rights to fight for them. The closing sentence of the Declaration portrayed their level of commitment:

> ... and, for the support of this Declaration, with a firm reliance on the protection of divine providence, we mutually pledge to each other our lives, our fortunes, and our sacred honor.

The colonists fought the Revolutionary War *with a firm reliance on the divine providence.* The man chosen to take command of the Continental Army of these new United States believed that the only way we would win this war was with God's help. The day after General George Washington took charge, he issued the following order to his troops:

The General most earnestly requires and expects a due observance of those articles of war established for the government of the army which forbid profane cursing, swearing and drunkenness; and in like manner he requires and expects of all officers and soldiers not engaged in actual duty, a punctual attendance of divine services to implore the blessing of heaven upon the means used for our safety and defense.

(A soldier who couldn't drink and curse?... what was this army coming to?)

Early in the Revolutionary War, the Continental Army should have been defeated. By any gambling odds one could compute, that was a certainty. About the same time the Declaration of Independence was being signed, the British general, William Howe, was assembling an army on Staten Island. Less than two months after the signing, Howe had a well-disciplined fighting force of over 32,000 troops on that island. The British knew that if they could control New York, they would control the Hudson River. In those days the Hudson River split the colonies in half. And if the British could split the colonies in two, they could easily win the war. So our forefathers knew they had a fight on their hands but they also knew what the Scriptures said: that God blesses those who obey Him ... and a modern day miracle occurred.

The British General Howe had 32,000 men; our General Washington had barely 8,000, most of them untrained ragtags. The Americans were gathered near the town of Brooklyn near the western end of Long Island. The British moved in, and on the 27th of August, 1776, the entire Continental Army was surrounded. It was then that two of the strangest events of the entire Revolutionary War took place. First, General Howe did not attack on that day and, to this day, no one knows why he didn't strike when he had an obvious victory. If he had, the war would have been over. Then came an even more unusual event.

General Washington knew that to fight would be suicide and to surrender was out of the question. The only other way out was to transport 8,000 men across the East River, which is more than a mile wide, without the British hearing or seeing them. That night, as they crossed the East River by small boats, not a sound was heard, but time was against them. Before long the inevitable happened. The sun started to rise; except this day it would mean death for the Americans who had not yet crossed. Major Ben Talmadge, one of the American officers there that morning, described what happened:

"As the dawn of the next day approached, those of us who remained in the trenches became very anxious for own safety. When the dawn appeared, there were several regiments still on duty. At this time, a very dense fog began to rise out of the ground and off the river, and it seemed to settle in a peculiar manner over both encampments.

I recollect this peculiar providential occurrence perfectly well. So very dense was the atmosphere, that I could scarcely discern a man at six yards distance. We tarried until the sun had risen, but the fog remained as dense as ever. The fog remained until the very last boat carrying General Washington had departed,and then, as suddenly as it came, the fog lifted! When the British saw that the Americans were escaping, they began firing at them but, by that time, Washington's army was out of range. Then Washington and his army thanked God for His divine intervention. It was a blessing of Heaven realized."

"To attempt government without God," said Washington, "is impossible." Like it or not, twentieth century American, the Bible was once the main source of America's national identity.

The Americans continued to praise God as they fought their way through the war. Many more of these reports of providential acts of God were recorded in diaries and documents before the war ended. God rewarded their faithfulness with victory. On October 18th, 1781, British General Charles Cornwallis surrendered to Washington. While the fighting would not die out for some time yet, the war was over. There was a lot for which to be grateful. While the country celebrated its victory, our founding fathers saw the need for a stronger republican form of government than they had under the Articles of Confederation. This led to the Constitutional Convention of 1787.

For awhile it appeared that there might not be a Constitution at all because each colony was concerned with its own special interests. Disagreements led to the delegates from New York walking out in disgust. When things looked the darkest and the convention seemed doomed to failure, an eighty-one-year-old man, not known to be a Christian, rose to speak. His name was Benjamin Franklin:

> In the beginning of the contest with Britain, when we were sensible of danger, we had daily prayers in this room for divine protection. Our prayers, sir, were heard, and they were graciously answered. All of us who were engaged in the struggle must have observed frequent instances of a superintending providence in our favor. And have we now forgotten this powerful friend?! Or do we imagine that we no longer need his assistance? I have lived, sir, a long time ... and the longer I live the more convincing proofs I see of this Truth: That God governs in the affairs of men. And if a sparrow cannot fall to the ground without His notice, is it probable that an empire can rise without His aid?
>
> "We have been assured, sir, in the sacred writings that except the Lord build the house, they labor in vain that build it. I firmly believe this. I also believe that without His concurring aid, we shall succeed in this political building no better than the builders of Babel. We shall be divided by our little, partial, local interests. Our projects shall be confounded, and we ourselves shall become a reproach and a byword down to the future ages. And what is

worse, mankind may hereafter from this unfortunate instance, despair of establishing government by human wisdom and leave it to chance, war, or conquest. I, therefore, beg leave to move that, henceforth, prayers imploring the assistance of Heaven and its blessing on our deliberation be held in this assembly every morning before we proceed to business.

The convention later voted *not* to have prayer because they could not afford the pittance charged by the ministers. Our own political buildings that *are* Babel proves that Franklin was right; that the USA was later built without God's concurring aid, but that makes for another whole book.

From inevitable collapse to a constructed republic, the convention, with God's direction and in a very short time, then produced the greatest civil document ever put on parchment. A land governed by "We the People" ... or so we thought. My research and study kept turning up reference after reference to God by our leaders, and, after Washington's Inauguration, at which he gave still another speech praising the Lord for our nation's creation, America enjoyed over seventy years of success and prosperity.

But as we grew as a nation, we also grew too self-sufficient and forgot the God who had blessed us. We allowed our sectional interests to come between us. I can't help hearing "The Battle Hymn of the Republic" echoing in the background each time I read this stirring plea from Abraham Lincoln to the people appealing to them to recognize the true cause of the national calamity:

> ... And, inasmuch as we know that by His Divine Law, nations, like individuals, are subjected to punishment and chastisement in this world. May we not justly fear that the awful calamity of civil war which now desolates the land, may be but a punishment inflicted upon us for our presumptuous sins? To the needful end of our national reformation as a whole people, we have been the recipient of the choicest bounties of heaven. We have been preserved these many years in peace and prosperity. We have grown in numbers, wealth, and power as no other nation has ever grown, but we have forgotten God. We have forgotten the gracious Hand which preserved us in peace and multiplied, enriched and strengthened us. And we have vainly imagined in the deceitfulness of our hearts that all these blessings were produced by some superior wisdom and virtue of our own. Intoxicated with unbroken success, we have become too self-sufficient to feel the necessity of redeeming and preserving grace. Too proud to pray to the God that made us. It behooves us then, to humble ourselves before the offended power to confess our national sins and to pray for clemency and forgiveness."

Intoxicated with success, we are too proud to pray to the God that made us. Is that still true today? Well, yes and no. Millions of Christian Americans may still be praying everyday, but if the government has locked out the God of our founders, what god is hearing? With most of the churches having incorporated and receiving a "501(c)[3]" tax status from Caesar, who really governs what is taught here?[2]    In 1962 the Supreme Court of the United States of America removed State sponsored prayer from our schools. The following year that same court decided that the book which was the very blueprint for the success of this nation could no longer be taught in the public classroom as anything other than an ordinary piece of literature. That book, of course, is ... the Holy Bible.

I was astounded to learn that our nation was born, and grew, on the laws of God. Many of our founders said that they wanted our nation to be a society based on the Word of God. If one needs more evidence of that fact than the historic Declaration of Independence, let him look at *The Federalist Papers* by three of our most prominent founders. But we seem to have lost sight of that vision, and we act like a nation that has lost its memory; a nation that has forgotten what it means to be governed by Biblical principles.

It appears that the only thing we learn from history is that we don't learn anything from history. God has never turned away from us but, evidently, every few generations, we have turned away from Him. Our schools, public and private, teach not that our nation was founded as a Republic, under God, but as a Democracy with the wisdom of man.[3]  I am sad to report that today, as learned at the end of the previous chapter, a democracy is exactly that to which we have evolved. It is praised by our national leaders as something wonderful, but it is doomed to failure. Democracies have never been more than stepping stones to another, more drastic, form of collectivism ruled by one sort of tyrant or another.

It is a note of interest that in 1789, when George Washington became President, there was a king of France, a Holy Roman Emperor who ruled much of Europe, a czarina in Russia, a shogun ruling Japan, and an emperor of China. Of all of these powerful offices, only the Presidency still exists, and his office is not just the head of the executive branch of a Constitutional Republic

---

[2] 501(c)[3] has federal jurisdiction and grants non-profit status. It says that tax-exempt organizations may not conduct any activities which may influence political campaigns/elections. A corporation is a state-created entity which binds a church corportation to any and all state statutes applicable to corporations. One can see why today's preachers chirp: "We should render unto Caesar.." whenever the question comes up.  Yet Section 501(e) tax-exempted churches anyway.

[3] During one of our many incidental conversations, I asked Tupper Saussy, "Just what is a Republic, anyway?" His inconoclastic reply was, "A Republic is what a dictator calls his Oligarchy to make the slaves feel important. As the slaves crave more attention, he calls it a Democracy."—J.P.S.

anymore. It is a ruling throne as powerful as any of the aforementioned, with the ability to manipulate its democratic subjects like puppets on a string.

* * *

From the gloomy streets of London after World War II came a warning of a doomed world of the future. A future of technical marvels that in the hands of ruthless dictators had turned the people into soulless robots. The year was 1984 and though that year has chronologically now come and gone, how close are we? How close?

In the last decade, there has been nothing subtle about the repression in Afghanistan, Iran, or El Salvador, but there are threats to liberty in the West also .... threats of a more subtle kind. There are combinations of repression and computer invasions of privacy; new technologies of surveillance, behavior modification research; things that make people think of words like "Orwellian" or the novel *1984*. Since its publication in 1948, *1984* has been translated into thirty different languages and each represents another nation which has been given a new term for tyrant. He may be "Der Grose Bruder," "Il Grose Fratello," "Grotebroer," or "Big Brother," but the world knows him as the ultimate dictator. He has made his way into the headlines as newsmen try to describe total tyranny. As a synonym for repression, George Orwell's name has been turned into an adjective and enshrined in the dictionary. Behind all of this is a novel that is half satire and half sermon.

Orwell set the story in a future called *1984*, in a city called London and in a country called Oceania. Its ruler was Big Brother. He was never seen in person but was the figurehead for the ruling elite and the focus for the love, and fear, of the people. One of those people was 6079—Smith, W.

Winston Smith worked at the Ministry of Truth revising back issues of newspapers because even the past was under the control of the State. The world was at war in 1984, constantly, as three superpowers and shifting alliances fought for land and resources. A kind of permanent martial law existed everywhere. Police enforced absolute loyalty; sex was unpatriotic; privacy disloyal; and the televisions were equipped to watch back. For Winston Smith, adequate food and cheap government gin were not enough. He fell in love with a woman named Julia and tried to become a traitor to Big Brother, but the Thought Police had their electronic eyes on him, and he and Julia were arrested.

Under the electronic pain machine, Winston learned to believe that if the State wished, two plus two could equal five. Finally he was taken to Room 101 where torture was planned to play on a person's deepest fear. For Winston, they had prepared a mask filled with live, hungry rats, and his last defenses fell. "Do it to Julia," he cried, "Not me. Julia!" They released him then to drink his gin under the watchful eye of the telescreen. The struggle was finished. Winston was cured of his insubordination malady. He loved Big Brother .... even more than Julia.

That's the outline of George Orwell's novel, *1984*. He seems to have been on target with everything and, maybe, miscalculated only with the subtlety and covetousness with which governments carry out their terror. It is a portrait of the complete political evolution from God's law to man's law. He said that if you want a picture of the future, imagine a boot stamping on a human face forever.

Best-selling author Michael Crichton writes that biotechnology promises the greatest revolution in human history. By the end of this century, he says, it will have outdistanced atomic power and computers in its effect on our everyday lives. In the words of another observer, "Biotechnology is going to transform every aspect of human life: our medical care, our food, our health, our entertainment, our very bodies. Nothing will ever be the same again. It's literally going to change the face of the planet."

Efforts to engineer paler trout for better visibility in the stream, square trees for easier lumbering, and injectable scent cells so you'll always smell of your favorite perfume may seem like a joke, but they are not. Indeed, the fact that biotechnology can be applied to the industries traditionally subject to the vagaries of fashion, such as cosmetics and leisure activities, heightens concern about the whimsical, and often times terrifying, use of this powerful new technology. For nearly a half century a primary influence upon all our lives has been the fact that Russia exists as an implacable, unswervable danger to our way of life.

This fear justified confiscatory taxes, mushrooming government spending, various "police actions" in which a good many "policemen" died, for a long time a peacetime draft, and, although they are much less in the public spotlight, spy satellites. I believe most Americans would be surprised to learn of the enormous size of the satellite network, not only in terms of the hardware in space, but also the hardware on earth required to service it, and the large numbers of people involved in the systems.

Of course, all of this expenditure is justified by that old bugaboo, Communism. But now that we are to believe Communism is being "discarded"—at least in its most obvious and inefficient form—won't this satellite network be allowed to fade away? Of course not. In fact, as the idea of one-world government becomes ever closer to reality, the existing satellite systems fit into the picture so perfectly that one might almost believe that surveillance of our Russian "enemies" was merely a ruse to get the stuff into space in the first place. We are assuming that gathered under one super-government, by means of one-world currency, there might be among us at least a few individuals who feel sufficiently oppressed to attempt to regain their freedom with the use of a sort of underground.

But Big Brother is watching, and far more efficiently than George Orwell ever dreamed. The enemy is not at our door. It is inside our homes and has been for a generation or more.

For almost twenty years now, a satellite named Rhyolite has been able to monitor telephone calls from space. In fact, it can monitor 11,000 such calls simultaneously. Additionally, it can listen in on walkie-talkie communications and intercept telemetry signals. Newer satellites of the same type, over twenty-two thousand miles in space, can intercept microwave transmissions and radio traffic.

Of course, there are the old plain-Jane photographic type spy satellites, too. Armed with image-enhancement devices, these can give incredible data. For instance, the KH-11 satellite, equipped with something akin to a telescope with flexible mirrors to adapt to the distortions of the atmosphere, can read the license plates of the cars in your driveway. You should be careful not to leave any material critical of government, such as a copy of this book, in your yard or in the back window of your car. The reconnaissance expert who studies the images from this satellite may be able to read the cover and have you and your family put on the "enemies" list.

So we are free men and women, right? Sure we are. Of course, the government can keep track of our spending via the paper trail we leave with checks and credit cards. When the magnetic stripes are put into our new currency, it will even be able to tell the amount of money we are carrying as we pass through detectors, without our being aware of it. If we attend a seminar on, let us say, "personal freedom," our license plates may be detected and recorded from hundreds of miles in space. Our phone calls can be overheard without the clumsy and detectable addition of a "bug" to our line; and should we become so paranoid as to communicate by walkie-talkie, even that will be heard by Big Brother. Don't even consider using the ham radio for privacy. An ordinary police scanner can be set to pick up any cellular telephone conversation within the immediate proximity.

It is especially galling that all of this is justified by the need for "security." Does the chicken feel more secure knowing that the hen house is being guarded by the fox? Louisiana Governor Earl Long, little brother of the fabled Huey and who was once railroaded into the insane asylum by his political adversaries, may not have been so crazy the day he advised: "Don't write anything you can phone. Don't phone anything you can talk face-to-face.

Don't talk anything you can smile. Don't smile anything you can wink. And don't wink anything you can nod."

I was not so diffused anymore. I believed I was beginning to see the light. Disgusting as I found the conclusion to be, I realized, as Pogo told us, that "we have met the enemy and he is us!" Or, as Cassius, "The fault, dear Brutus, is not in our stars, but in ourselves."

Today the church is only an embellishment. The churchgoer, all too often, merely decorates his life with occasional attendance. Most have to refer to the dollar bill (FRT) to recall our national motto, "In God We Trust," and the worship of money—rather than God—has become ingrained. Villages are no longer born around a central church, but wherever a bank is built.

*If governments would refrain from regulation (taxation), the worthlessness of the money becomes apparent and the fraud upon the public can be concealed no longer.*

—John Maynard Keynes - 1920

# CHAPTER EIGHT

# BOGUS MONEY, THE ROOT OF ALL EVIL

*He that sacrificeth unto any god save unto the Lord only, he shall be utterly destroyed.*

—Exodus 22:20

The *Communist Manifesto* was written in 1848 by Karl Marx, in some part, and Frederic Engels, probably in a larger part but without the historical credit. There is some evidence to suggest that Marx was an irresponsible bum who spent his life being subsidized by others and lacked the mental fortitude and political background (his greatest ambition being to become a renowned poet) to have created such a document, but was clever enough to steal the authorship after its completion.

On the other hand, if he honestly earned the credit he received for writing *Das Capital* in 1863, then the negative publicity for the previous writing is unwarranted. Whichever is true is not really important in the 1990's, but a basic understanding of the Manifesto is fundamentally necessary for any American attempting to grasp the magnitude of the tyranny that has already enveloped his country. Please bear in mind, this is not another John Bircher screaming about the bogeyman "Communist under every bed," nor do I feel you should harbor the slightest fear of Russia or Red China taking us over ... or even Japan, for that matter. Whoever invented the Kamikaze can't be too smart ... or dangerous.

The world was once believed to be divided into two parts: the Communist world and the non-Communist world. This distinction is made more vivid by the Communists' view that outside of their world nations exist only temporarily, destined one day to be absorbed into their empire, as has happened. It is their creed that this "New World Order," "the wave of the future," is inevitable for all humanity. Over a billion people in this century have been captured or seduced into living out their lives under the "dictatorship of the proletariat." This is enough reason for every American to examine the fundamental doctrine on which Communism was founded.

An even stronger reason would be that Communism consists of ideologies which are completely *contrary* to those of our Christian civilization. Just such a principle as "The end justifies the means" is sufficient to illustrate the point. It is by this principle that the Communists rationalize, without any qualms of conscience, every inhumane and perverse act of cruelty imaginable. Of course, we know that "this could never happen in America." Ask any congressman or schoolteacher, and you will be satisfactorily reassured with a manufactured piece of rhetoric that sounds something like: "Well, with all our problems, this is still the best place on earth to live." How do they know that? And what if it is? Is the west side of hell cooler than the east?

Let's examine the Manifesto's ten planks and decipher them into American life today.

1. *Abolition of property in land and application of all rents of land to public purposes.*

   If the American government wants you off your property, they can either raise the taxes so you can't pay, or the IRS can seize it without benefit of a court order. They may not get your property directly, but you will spend so much time and money defending against them, they will get it eventually.

2. *A heavy progressive or graduated income tax.*

   The colonists started shooting when the tea tax reached fourteen percent. Nearly every American today is burdened by multiples of that with the income tax alone—a "tax" that funds nothing—and yet a tax to which nearly everyone passively submits.

3. *Abolition of all right of inheritance.*

   Probate and estate taxes destroy most of what the next generation expects to inherit from their family's efforts. These taxes serve the same function as income taxes—to take away the excess credit before it can be bid against other hard goods.

4. *Confiscation of the property of all emigrants and rebels.*

   Elden Warman's story is not an isolated case; it is one of thousands. A simple "letter to the editor" criticizing local, state, or federal government policy will be clipped by the IRS and placed in your file. Millions of people today have their names in such a file and are on the fringes of being elevated to "protestor" status as their file expands. Voltaire said, "it is dangerous to be right when government is wrong."

5. *Centralization of credit in the hands of the State, by means of a national bank with State capital and an exclusive monopoly.*

   Money is counterfeited into existence today and loaned to credit-worthy recipients. We have a centralized national banking system known as the federal reserve system. It was funded with state capital and, privately controlled, enjoys an exclusive monopoly.

6. *Centralization of the means of communication and transport in the hands of the State.*

The agencies of government—FCC, FAA, DOT, et al—license and control communication and transportation. Executive order 10995 provides for the takeover of all communications media and 10999 permits the takeover of all modes of transportation.

7. *Extension of factories and instruments of production owned by the State, the bringing into cultivation of waste lands, and the improvement of the soil generally in accordance with a common plan.*

The United States government is prohibited by the Constitution to own land yet it does own enough to equal all the acreage east of the Mississippi River. Corporations are controlled by government because they are created under its seal; government reclaims wastelands and cultivates them, and operates soil improvement programs (which are spoiling more than improving the soil). The federal government is now in more than 850 businesses competing with private enterprise while it also taxes and regulates that competition right out of business.

8. *Equal liability of all to labor. Establishment of industrial armies, especially for agriculture.*

Many mothers have to leave their homes and join the external labor force in order to survive financially (their take home pay usually just about equals the taxes on the dual incomes of the household). Of course, most girls today aspire to careers rather than motherhood. Labor unions and social security form a vast national army of workers. Passage of the equal rights amendment would compel women to do what men do including soldiering in "no-win" wars.

9. *Combination of agriculture with manufacturing industries; gradual abolition of the distinction between town and country by a more equable distribution of population over the country.*

Urban renewal; population control; metro councils; regional government and planning programs; bussing of the school children. Before this century most foods went directly from the earth to the table. Now, most foods pass through processing plants, where they are denatured and divided into as many as one hundred different products, all packaged and distributed for sale in supermarkets. This development has abolished the distinction between town and country, evening out the population nationally. (Paralleling the increase in processed foods is an increase in doctors, medicines and hospitals, all rigidly controlled by government.)

10. *Free education for all children in public schools. Abolition of children's factory labor in its present form. Combination of education with industrial production....*

The public schools are free, making it easier for the children to be indoctrinated with only what the government wants them to know. For example, democracy, abhorred by our founders as an evil form of government, has been taught in the public schools for most of this century as "American," yet the word cannot be found in our constitution or declaration or any founding documents anywhere. We have been educated into ignorance.

Private schools are of little or no improvement. These schools, teachers, books and materials are also approved by the department of education. Government schoolmeisters do not want us strong or free. Even education secretary, Lauro F. Cavazos, termed the reading and writing abilities of U.S. students "dreadfully inadequate." With only six percent of high schoolers capable of computing simple interest and twenty-six percent able to find Greece on a map, "dreadfully inadequate" seems a dreadfully inadequate understatement.

Let us next consider the following Executive Orders, now recorded in the *Federal Register* and therefore accepted by Congress as the law of the land, that can be put into force at any time the President wants to declare an emergency:

| | |
|---|---|
| 10995— | All communications media seized by the Federal Government. |
| 10997— | Seizure of all electrical power, fuels, including gasoline and minerals. |
| 10998— | Seizure of all food resources, farms and farm equipment. |
| 10999— | Seizure of all kinds of transportation, including your car, and control of all highways and seaports. |
| 11000— | Seizure of all civilians for work under Federal supervision. |
| 11001— | Federal takeover of all health, education and welfare (as if they hadn't already). |
| 11002— | Postmaster General empowered to register every man, woman and child in the United States of America. |
| 11003— | Seizure of all aircraft and airports by the Federal government. |

11004—     Housing and Finance authority may shift population from
            one locality to another.

11005—     Seizure of railroads, inland waterways, and storage.

11051—     The Director of the Office of Emergency Planning is
            authorized to put Executive Orders into effect in "times of
            increased inter-national tension or financial crisis." He is
            also to perform such additional functions as the President
            may direct.

Democracy is not only communism in the embryonic stages, democracy is
communism is democracy.

The American Republic was seduced by gangsters and artificially
inseminated with paper money. She carried her baby called "socialism" full
term and has already given birth to a bastard child who masquerades under the
name of "Democracy" and has twin brothers all over the world. Sometimes
these brothers fight, but only for as long as their omnipotent "Big Daddy"
allows them to. We have arrived at a point where it is now inevitable that this
country will go through a decade or more of most of us picking rags, and we
will not even have hanged the ones who did it to us.

> When the ship has sunk, everyone knows how she might have been saved
>
> —Italian Proverb

Surely there are individuals and groups of individuals that are working
together in a cartel to deprive their fellow men of their property and perhaps
even their lives, but that is nothing new. There have always been men of
criminal mind, and there always will be. Are they just a handful of
international bankers who have usurped unbelievable power through the
control of our money?

Is it a group whom we can label like the CFR (Council on Foreign
Relations), The Trilateralists, the Masons, the Catholics, the Mafia, or a
tremendous spiderweb combination of all of the above and a dozen more,
controlled by one ultimate Grand Ding-Dong who will evolve into the
Anti-Christ and eventually butcher all God-loving people? Or has the whole
"conspiracy theory" been blown out of proportion because someone suggested
it years ago, and it made wonderful typewriter fodder the last couple of
generations?

Who cares? You can spend a lifetime in that swirling eddy of confusion
and never be any farther down the road to Truth than when you started. The
conspiracy theorists have been observed for years. Some of them approach the

problem with reasoned argument; others with frenzied speech filled with invective and hatred. Both want to "expose" the conspirators, but to what goal? What has the "conspiracy" (whatever its size) to fear from exposure? Are the enlightened citizens going to come out and kill them in their anger? Not likely. Are they going to form vigilante groups and arrest the conspirators? In what court would they be tried? And by their own judges?

Does the Mafia quiver and quake and withdraw from its plans because newspapers print distasteful articles about their activities? Hardly. And neither will any criminal government group. They have no reason to fear exposure. They do have reason to fear the use of force against them and that is the sole reason for the strengthening and interminable movement towards gun confiscation from the people.

So what is the point of a captured nation fearing invasion by a foreign "power?" None; unless the people of that nation are unaware that they are already captured. In that case, the fear factor can be very useful in the collection of "taxes" for their "protection."

* * *

I lucked out and grabbed a gig in Denver at the Hilton while the August weather was so unbearable in Arizona. The reception was such that I managed to extend it through September. Then, before the snow flew, I picked up another month in St. Louis before my booking agency, ABC out of Chicago, got my winter set up the way I had hoped they would: two weeks in Atlanta in December, three weeks off for the holidays, and six weeks at "The Jolly Coachman" in Fort Lauderdale. This would take me out of any serious frigid weather anywhere this season and ended my paranoia, for at least another year, of having to spend a winter in a snowbank in Calgary.

While in Denver, I had the pleasure of getting to know the soft-spoken but hard-nosed Director of National Commodity and Barter Association (NCBA), John Voss, who was very helpful with the supply of new information and literature. The National Commodity and Barter Association was founded by John Grandbouche (now deceased) about a decade earlier as an alternative to the Federal Reserve banking system. The legalities of it were obvious.

The First Amendment protects the right of people to associate, and, as members of NCBA, these people could exchange ideas, become politically active and, if they wish, exchange "money" for money ... or fed notes for gold and silver. The government has no power to compel anyone to do business with a private corporation such as the Federal Reserve Bank. Perhaps it would be more accurate to say that they do not have the authority to do so.

If you know John Voss personally, you are sure to give a double-take any Saturday afternoon you tune in a CBS-TV sports program and see Al Trautwig giving the scores in back of the sports desk in New York. Trautwig could have been his twin brother. I took John Voss to lunch one day in late August, and he told me of their upcoming convention on Labor Day weekend to be held at a local church college on the southwest side of town. I paid him my fifty bucks and agreed to come for everything except the Saturday night banquet because, of course, I had a previous commitment.

Before we left, John told me a little about the famous "Good Friday" raid of the NCBA, when the Feds came in and confiscated "around two million" in gold and silver from their offices and two other locations in 1985. He said he had just had a visit from a friend that morning who had repaid a loan of nine hundred dollars which was in an envelope lying on the desk at the time the SWAT team arrived. The cash was taken too, in addition to many, many things which were not named on the warrant. John protested to them that he was familiar with procedure on "Fourth Amendment" raids, and he was retaining his right to stay and watch exactly what was being bundled up, labeled only "miscellaneous," and hauled away. With a cocked .357 magnum placed on his temple, he was told that he had just relinquished that right and was escorted into the hallway.

Some wit somewhere once wrote a short parody to the Golden Rule: "He who has the gold, rules." Further to that might be, I thought, "He who has the guns, takes the gold ... and rules."

John Voss drives without any driver's license. Rather, if you ask him, he *travels* without any license because that right is protected by the U.S. Constitution. A license, I learned, is something that is issued as permission to do what would otherwise be illegal. A driver's license is required in order to transport people or products from place to place but if one desires to *travel* from place to place, by foot, bicycle, horse or even an automobile *no license is required.* The supreme court has ruled numerous times:

> The right of the citizen to travel upon the public highways and to transport his property thereon, either by carriage or automobile, is not a mere privilege which a city may prohibit or permit at will, but a common right which he has under the right to life, liberty and the pursuit of happiness.

—Thompson v. Smith, 154 SE 579.

—Chicago Motor Coach v. Chicago, 169 NE 221.

—Kent v. Dulles, 357 U.S. 116, 125.

—Schactman v. Dulles, 96 App D.C. 287, 225 F 2d938 at 941.

To name just a few.

The State Motor Vehicle Codes constantly refer to the UCC, the Business and Professional Codes, the Revenue and Taxation Codes, all of which are totally commercial in nature. Section 9303 of the California Revenue and Taxation Code (all state laws are almost the same) states:

"Operator" includes someone who hauls passengers or freight on the highways for hire.

But 9303.3 clarifies the difference: "operator" excludes someone who hauls passengers or freight on the highways as long as it is *not* for hire.

It also tells us that an "operator" must pay three percent of his gross receipts and that an "operator" must have a driver's license, all of which, once again, are commercial in nature. John Voss is not an "operator" and, apparently, neither was I and had never been.

The statutes are written by masters of gambit. So why do you and I carry a state drivers license ... and even pay tribute every few years to acquire one? The only answer I could come up with was fear. We are so enveloped in tradition and comfort and ignorance that we fear what the repercussions might be if we do not conform. Isn't that the same reason we file income tax forms every April? Have you ever seen the law that requires you to do so? But isn't compliance with non-laws living a lie?

"The purpose of the State driver's license is not to protect the citizenry against incompetent others who are underaged, overaged, blind, deaf, or crippled," John said, "and I proved it." The purpose of the 'driver's license is to gather more revenue for the State and for control of the people, most of whom are not legally 'driving' anyway and the judicial system knows it.

"A judge in Denver traffic court spilled the beans a few years ago when she told me that because I had applied for and received a driver's license, my Constitutional rights did not apply there. I did some checking in the law books and found that she was absolutely right. The license is a contract which places one in an *equity* jurisdiction, and that supersedes any common law protection. The jurisdiction is pre-decided by the contract and 'rights' never enter into it. In other words, did you or did you not speed or run the stop sign? And, of course, if it comes down to your word against the cop's, as it usually does, guess who wins?

"So I decided, when renewal time came up, not to voluntarily submit to their contract and told the licensing bureau, by certified letter, that I would be happy to take their standard operator's test to prove my competency, but I would not sign any contract or agreement that would cause me to waive any of my God-given, Constitutionally protected rights. When I got no answer, I submitted a second letter with the same request. To this date, five years later, they still have not replied.

"This causes me a little harassment whenever I am stopped for some infraction because the copy of the letter that I carry over the visor of my car makes little impression on the cop. But every time I have taken it to traffic court—four times now, I believe—the judge has ruled in my favor.

"Today, most Americans would go to the courthouse and purchase a *walking license* if some agent of the government demanded it. If their masters demanded, through ordinances, that they purchase a permit to wash their cars, most would comply."

"Not a bad plan for the car wash industry, I thought. Either buy a permit or bring your car in for the professionals to clean it for you. It worked for the insurance companies. Very few states today do not require car owners to purchase automobile insurance.

"How well do you know Tupper Saussy?" I asked.

"Oh, very well. He has been one of our guest speakers at almost every convention we have had since 1982. This will be the first one that I can remember that he has missed .... unless he shows up, of course." He then paused, gave me a baleful eye and said, "Are you looking for him? You're not a government agent, are you? I wouldn't tell you where he was even if I knew."

"No," I chuckled, "I'm not looking for him and I'm not an agent. I did know him in one of his previous lives, however. We used to play a little music together. His plight and flight is what has turned me on to all this. I wish I knew more about what he has discovered and that's why I want to attend your convention."

"When you get to St. Louis, look up Dave Wilber," John said. He spent a year or so at Leavenworth as a political prisoner and can tell you a lot about doing battle together with Saussy. Get him to tell you about Amos Bruce, Tupper's renegade researcher who just died last year. There was a character from the story books. I don't have Dave's phone number, but he's in the book; he's in the real estate business on the south side."

The NCBA convention that weekend was refreshing. I met Connie Jansen, wife of the former Congressman who was still incarcerated at the time. She was one of the speakers and gave us an update on her husband's case and condition. There was a lawyer named Jeffrey Dickstein who had had some success defending tax patriots and was currently testing the validity of the 16th Amendment in the Kentucky courts.

The most entertaining, yet disturbing, speaker was Larry Lopez-Alexander, a former Denver County Judge who had been drummed out of the job by his own peers—lawyers who had become infuriated at him for refusing to accept "plea bargains" because he had continued to mete out harsh sentences against drunk driving offenders. That action brought a quick response. In 1982, various defense attorneys periodically delivered a message to the judge. The aim of those lawyers was simple and direct: "We are going to get you!" Three years later, they succeeded. Judge Lopez-Alexander was ousted from office.

In addition to his staccato delivery and entertaining wit, I was particularly impressed with Larry's Biblical knowledge. Here was a judge who understood what the real law was and how to administer it, and when he did, the heathen lawyers couldn't stomach truth. That he could be kicked off the bench was a shocking reminder of how much the lawyers run things in our society. When I introduced myself, I reminded him of II Timothy 3:12 (see Chapter 3) and he not only recited the scripture to me with a big smile, but reminded me of the previous verse and recited: "What persecutions I endured; but out of them all the Lord delivered me."

And then there was the indomitable Peggy Christiansen. Someone should write a book about her exploits someday. Peggy has more fun doing battle and using the law to her advantage than anyone I have ever met. Once, she told me, a local motorcycle cop stopped her in downtown Missoula, Montana, where she headed up an organization called The Golden Mean Team helping people with tax problems. It seems that this day, Peggy— fortyish, mentally and physically tough, and with the size to go with it—was travelling without benefit of license plates displayed on her automobile.

The local gendarme, who at about 250 pounds. was not a lot heavier than she and not as tall, finally told her that she was going to have to come down to the police station with him. Not the correct wording to verbalize to Peggy. "Okay," she said, leaping onto the back of the motorcycle seat with him, "let's go!" "You should have seen our two big butts squeezed and straddled over that little seat," she said. "The big, fat sumbitch got so flustered, he let me go!"

I came back on Sunday for another eight hours of instruction on the problems and solutions and decided that I never wanted to miss another convention. Even Tupper Saussy's books were still on sale there, and, when I mentioned to a group of people that he and I used to be good friends, I was again overwhelmed with the love and respect he commanded from people that had never even met him. His disappearance was only serving to make him more legendary. I had to bite my tongue when one of them asked me if I knew where he was.

"Of course not," I said. "I just *used* to know him when we played music together. I haven't seen him in years." Whew. Is it a sin to tell a lie? The Holy Rule Book says that it is. But it also tells us of situations where the deceivers were actually blessed when they intentionally fabricated untruths to confuse the enemy in order to protect the Godly.

Moses was hidden for three months by his family in defiance of the king's order; an "illegal" action by his parents which, of course, saved his life. Joseph and Mary were warned by God in a dream to take the Christ child and flee into Egypt from Herod who would destroy Him. In defiance of man's statutes, they followed this divine instruction, and there they remained until after Herod's death. (Matt. 2: 12-13)

Did Corey Ten Boom, a Dutch Christian (her biography was *The Hiding Place*, sin when she hid frightened Jews from the Gestapo in her homeland of Holland during World War II? She lied numerous times to protect human life. A lesser known but similar story is that of Giorgio Perlasca.

Giorgio Perlasca had been a soldier in the Italian army who fought for Franco in the Spanish Civil War. He carried with him a document he had been given when he left Spain, entitling him to seek protection in any Spanish embassy anywhere in the world. During World War II, he was the Budapest representative of a company that supplied meat to the Italian army, and he turned against his former German allies when Mussolini was overthrown in 1943.

From October of 1944 until the following January, Perlasca used his plenipotentiary credentials to pose as Spain's top diplomat in Hungary, confronting the country's cabinet ministers, the generals of the occupying German army, and the Nazi thugs who roamed the streets; once even shouting down the dreaded Adolph Eichmann who was about to seize two children and place them in a railroad car headed for the concentration camp. Instead the two children, a brother and sister about twelve years old, were boldly ordered by Perlasca to get into his car, which bore diplomatic license plates, and their lives were saved.

Perlasca's ploy was eventually expanded to allow him to place literally thousands of Budapest's otherwise doomed Jews and Christians under the Spanish government's protection. He never was found out and only stopped his charade when the Russian army reached Budapest and the Nazi threat was thwarted. Was the deceitful Giorgio Perlasca a sinner or a saint?

* * *

The month I spent in St. Louis brought on a further education on money. After a few nights of playing at the Downtown Marriott, I gave a call to Dave Wilber, St. Louis real estate broker, a monetary realist, and a walking encyclopedia on the Federal Reserve. Like most of the "patriots" that I have met, he doesn't drink or have much interest in night club life, but he was happy to meet me for lunch the next day.

Of average height, pudgy, nearing sixty, and with a bespectacled, cherubic face which belies his truculent personality, Dave kills flies with a sledge hammer. If you have a limited education on hard money, you will walk away either completely convinced that Dave Wilber is a kook, or, like myself, will ask questions and sit back in awe of the unbridled answers that will flow forth. When it comes to government issues, everything is either black or white with Dave; there is no room for compromise with as to whether or not bureaucrats should obey the law. He is not long-suited in tact and freely admits it. "Those bastards are the criminals." he says. "Where does the law say we have to be nice to criminals just because they wear a government title?"

This day, taking sympathy with a neophyte, he kept it simple for me—as simple as he is capable, which still gets pretty confusing sometimes to the newly initiated.

"Look," he told me, "I can tell that you have been around this money circuit a little bit, so let's not waste a lot of time jawboning about stupid things like the 'deficit,' 'taxes,' 'money,' 'inflation' and other bullcrap. It's all illusory. The fact that there is no money makes null and void all the other related terms that the government people use. These boneheaded patriots aid their own destruction by using the same Orwellian terms that politicians use ... like 'Taxpayers' money.' There is no taxpayers' money. There is no tax and there are no taxpayers because there is no money."

"What about that ten thousand dollar extraction from me last year," I asked. "If that wasn't a tax, and I'm not a taxpayer, and that wasn't money of mine that they got, then explain the illusion, because they sure fooled me!"

"Okay," he replied, "but listen closely and don't interrupt unless I lose you. I wanna' pursue just one train of thought, and I don't want you to think about anything but facts and law and not any political ideas which you have been inundated with by TV and newspapers the last twenty years. Okay?"

"Okay," I agreed.

"No lawyer can show you a law that requires individuals to file income tax returns because Congress is prohibited from passing such a law, but let's understand the money fraud first."

He took out a dollar bill and said, "If I get all of these I want for nothing, and I can hire you to work for me in exchange for an agreed amount of these, have I not stolen your labor? What's the difference if these were leaves, bark, tallies, tokens, or paper? If I am the only source of the so-called money, and this is the only 'money' that your grocer and other merchants will accept, have I not enslaved you? Are you not working for me for nothing? How much am I paying for your labor?"

"Nothing," I had to agree.

"This is what has happened to us in America," he went on. "A dollar was defined as a measurement in the 'Coinage Act of 1792.' Just as a quart is a measurement of liquid or a mile is a measurement of distance, a dollar is a measurement of silver—371.25 grains to be precise—or 25.8 grains of gold. Anything less is not a dollar; it is a fraud, counterfeit, a lie." He showed me a book called *The Making of a Nation*, published in 1895. On page 22 he pointed out the underlined script concerning the Constitutional Convention: "... Now if anything was certain, in regard to a new Constitution, it was that it would prohibit paper-money issues by the states."

"Do you know what Article I, Section 10 says,?" Dave asked.

How could I know Tupper Saussy and not know that? The words will probably be emblazoned on his tombstone. "No State shall make any thing but gold and silver coin a tender in payment of debts." I recited the seventeen words from memory.

"That's the law," he said. "Have you ever seen that Article amended anywhere? There are twenty-six amendments to the Constitution now, and none of them comes anywhere close to even suggesting any change in the substance of our money." Then he took out an unusual looking hundred dollar bill that had been folded neatly into the picture section of his wallet and spread it flat on the table. I did a double-take and then realized he was showing me one of the old Federal Reserve Notes—1934 Series. I hadn't seen one in years. I started to pull out one of mine for comparison but he stopped me. "Don't do that yet. I want you to concentrate on this one for a moment," he said.

"Now what does it say across the top?" "Federal Reserve Note" appeared in large letters, and I recited it.

"Okay," he said, "Now that means that it is a note issued by the Federal Reserve. Any sophomore law student can tell you that a note, in order to be a bona fide note, must have four integral parts. There must be a payor, a payee, a specified amount and a due date. When you go down to a bank and sign a note for a car, aren't all those parts present in your car note?"

I nodded without speaking.

"Okay, what do the next words say?"

"The United States of America," I read aloud.

"And the next line right under Franklin's picture," he said.

And I answered "will pay to the bearer on demand."

He said, "There's your payor and payee and due date. Now what is the specified amount?"

"One hundred dollars," I read right there in bold print across the bottom.

"Right," he said. "Now to determine one hundred dollars of what—a dollar being a measurement—let me read the smaller print to the upper left of Franklin's picture: 'This note is legal tender for all debts, public and private, and is redeemable in lawful money at the United States Treasury or any Federal Reserve Bank.' So, is this lawful money?"

"Looks official enough to me," I said.

"No, hell no," he barked. "Aren't you listening? It just told you that it was *redeemable* in lawful money. So if it is only redeemable in lawful money, it can't be lawful money; it is the receipt for that lawful money. To find out what that lawful money is that is waiting to be redeemed at the U.S. Treasury or any Federal Reserve Bank, we can go to 12 USC 152," and he read from the United States Code:

The terms 'lawful money' and 'lawful money of the United States' shall be construed to mean gold or silver coin of the United States.

I sheepishly swallowed the reprimand and, staring at the note, said, "Oh."

"So what you are holding in your hand, my friend, is a legitimate, bona fide but dishonored note issued by the Federal Reserve Bank. They found it necessary to renege on their promise-to-pay back in 1968, because they had issued a few billion too many and redemption was impossible. But now pull out one of your so-called notes and let's compare."

I found a ten spot and noticed that it was of the 1985 Series. Placing them together on the table, I noticed how inferior, how less official mine looked; how ... counterfeit. Across the top it looked almost the same and the wording said "Federal Reserve Note" and "The United States of America" over Hamilton's picture. But underneath, instead of "will pay to the bearer on demand" and "Ten Dollars," it just said "TEN DOLLARS" in giant print, indicating that this piece of paper *is* ten dollars. The upper left said nothing about this being redeemable in lawful money but only that "This note is legal tender for all debts, public and private." Suddenly paper was money.

"How can this be a note?," I asked Dave, "It has no payor, no payee and no due date?"

"You learn fast," he said, "and the specified amount is not ten dollars of gold or silver, but no thing. Our problem began years ago when our ancestors were conditioned to say 'silver dollars' which is akin to saying 'milk quarts' or 'bread pounds.' Correctly speaking, just as you would say 'ounce of silver,' you would say 'dollar of silver.' Ten dimes would weigh one dollar and so would four quarters or two halves. Now that all of that has been stolen from us, this is not a note for anything, it's a token; just a piece of paper with more lies printed on it. Ludwig Von Mises, the famed Dutch hard money man, said that only governments can take a perfectly useful commodity like paper, slap some black and green ink on it, and render it perfectly worthless.

"The reason for having substance for money, like Jefferson said, is that when the government needs taxes, it must get it from the people; not just print it into existence thereby diluting everyone's purchasing power ... or worse yet, having a private corporation lend it into action at interest. People can not be self governing and free unless public servants are dependent on being paid with something the people produce. When the people become dependent on paper their servants print, the roles of master and servant are reversed."

"So instead of FRN, it's FRT—Federal Reserve Token," I said. Instead of 'ferns,' we should call 'em farts!"

"Perfect," he yukked. "And they stink up our economy worse. Someday we'll use them for bumfodder because that's all they'll be worth."

He went on to tell me that those who accept counterfeit paper have been robbed, and it's the same with the coins. The Fed stole the silver out of the dimes and quarters after 1964, and the halves in '68. Our last inkling of lawful money left us in 1981 when the authentic looking pennies were actually produced with copper-coated zinc ... tokens.

"By the way," he said, "did you know we have no laws against counterfeiting in this country? The laws prohibit 'Illegal Counterfeiting.' They were changed in recent years, I guess, when they figured some smartass like me would take them to task on the subject. Now it means that you and I cannot counterfeit, but they can! We go to jail for what they do legally. But the 'legal' reasons for that are obvious: If we all printed our own money, the stuff would become worthless as it flooded the marketplace and merchants would soon refuse to accept it. But with the printing of counterfeit permitted to only one select group, the process will take longer. The devastation will be just as complete, only longer in coming. There is no alternative to that collapse short of a complete and prompt return to a tangible money system and there seems little likelihood of that.

The Founders were so vehement on the subject that when the Coinage Act of 1792 became law it also legislated the death penalty for anyone found guilty of debasing the currency. Today the debasers want to kill anyone who challenges the debasement. If you want to get on the government's secret "most wanted" list, just write a book about the subject. Everyone who has, has been indicted for something; usually "Conspiracy" to do something vile. Tupper Saussy knew and wrote all about this subject and that's when they went after him."

I made a mental note to be sure not to ever write a book about the subject as I thought: "Is it any wonder to thinking Americans that the private individuals who now enjoy power to create money spend hundreds of millions of their chimerical dollars upon false teachings and propaganda to prevent the people from understanding the gross dishonesty in the system actually operated?" How many honest Americans have ever been permitted to learn that if one obtains a "dollar" for his labor and spends it for food, that "dollar" has been paying tribute to the banking system for its very existence? Would they permit it if they knew?

Andrew Jackson said they wouldn't; that "... there would be a revolution by morning."[1]

But, today, I don't know. Americans are awfully content with their televisions, ball games, beer and the sexy movies that they acquire with their Fed tokens. Will enough of them even whimper at anything less than total collapse?

"Hell no, they won't," said Dave. "The money powers have exercised great patience in mis-educating the people with this disinformation. I am surprised that the whole thing has lasted this long without blowing up, but the truth is— and the church-going, right-wing conservative can sing 'land of the freeee and the home of the braaave' until donkeys fly—but the truth is" he repeated, "this

---

[1] "Gentlemen," Jackson told the bankers, "I have had men watching you for a long time, and I am convinced that you have used the funds of the bank to speculate in the breadstuffs of the country. When you won, you divided the profits amongst you, and when you lost, you charged it to the bank. You tell me that if I take the deposits from the bank and annul its charter, I shall ruin ten thousand families. That may be true, gentlemen, but that is your sin! Should I let you go on, you will ruin fifty thousand families and that would be my sin! You are a den of vipers! I intend to rout you out, and by the Eternal God, I will rout you out. If the people only understood the rank injustice of our money and banking system, there would be a revolution by morning." Later, there was an assassination attempt on President Jackson. on the steps of the Capitol Building, but the assailant's gun misfired, and Old Hickory thrashed him with his cane.

nation is already bankrupt and has been since 1933 when Congress declared it so with HJR-192.

But don't confuse reality with the lyrics of a song. When you and I are obligated via legal tender laws to accept scrip for our goods and services, then we are under the thumb of the printer of that scrip and we are slaves to them. What we used to trade for gold and silver, we now give away for pieces of paper signifying nothing; but there is no power on earth that will compel people to continue to do this once they realize the true nature of the exchange. Unfortunately, most of us, who are yelling, find our words falling on deaf ears. I am glad you want to listen because now we not only have one more who has heard and understands but one more who can now tell others."

I looked at a copy of a newspaper called the *National Educator*, the house organ of a national association known as "Redeem Our Country." It is headed by Jim Townsend in Fullerton, California and is dedicated to abolishing the Federal Reserve. He wrote: "The Federal Reserve banks are privately owned, locally controlled, separate corporations.[2] Who says so? In Lewis v. United States, the Ninth Circuit Court of Appeals says so:

Thus, after years of senators and members of the House of Representatives denying that the Fed was private, the court has exposed their seventy years of lies. But how will this piece of information impact the paper issued as Federal Reserve Notes? As private bankers, they have no more right to issue and circulate their credit and paper than does the local counterfeiter. In fact, the local counterfeiter's "money" would be more desirable because he charges no interest on his paper. The Federal Reserve counterfeiter not only distributes worthless paper and credit, he collects interest by loaning it into circulation. Incidentally, neither the printed nor electronic media found this court decision to be a newsworthy item.

"Tell me more," I said, "about this Congressional 192 thing, and Congress declaring us bankrupt."

"HJR," Wilber said slowly, "House Joint Resolution, one ninety two. It was the legal tender act that suspended dealing in gold, made it illegal actually *in the public interest*, because of public policy. Who was this public they talked to? Nobody. At the height of the depression, it was the perfect time to start creating gigantic amounts of credit so as to 'pay' for WPA projects and the bureaucracy that was to be created.

---

[2] This same truth can also be found in about a dozen of the FED's own publications.

Anything that government ever does to us in the name of public policy or public interest, you can bet, is always in the government's interest. Of course those people who surrendered their gold were not actually paid, they just thought they were being paid because the next guy would take the paper too. But it is impossible to "pay" for anything with legal tender. You may retire the obligation with a note, but it cannot be lawfully paid without lawful money or barter of like value. The government was actually declaring, after nineteen years of issuing paper notes, that there was not nearly enough lawful money to redeem them.

With the passing of HJR-192, the nation declared bankruptcy, but don't take my word for it, listen to what the rattlesnake, Senator Carter Glass, who was there from the inception of the Fed, said." He fumbled with papers for a moment, then pulled out a single sheet and read "I had never thought the Federal Bank System would prove such a failure. The country is in a state of irretrievable bankruptcy!" That remark is dated June 8th, 1938.

"So, back to your so-called 'tax' of ten thousand bucks last year," he went on. "Granted, they took it from you, but what do you think that funded? If they can create all the 'money' they want with the push of a computer button, do you think they really need your 'tax dollars' to fund anything? Your money is worth no more to them than a handful of sand to a beachcomber. They could create another ten thousand with a whole lot less trouble than trying to get you to part with it.

"The dual purpose of the 'tax' (he spits the word like a cobra) is number one, to restrict your consumption; and number two, to erase some of the credit that was created last year, before inflation becomes hyper, so they can maintain their sham until next year, when they do it again. If everyone were permitted to spend all the credit that was allocated, prices would be bid to the sky in no time, and the people would regain their financial freedom as they stopped using the credit."

"Is this why they deal so harshly with tax protestors,?" I asked.

"You got it! They can't afford for the truth to be known because if a few get away with it, the word will get out and the Fed's house of cards will come tumbling down on top of them.

"Endless lies of where our 'tax dollars' go hide the truth that no tax dollars go anywhere. When credit exists only in the minds of the people and the system works only with credit, they have to control the minds of preachers, teachers, publishers, politicians, and the public to work all of us with credit, do they not? In spite of the millions of checks coming from Washington, there is nothing going to Washington as taxes... nothing, nada, zilch, zero. When government spends nothing, there is no reason for anything to go to

Washington as taxes. Why should government spend money when you and I and everyone else will risk our lives for credit? A check sent to the Imaginary Revenue Scum is nothing more than an authorization for your bank to reduce your credit.

"These Tax Protestor clowns who pay a lawyer twenty-five or fifty grand to 'defend' them in the King's court are licking a hollow lollipop. How can they expect the judge to be an unbiased referee when he is a direct beneficiary of the very system that is being challenged? He is always part of the prosecution. And even the defense attorney is hamstrung throughout the whole trial because he knows if he performs a successful defense, his 1040 form is the next to be audited.

I am not a tax protestor. You might call me a 'Money Protestor.' Give me lawful money, and I will happily pay all lawful taxes. Let's forget all that crap about paying a 'fair share.' That's an IRS slogan that is designed to herd us into the shearing pen every April 15th. I pay my 'fair share' of cigarette taxes because I don't smoke. I pay my fair share of liquor taxes because I don't drink. And, I pay my fair share of income taxes because I don't have any 'income.' "

I pondered that for a moment and then asked, "So what does a guy do who has been indicted for Willful Failure to File if the deck is stacked against him before he ever goes to trial?"

"He must not use a lawyer. Clients are legally referred to as 'wards of the court' in regard to their relationship to their attorneys. A ward of the court is legally defined as 'Infants and persons of unsound mind.' The lawyer's first duty is to the courts and not to the client. That's from *Corpus Juris Secundum*, their law book that can be found in any library. "The only defense is to become educated enough to be able to explain to a jury yourself such things as the lack of jurisdiction on the part of the prosecutor and, more importantly, Jury Nullification."

"That's something I never heard of," I said.

"Most people haven't," he went on, "but it is an integral part of our trial system that is older than America. It means that the jury, not the judge, is the governing body of the trial, and they have the power to judge the law as well as the facts of the particular case. If the jury decides that government was trying to oppress a citizen into obeying a 'bad law,' they have the power to rule "Not Guilty" and, in effect, strike down that law. One of the most famous is the Peter Zenger case of around 1735, as I remember, and another is the William Penn fiasco in England in the 1670's. Jury Nullification was the governing force that finally ended Prohibition after thirteen years. When most of the jury members were attending the speakeasy of their choice, illegally, how could they vote "guilty" to incarcerate the one who was providing their booze every weekend?

"The people knew it was a bad law—you can't take from the people what the people want—and when they couldn't get convictions, the government realized it was bad law too. The juries nullified the law. "However, the problem today in the tax trials is that neither the judge nor the lawyers will tell the jury about their powers. In fact, in his jury charge at the end of the trial, the judge even tells the jury that they may only judge the facts of the case. Did the defendant do it or did he not do it? The jury is never told by the judge or lawyers that whenever man's law conflicts with God's law, the defendant's obligation is to the higher power.

"So even though millions of Americans realize that their peers are being prosecuted on a 'bad law' in these tax trials, they continue to come back with 'guilty' verdicts. Hosea 4:6 says, 'My people perish for lack of knowledge.' "

"So it is all cut and dried," I said.

"It is if the defendant is foolish enough to use a goddamned lawyer. That crap about 'He who defends himself has a fool for a client' has been brilliant PR work perpetuated by the lawyers. But who would ever hire a lawyer whose first loyalty was to someone other than the hirer? Are you a person of 'unsound mind' who wants to be a 'ward of the court?' That is how the law books define a client of a lawyer.

"The public has been hoodwinked and mesmerized into believing that ordinary people are not smart enough to correctly handle anything having to do with the law; that an attorney is some kind of wizard know-it-all without whose advice one is doomed to failure. You should talk to Dan Gibson over in Kansas City sometime. He has put together a hundred-plus hour course on video-tape to teach the ordinary guy how to baffle the bafflers. It is based on Biblical Law and teaches one to challenge successfully the jurisdiction of the courts that would try to force man's law as supreme.

"I understand that ordinary people with absolutely no legal training prior to this are going into courts and either winning, or hanging the jury, which often is as good as a win. Dan is turning the tables on them. This way the county has the legal expense and the defendant has little or none. The county would end up spending thousands on a case that would bring them only a hundred or so in fines, even if they won ... so they end up dropping the charges.

You should look Dan up the next time you play Kansas City. Here is his phone number. Don't lose it because he is listed under some guy who has been dead for fifteen years."

"Why is that?"

"Just for privacy. The patriots have all kinds of ingenious ploys for avoiding government snoopervision. Utilities in the name of a friend or relative makes it rather difficult for someone to locate you if they don't know you. You know, it is not against the law to use a different name as long as you don't use it to defraud someone. In the common law, you are who you say you are."

"By the way," I said, "when I was in Denver, John Voss told me I should ask you about a man named Amos Bruce. Who is he?"

"Until a year ago," Dave said, "he was one of the most remarkable people I have ever known, and I knew him well. Unfortunately, he died last summer. Just woke up dead one morning just like we all told him he would someday. I am sure the underlying cause had to be the few million Camel cigarettes he sucked on all his adult life and most of childhood. Amos and I spoke at gatherings in Chicago, Milwaukee, Rockford, Oshkosh, Dodge City, Manitiwoc, Fon Du Lac; all over the Midwest."

"He was one of the front line patriots then," I guessed.

"You better believe it. The guy went to the fifth grade, became an accomplished safe cracker as a young man, and got caught here in St. Louis and served a lot of time; ten years or more. When we all knew him, he was reformed of his life of crime but took special delight in agitating Caesar and spent the rest of his life in study of the law and exercising his rights. Of course, the government people called him 'seditious and insurgent.' Tupper Saussy loved his crankiness and labelled him 'the irascible but distinguished St. Louis cabdriver and Main St. Journal's legal director!'"

"He was a taxidriver?"

"Sure. That's what he did for a living, but his time and money were almost exclusively spent in doing battle for Truth when he wasn't driving the cab. Sometimes even in between fares.

One afternoon when he was invited to Centralia, Illinois, a little burg across the river, to do a radio show, he asked me to ride along with him. Now bear in mind that, in spite of his background, this guy was an articulate debater with more knowledge on lawful money and taxes than any lawyer in town. Once he debated with the head of the local Federal Reserve Bank on the air and utterly destroyed him. The guy would never do it again! Amos was the only non-lawyer I ever knew who was actually allowed by the courts to represent someone else as both counsel and spokesman. He impressed the hell out of the judges.

"Anyhow, on the way over there, we had been listening to the local station that he was to speak on. We decided that I would sit in the car, listen to the radio, and tape the interview while he went in to do the show. Strange thing. I kept waiting and waiting for his program to come on. I spun the dial and couldn't find the station again. You know what happened? You wouldn't believe it. The power went off before he went on and did not return until he was finished. I didn't hear a damned thing! You figure that one out."

He showed a copy of the Main Street Journal that I had not seen wherein Tupper had written the obituary and fitting eulogy for his sixty-year-old friend:

> Our favorite curmudgeon, the irascible but distinguished St. Louis cabdriver Amos W. Bruce died last July 27th. The MSJ's Legal Director's body was discovered July 29th on the floor beside his bed. Death was attributed to a respiratory illness, which is plausible, given Amos's dedication to cigarettes and biscuits with white gravy, and his aversion to healthful living. Although some would say he established quite a record as a sinner, the Amos we knew was a staunch foe of all liars, evil-doers and workers of iniquity. Delicately avoiding religious classification, he nevertheless scourged the money-changers more thoroughly than any contemporary minister of gospel we can think of offhand.

> As we sit here trying to comprehend Amos's passing, the sensation comes over us that his sins—which he gleefully confessed to thousands through The MSJ and the St. Louis papers—have been forgiven, and that his fruits, as well as his cantankerous demeanor, have been found highly pleasing if not downright amusing to the Lord. Amos's funeral was a gathering of Monetary Realists and family and fans. The atmosphere was full of that bold, unsuperstitious Bruce mood and that bold, unsuperstitious Bruce laughter, and tender emotional reconciliation and spiritual communion and, yes, lots of trifling over fine legal monetary points.

"Amos had one idiosyncrasy," Dave went on, "He loved to taunt people. Not just his adversaries; his friends, too. It didn't bother me, I knew him too well. But he would taunt government officials when he had nothing to gain beyond exposing truth ... or their bullshit.

"Once, after he had done considerable research and discovered that the tobacco tax laws were flawed in Missouri and nobody had ever been convicted under them, he took off in his cab for North Carolina with a trailer to buy cigarettes which he then sold without taxes at a bargain price back in Missouri right in front of the state revenue office.

"If his only concern had been money, he could have continued indefinitely with no problem but, as I said before, he loved to taunt. He would park his van full of untaxed cigarettes in front of the Revenue Building, tell them what he had and what he was selling them for, and ask them what they intended to do about it! The State agents wanted the IRS to get him. The IRS told the State that Amos was 'their baby.'

"Meanwhile, Amos wouldn't stop. If he had only bugged them once, they would have ignored him, but when he ran out of cigarettes and they hadn't arrested him yet, he took off for Kentucky and got another load. Eventually, the State took him to court for failure to file a sales tax return. The trial lasted three weeks, and the testimony that Amos drew out of the local bankers that he had subpoenaed as well as the Chief Counsel of the St. Louis Fed was just fantastic. Three prosecutors quit their jobs rather than risk being whipped by a non-lawyer, let alone a cabdriver. The fourth wanted to quit, too, but the judge said, 'Nothing doing, we are stuck with him.'

"With all the Truth that Amos exposed, he still lost. I couldn't believe it. But as I analyzed it, I realized that the jury just couldn't relate the money issue to the charge. He spent a few months on the State Prison Farm, and we gave him a 'Going-to-Prison' party complete with a cake on the front lawn of the work house. But this was the price he was willing to pay for his penchant to taunt. Amos and I both knew that you could not teach Irwin Schiff anything. When Amos returned from a meeting with Red Beckman for the first time, his comment was, 'He's worse than Schiff.'[3]

"I learned a great lesson from Amos," said Dave, "even though it took me two or three times of hearing it to understand it. Once when I had dropped by his house and was mildly criticizing him for reading books written by obvious fools, he said, 'Dave, you can't learn anything from anybody that you are in total agreement with.' It made a lot sense."

Dave Wilber made a lot of sense to me, too, and I am still learning a lot more from his periodic newsletter when he remembers to mail it to me. I will never forget the horrified look on the cashier's face as I was paying the check, when Dave said to him, "Watch out! He may put a fart or two on you." I was giggling much  too uncontrollably to be embarrassed or to even attempt to explain about frns and frts and federal reserve notes and tokens.

*When a bank makes a loan today, it creates a checking account balance which the borrower then spends, thereby adding new money to the total money supply.*

—Federal Reserve Bank of Boston

---

[3] Both Schiff and Beckman are excellent researchers and authors in their own right, and both are credited with uncovering little known Truths that would have, otherwise, remained buried under government subterfuge.

*The Federal Reserve System works only with credit.*

—Federal Reserve Bank of New York

*Deposits are merely book entries; demand deposits are liabilities of commercial banks.*

—Federal Reserve Bank of Chicago

*A wise man feareth, and departeth from evil; but the fool rageth, and is confident.*

—Proverbs 14:16

One of the great St. Patrick's Day celebrations in the world is in Kansas City. I had drunk the green beer in Denver on March 17th in the sixties and sung all the Irish songs with the southern descendants of the old sod in Savannah in the seventies, but those, and the other celebrations I had attended through the years, did not quite reach the blarney level that one can find on that day in Kansas City. New York still has the largest parade, and while I have never personally participated in that shindig, I am sure it cannot be more inane and uncivilized than what I found in the midwestern city. For good, clean, utter foolishness, these people take the trophy.

I had just returned from spending the winter in Fort Lauderdale and this week had been unusually warm; just slightly cooler than Florida but with a light drizzling rain all day long on the holiday. Another good reason for people to stay inside and just drink. Mike Murphy, a talk show host cut from a different mold than Nashville's Dan Hoffman and quite a popular personality in Kansas City, organized the city's first St. Patrick's Day parade in the early seventies. It has grown in popularity and with participation each year to the point where he now boasts that it is the third or fourth largest in the country ... or, maybe, the world. It definitely is the longest, loudest, wildest party anytime to be found between Tulsa and Omaha, St. Louis and Denver.

Mike Murphy, as chief organizer and Grand Poo-Bah, rides in the last float every year along with his special celebrity guest who is designated the Grand Marshall. Sometimes it's the mayor, a local hero, or a show biz personality, and, when it's all over, Mike always brings his entourage to his favorite watering hole, naturally, called "Murphy's Landing." This also happened to be my location for a three week stand.

It was early evening when I launched into some of my favorite frivolity and sang something called "Be Prepared," a slightly risqué satirical aspersion lampooning the Boy Scout's century-old tradition. Before I got halfway through, Murphy was away from his table in the back of the room and standing next to my piano singing along and not missing a lyric.

"I thought I was the only guy in town who knew Tom Lehrer's stuff," he yelled over everyone else, and somehow I heard.

"Maybe you were," I grinned back. "I ain't been in town long."

"Can you do 'Poisoning Pigeons in the Park?'"

When I did, he bought me a drink, placed his beautiful emerald green top hat on my head, sat down on the bench beside me, and the party was on! For the next hour the crowd heard all or part of every Tom Lehrer number of which Murphy and I had ever heard, and that must have covered them all.

I don't usually participate to a great degree in the imbibing as I am expected to entertain the whole night, and such participation greatly diminishes my staying power, to put it mildly. I had witnessed enough middle-aged entertainers, sloshing their profits down their improvident gullets, as a young man to be well aware of the risks of substance abuse and had long since learned to keep consumption at a minimum. (Hard drugs had always been out of the question for me. Unlike many show people who suddenly end up with more dollars than sense, I have never even considered sniffing poison up my nose or sticking needles in my arm.

David Crosby says that anybody who remembers the sixties wasn't there. Funny line for all former potheads, but I was there, and maybe this is why I can remember detailed conversations with his future partner, Steve Stills, while Crosby couldn't find his butt with both hands for a decade or more afterwards.) However, it was one of those days when everyone was already going strong by noon and by sundown, "carrying more rum than their heads could handle." Falling off the wagon just seemed to be appropriate. Staying on the wagon this night would have been most unpatriotic, face-slappingly anti-Irish, and disgustingly out of place. I succumbed. The next morning I was paying the normal price.

A voice on the TV says that there are nine million alcoholics in the United States. If that's all there are, I am sure I have met them all; most of whom must show up in Kansas City every St. Patrick's Day.

I was staying in a new condo in one of those urban renewal projects in an old section of downtown, just a couple of blocks walk from "Murphy's Landing." (I forgot to ask Mike if he was one of the behind-the-scenes owners of the joint.) I didn't even need to use my rental car to get to work each night. The short stroll through the coffee district this sunny morn was a refreshing respite to my lungs and spirit after breathing the stale smoke of a night club for so many hours the day before.

It was such a great "recovery room" that I considered walking around the block a couple of more times just to inhale more of the caffeine-flavored oxygen, but my body rebelled at the last second and directed my feet up the short stairs to Murphy's and a late breakfast. I had just sat down at a table by the window with my morning paper and large mug of coffee when I heard the unmistakably familiar brogue of Elam, the authentically-Irish bartender from Galway Bay, barking my name from behind the bar.

"Yew've gaat a cawl on thee phaone, mayte," he said, his reverberating voice piercing my reveries like tiny hand grenades.

"Who is it?" I said, not wishing to be interrupted for a few hours, at least.

He returned to the phone for a moment and then yelled back, "Jim Gorr-tonn."

It had been eight months since I had heard from him, and, for a second, the name didn't even register. Just as I was about to tell Elam to take the number, and I would call back later, it hit me who "Jim Gordon" was as I did a double-time pace towards the phone with my thoughts divided between yelling to the cook to stick my plate of eggs in the microwave to reheat them later and wondering how he had found me. I had told Juan to pass on my number to anyone when I went to Denver, should they call, and had even called Tempe when I didn't hear to let them know where I was in Florida. But I hadn't touched back since I made the Kansas City booking, and there were very few people in the world who knew where I was at this time.

With as much cheer as I could muster through the mental fog, I heard my gravelly voice say, "How-the-hell did you find me?"

"It only took three calls, it wasn't so tough. The third one was my ace in the hole. I called your dear sweet mama." That figured. A Mafia hit man could call her and say that he needed to find me because I had just won the lottery, and she would comply. I made a mental note that if I ever got on the lam like Tupper, I would need to tell Mother that I was doing an extended tour with the Moscow Circus.

"It's great to hear your voice, old friend," I said with a friendly growl, "I've been wondering if I'd ever hear from you again. Where is the peripatetic Mr. Gordon these days? Still in California?"

"Well, yes and no," he said vaguely. Currently I am in Utah doing some research for my new book, but I will be headed back to that same place—you know that same place where I was headed when you last saw me—in about a week. I just decided last night that I would attempt to track you down and see what's going on. How are you doing?"

"Well, right now I feel like somebody whupped me widda' boat paddle," I said as I drifted into, and then quickly out of, my Eddie Murphy rendition, realizing I really wasn't quite in a lighthearted mood yet. "Yesterday was St. Paddy's Day, you know, and it got pretty foggy around here."

"That's what you get for drinking the devil's brew and celebrating pagan holidays," he cackled, mocking a mountain preacher.

"Naa, it wasn't last night's party. It's just that the smog in the air, the coal tar in the cigarettes, the insecticide residue in my bread, and the strontium 90 in my milk are all getting me at once. Hey, I'm headed back to the Casa Loma in Tempe after next weekend. Why don't you come down and stay for a few days before you head north?"

"Thank you. That's a most tempting invitation. However, I don't think I can afford the time. I have some pressing things that need to be tended to up north, and I was planning to leave about that time. When do you start in Tempe?"

I had to think for a moment. "Let's see, it's the Tuesday after Easter. I think that will make it April 5th. I finish my three weeks here next weekend and leave on Sunday the 27th. That gives me the whole week off before Easter."

"Hey," he said, "I've got a better idea. Why don't you fly out here and travel with me for a week and then you can buzz on down to Phoenix? We can sleep in the motor home so you can make it a cheap vacation."

He knew how to pull my chain with my weakness for a bargain, and I agreed that that would be fun because I really hadn't made any plans for that gap in my schedule. For logistical reasons, we decided that I should fly into Las Vegas a week from Sunday, and he would pick me up. He gave me a number where I could call him back in a few days with my flight times, when I had them, and he would then plan to be outside of the baggage area twenty minutes after my arrival. Good plan I thought. Before we rang off I said, "Oh by the way, Jim, I've been doing a lot of study like you recommended, and I just want you to know that I believe you are right."

"About which part?"

"All of it! The facts, of course, are indisputable, but I think you are right on, too, with your ... uh, shall we call them your ... assumptive conclusions."

"Great. I knew you would see it if you just exercised your keen eye of discernment. I am delighted. We'll have plenty of time to talk about it more when I see you." We were learning to communicate the delicate subjects while on the phone without going into too much detail for any unwanted eavesdroppers who, by some longshot, might figure out exactly who was participating in this conversation.

*Currently I am in Utah writing and doing some research for my new book,* he had said. His is the epitome of the truly creative mind about which Pearl Buck wrote:

> A human creature born abnormally, inhumanly sensitive. To him a touch is a blow, a sound is a noise, a misfortune is a tragedy, a joy is an ecstasy, a friend is a lover, a lover a god and failure is death. Add to this cruelly delicate organism the overpowering necessity to create, create, create—so that without the creating of music or poetry or books or buildings or something of meaning, his very breath is cut off from him. He must create, must pour out creation. By some strange, unknown, inward urgency he is not really alive unless he is creating."

This is F. Tupper Saussy.

I hadn't talked to Dan Gibson yet and didn't want to miss him before I left Kansas City, so, the following week, I gave a call to that number Dave Wilber had given me back before Thanksgiving. When the machine answered, I left no message but made a mental note to write to him about the information on his school. It had sounded like something I wanted to own.

\* \* \*

The morning of Sunday the 27th was cool and sunny in Kansas City as I unloaded my things from the trunk of the taxicab at KCI, and warmer and sunnier in Las Vegas three hours later. The flight was five minutes late at 9:55 a.m. so I expected him to be out front at 10:15. After a very short wait to scoop my bags—which arrived an unprecedented first—off the automated carousel, I was about five minutes ahead of our proposed schedule and already seated on the bench outside of the Northwest baggage gate when I saw what appeared to be him approaching only a couple of minutes later. Precision timing.

I gathered up my things as the faded-out gold and white, ancient Dodge motor home came chugging over hill and around the bend. There were few people and cars out there at that time of day—most people were leaving, not arriving—and he spotted me immediately as I stepped to the curb.

The door swung open, and, with his big smile, he chimed, "Welcome to Gordon Guided Tours! Just leave the driving to us," he crowed as the big door swung shut. He was as happy as a kid with a new train set and couldn't have been prouder of his new acquisition had it been a quarter-million-dollar Eagle bus. Immediately sensing this, I saved my denigrating remarks about the age of the old relic for later. I dumped my guitar case on the floor in the back under the table, threw my hanging bag over the horizontal pole, parked my suitcase underneath in the closet, and settled into the co-pilot's seat.

"Good thing you don't travel with your Steinway," he wisecracked as he put it in gear, and in a moment we were rolling down the ramp out of the airport.

We stopped at Denny's for a quick breakfast. I had their "Grand Slam" and he his favored strawberries and cantaloupe. We shared what we had been doing since last summer. He had arrived safely in Placerville, California, as planned, after an uneventful air cruise in the Beech Baron to Sacramento to pick up his motor home. His benefactors were "some wonderful people," Kevin and Linda Wilson, who had a few acres outside of town, and who had graciously provided a space for him to park the rig. Jim had done some paralegal research work in their office to earn a few bucks until Thanksgiving when some heat had come down.

When I asked what kind of heat, he told me, "One afternoon a U.S. Marshall came to the MBA office in Placerville, flashing his badge in one hand and an unrecognizable picture of me in the other. The receptionist told them no one of that description had been in the office. The marshall said the man was a little over six feet tall with gray hair, from the South. She said the only new person close to that was 'Jim Gordon,' but Jim certainly wasn't the man in the picture."

Although he was born and raised in the south, Tupper, with his articulate capture of the English language, has never allowed himself to acquire that lazy accent called a "southern drawl." He also has spent enough time in New York, around the country, and in Europe that his patois is really sort of neutral; the kind that people cannot pinpoint.

"I was visiting in southern California at the time, and she honestly told them she didn't know when to expect me. When I did return in a few days, Kevin and Linda told me about the visit and were afraid for me, even though they thought it only concerned something about my 'non-payment of child support.' As far as they know, I had domestic problems, and they had never asked much about my 'divorce' and were sympathetic to my created problem of not being able to pay. Anyway, I didn't want to cause these nice people any trouble, so we decided that it would be a good idea for me to go elsewhere for awhile. That's when I went to Utah."

"So what have you been doing for three months?" I asked.

"Just reading, reflecting, and writing. I've been editing a new publication called the 'Freedom Guide,' under a nom de plume, of course. I want to do another book telling my whole story. Maybe both sides will learn something.

You know, I don't mean to abruptly change the subject," he said as he abruptly changed the subject, "but it's going to take us all day to get where we're going. We need to get rolling."

As we walked across the asphalt parking lot towards the bus, I asked, "Where are we bound for first?"

"Placerville. I want you to meet my friends."

"The heat's off then, I presume?"

"Oh yeah. I called up there yesterday. They've had no more visits since the one in November. They're looking forward to meeting you."

"You don't think we'll need to put me in the gun turret of this tub with a Gatling gun and hand grenades so we can blast our way into town then," I joked as we climbed in, but he just smiled and didn't flatter that absurdity with a comment. Later, headed up U.S. 95 towards Beatty, I asked him seriously, "Do you even own a gun?"

"Nope."

Knowing his reputation as a mild-mannered pacifist, I pursued it a little further. "Have you *ever* owned a gun?"

He thought for a moment or two and said, "Yes, the first and last gun I ever owned was a 12 gauge at age 13 or 14 when I went on a dove shoot in south Georgia, which I did not enjoy. I don't know where it is today ... and I don't care. A gun would be what they would want me to have if they ever confronted me, and if I didn't, I am sure they would provide one, after the fact." I agreed and thought we had dropped the subject.

He paused pensively, and then began to tell me of another episode in his younger days which had perpetuated his distaste for guns. He had had a college friend, the son of prominent Tampans in his hometown, who craved jazz and knew every bar in town. Wherever his friend took him, Tupper played, and the drinks were on the house.

"Blackie got me popular. He almost got me shot. We always made the Sunday afternoon jam session at Jimmy White's *La Concha* tavern, on what is now Kennedy Boulevard. This session enabled me to play with several great California jazz players stationed at MacDill Air Force Base.

"One Sunday, Blackie left early. I was to ride to the beaches with another carload of people who arrived a little later to pick me up. I thanked the band and the audience, and left the stage through the back storage room. Jimmy White was sitting at the table with his girlfriend, a stripper from one of the skid row clubs. Both of them were smacked-out blasted. His eyes were wild, man. He asked me where the hell I was going. 'To the beach,' I said timidly. 'People have come for me.'

"The stripper was making faces—not at me—just making faces generally like bugs were swarming around her, and she kept licking her lips. She and Jimmy were crazy. Then Jimmy pulls a revolver from his pocket and ordered me to get back in the club and play. 'Fine, okay, Jimmy,' I tell him, and turn around and head back into the club. 'Hey, waitaminnit,' he snaps, and I stop. Now he was wobbling the gun toward the back door and says, 'Get your ass outa' my club.'

"I prayed for coolness. 'Jimmy, do you want me to play or not?'

"The stripper said, 'Make him play.' 'You heard the lady, go play,' he says.

"He leveled the gun right at me—I can still see those slugs in the chamber—and in one breath he tells me to leave, the next to get back in the club and play. This went on for a half a minute and seemed like half a lifetime. It almost was a whole lifetime. As I walked towards the clubroom door again, I measured the consequences of diving for the door and the safety of the crowded room. 'On second thought,' he says, and now they both are laughing like maniacs, 'maybe she's had enough of your music.' I halted. 'Yeah, I've had enough, Jimmy, get him outa' here.' 'You heard the lady, get the hell outa' here,' he said.

"At this point, a power I have tried unsuccessfully for years to describe *lifted* me from this situation. It felt as if I had been made temporarily invisible to Jimmy and his girl. My eyes were resolutely fixed on the brass handle of that door to the outside. I now walked past the two of them as if they didn't exist. I neither heard nor said a word. I deliberately opened the door, went out, and let it close by the action of its own spring-loaded mechanism.

"My friends chastised me for taking so long and had trouble believing what I told them. But the next morning, back at my summer job of running documents for Tampa Abstract & Title Company, the reality of the incident was eerily manifested. At the corner where I usually purchased the paper, I dropped a coin in the slot and picked up my copy of Monday's *Tampa Times*. The headline shook me to my ankles: 'Jimmy White kills Girl, Self.'

I empathized with his predicament at the time but pointed out that such a situation would have motivated me in exactly the opposite way—that I would rather have a gun than not, if the situation dictated it. Jimmy White had been in control of Tupper's life for a few minutes that day for one reason only. It was a similar situation that happened to me in New Orleans in 1964, which motivated me towards the opposite attitude concerning gun possession.

After moving out of the Exchange Alley flat that had been Lee Oswald's as a child, I had a roommate on Governor Nichols who had an "honest job" and went to work at 8 o'clock each morning, a couple of hours after I was just getting to sleep. The bedroom was windowless between the kitchen in the back, where the entrance was, and the living room and verandah overlooking the street in the front on the second floor. There was a bureau between the two beds where I kept a small .22 revolver (the same 8-shot Iver Johnson model carried by Sirhan Sirhan at the Ambassador Hotel in 1968 which he supposedly fired eleven times) in the bottom drawer on my side.

About 10 o'clock one weekday morning, I awakened to see two strange men standing just inside the kitchen doorway at the foot of my bed. Only the light from the kitchen shone in, and I could tell immediately that they were unaware that I was there. I quickly collected my thoughts but didn't move, as one of them stepped forward into the bedroom slowly walking towards the living room.

*Are these friends of Billy's,* I wondered. I had been there only a week or two and didn't know all of his acquaintances, and certainly shouldn't react too fast if they were only there looking for him. I contemplated going for the gun when the time was right and mapped out my strategy in my mind. I would pop the guy in the doorway on my right first before he could disappear back into the kitchen, and then I would have the other one trapped between me and the door. His only other escape would be by diving over the verandah into the street.

One slowly crept past the end of my bed from my right to left towards the front room while I was still trying to determine in my sleepy state whether or not they belonged there. On his right on the far wall away from me was a large bureau, and, on his way by, he pulled open a drawer, which was my final signal that he was up to no good. I made a startling move for the bottom drawer next to me, alerting both of them to my presence, pulled it open, and began to sling handkerchiefs, socks, and underwear three feet high as I searched for the weapon.

"Whereinthehell is my gun," I began to wonder as they scattered like scared deer. By the time I had nearly emptied the drawer, about one second, I realized: "Oh sheeeit, it's in the glove compartment of my car." I had forgotten to bring it upstairs when I came home a few hours before.

Regardless, the crisis was over. Seconds later, I stood in boxer shorts on the outside verandah, squinting my eyes and trying to adjust to the new sunlight, as I watched their candy apple red Pontiac pull away from the curb. The fact that they had *thought* I had a gun was enough. I had been in control.

"Oh, I agree with you," Jim said when I finished my story. "I am all for the Second Amendment and your right to keep and bear arms. I just don't choose to exercise that right personally. Don't forget that I have the right *not* to own a gun, too.

* * *

It was an absolutely perfect day for traveling, and we did it just the way I love it most but so seldom get to do. We would roll awhile and stop whenever we felt like it to see whatever was of interest. A vacation, like life, should not be a destination, but a journey. I always enjoyed small stakes gambling and suggested we pause for a half hour or so at some of the offbeat, Nevada casinos so I might pick up a little gas money as we moved north.

Many years ago a California mathematician by the name of Edward Thorp had written a book called *Beat the Dealer* in which he described how and why he had been banned from all of the casinos in Nevada after working out a method on his computer for throwing odds slightly back in favor of the player instead of the house. Although he had chapters of instruction on every casino game, his specialty was Blackjack which involved a fairly simple system of counting the spent cards.

It was his book that provoked the current custom of casinos dealing five decks out of a "shoe." I recently got a great kick out of watching Dustin Hoffman playing "Rain Man" in the scene in the Las Vegas casino as the mathematical genius who, apparently, was the only person in history who could successfully count in his head the remaining cards in a five-deck shoe.

It was the same system that I had learned from Thorp and used for years but, being mortal, I never attempted it when my adversary had more than two decks and was usually not successful with more than one. The smaller casinos, in recent years, have begun to advertise "Single Deck Black Jack" again. Their defense against "card-counters" today is a dealer trained to spot it who then counters the move by reshuffling halfway through the deck. My attack was to be as unobtrusive, even bungling on occasion, as was feasible and win as much as possible before being detected.

Once the early shuffling would begin, I knew I, or someone else at the table, had been spotted, and it was time to move on. Our first stop was in Beatty when Jim said that he needed to gas up anyway, so if I wanted to try my luck across the street, he would be over shortly. Fifteen minutes later, I was already in the parking lot when he drove in and before he could get out I jumped in, handed him a twenty spot and said, "Here, put this towards the gas-up!"

"How did you do that so fast?!"

"Got lucky. The system is simple," I said. "Sometimes it works early and sometimes it works later, but it always works. I didn't see any point in sticking around any longer once I had jumped out ahead. I was only playing two dollar chips and I reached my goal. Let's try another one up the road."

"You, betcha,' Red Ryder," he guffawed, and like the James Brothers, we galloped up the road towards our next "bank" hit.

In Tonapah, we stopped again. Sitting at the first bar stool was a weather-worn, bleached blond whose best years were behind her. The only thing covering her colossal, bra-less chest was a skin tight T-shirt advertising the name of the place. Emblazoned on the front side was "Liquor in the front," and on the back, "Poker in the rear." The rotten teeth behind her inviting smile cancelled the invitation. "A real classy joint," I thought, wishing I had my pocket Derringer, which I carry when I work the questionable sections of cities like New Orleans, Atlanta, and D.C. I would have felt a little more comfortable in this place with it in pocket instead of out in the van in my suitcase.

On the way up the road, I had explained to Jim the basics of card counting. The important cards are the ten counters—tens, jacks, queens, and kings. There are sixteen of them. That leaves thirty-six others, including the aces, which are important too, but not to the basic system.

After each hand, as the dealer is paying off, you can quickly calculate how many of each are spent. If the "tenners" fall early, the deck becomes "face card poor" and the bettor should play only with his original unit—say, two dollars. But, if the "bummers" fall early, the deck becomes "face card rich," throwing the odds in favor of the player and he should double, triple or quadruple his bet accordingly. A two to one ratio is when this increase should begin. So when I say to myself 28 to 14, for instance, it is time to double. When it reaches, as it does on occasion, an even spread of maybe 10 to 10, it is time to quadruple your bet (or even more if you are brave).

I suggested he stand behind me and watch but to be sure that his lips weren't moving when he counted ... not that I had any reason to think his would, but it is a common, unconscious habit of beginners. In twenty minutes, my twenty dollar purchase of chips was now worth sixty-five. I handed fifty of it to Jim, so that he might go cash it in for me. While he was gone, I shot five on one last play, lost, and cashed the last ten.

Heading up the road, Jim was ecstatic. "That was fantastic," he bellowed. Why don't you use hundreds?"

"Because I can't afford to lose hundreds right now and as soon as you more than you can afford to lose, your judgment gets clouded. This system can backfire on you too on occasion. Even Thorp admits that he cannot explain the phenomena of a 'run of luck,' good or bad. He just advises that when the house gets hot, go have some dinner or see a show. By the time you get back they will have cooled off. When we get up to Carson City, I'll show you my roulette trick. It is even simpler," I gloated.

The first thing any gambler had better learn is that no system is infallible and that is why the house loves people who come in with a new "system." Most are a joke. The fact that the whole state of Nevada not only banned Thorp from its casinos, but set up special defenses against his system, proved to me that this one worked and it was worthy of my time and study.

When we got into Carson City, it was getting to be suppertime and I was hungry enough to eat the hind end out of a diarrhetic goat. We hadn't had anything except beer in the casinos since that Denny's stop way back in Vegas, and I was craving one of those big, inexpensive prime rib dinners for which the casino towns are famous.

In the motor home, I had already received, with interest, a mild chastisement from Jim for being a carnivorous animal. "Don't you know that meat lies in your stomach trying to digested for eight hours?" Man's system wasn't made to handle that. It is the same with milk. The last milk you should drink is when you are weaned from your mother. All of the animal's milk is made for their offspring and not you." No wonder he stayed so slim and my weight was always fluctuating—gradually upwards—at the scales.

"The Arabs have an interesting philosophy about health," he said. "They say that health is the number one, love is zero, glory zero, and success zero. Put the one of health in front of all the others and are a rich man. But without the one of health, all the others are always zero."

"That's all very interesting, Jim, now may I remind you of a semi-famous piece of Irish philosophy?"

"Sure, go ahead."

"Let's go eat, drink and be merry for tomorrow we may die. The hippies of the sixties revised it to: 'Have a blast while you last.' "

"You are positively and irreversibly hopeless," he said, shaking his head.

At the "Motherlode," after I ate like a lumber jack, all of fat-laden foods that he would veto, and he had one of his disgusting salads, I took thirty-five of my newly found dollars (I call them "farts" now almost exclusively, except when I do not wish to take the time for a seminar with the uninitiated) and bought a five-dollar chip, a ten-dollar chip and twenty-dollar chip and said to Jim, "Watch this." I was getting cocky now. Mark Twain called it "the serene confidence which a Christian feels in four aces."

Everyone who plays Roulette for more than a short time develops some kind of system—most are grounded in superstition—and mine deals with only red and black on the wheel, disregarding the numbers. Initially, I just stand there as an observer and watch the wheel and wait. As soon as the same color comes up four times in row, it is time to bet the five on the other color. For example, if the wheel comes up black in four consecutive spins, I bet the red for the fifth. If it still comes up black, then I must double up—in this case, ten dollars—and bet red again. If it still doesn't come up red (and it usually has by now), which means six in a row of the same color, I have to double up one last time, twenty dollars. If it misses for seventh time in a row, which does happen sometimes, I just chalk it up to being snake bit and forget it until next time.

But the law of averages says that it should hit once out of seven, and by betting the last three, I am in a fair position to win. That's my theory Mathematicians say that the odds are the same with each spin. I say that that may be so, but what are the odds of hitting the same color on seven straight spins? I developed this in Atlantic City shortly after they opened it up for gambling and won four hundred dollars the first night. However, I did the same thing in Reno a few years later and got over six hundred dollars ahead, then blew my whole stack when the wheel turned eleven straight times without a red. I think they call that "staying too long at the party." There are more fun ways to play roulette, too. This one can get boring as hell, but it usually works.

This night it worked, and Jim, not an experienced gambler but one with an intellectual interest, liked it so much that he bought some twenty-five-cent chips and sat down beside me. He integrated my system with a sophisticated betting rotation of his own and improved it. In less than an hour, I was about a hundred ahead and so was he, so we decided to head north to Placerville.

En route, we began to share stories again and he told me an interesting anecdote that happened to him in Tampa way back in 1955 when he had one of his first entertaining jobs as a nineteen-year-old piano player in the lounge at the Ramada Inn. It seems that a middle-aged patron, a few fathoms too deep in his cups, wanted to hear "Charmaine" as he had heard this young virtuoso caress it through the piano on nights past. He stumbled up to Tupper and slurred, "Hey, boy, play 'Charmaine'." Tupper had not been appreciative of the drunk's deprecatory attitude, but had already learned that that comes with the turf, and he complied without a comment.

When he was halfway through it, the pest came up to the piano bar again and—right in the middle of his own request—shouted across it, "Hey, I requested 'Charmaine.' Are you going to play the damned thing or not?" So Tupper repeated the song, again without responding verbally and without pausing between. When he finished a few minutes later and was about to launch into something else, the man appeared a third time, and said "Hey, twit, I've been politely asking your for an hour to play 'Charmaine.' "

"Sir," said Tupper, ever the gentleman, "I just played it for you twice."

"You lyin', skinny sackashit, I've been sitting over there listening for it and you ain't played 'Charmaine' yet and if you don't play it right now, I'm gonna' stuff you in that piano box."

The mild-manner young Saussy had maintained his cool much longer than most of us could have, but still he had had enough. He stood up in what was now an assiduously quiet room as the attention of everyone was centered on this confrontation, and yelled in the man's face, "Why don't you just drop dead!" and stalked off the floor.

The next night, when Tupper reported for work, the bartender said first thing, "What are you, Saussy, some kind of wizard-witch?"

Tupper asked, "What do you mean?"

"You put a hex on that drunken old turd last night. He went to the parking lot to get in his car and dropped dead! They hauled him away in the hurry-up wagon about one o'clock this morning.

\* \* \*

On that last leg of the trip, coming out of Tahoe, I began to realize that Jim had logged a lot of miles behind the wheel this day, and I offered to drive. He declined, saying that he knew these precarious turns coming out of the mountains pretty well, and this was not the place for me to be learning to drive a strange motor home. It was probably a good thing because a little while later, he began to tell me the longest and shaggiest "shaggy dog" story ever, and I got to laughing so hard at the end that if I had been driving, we probably wouldn't have made it. His has always been a rare sense of humor that now and then steps completely out of character and just sends me into hysterics.

I retaliated with my Richard Pryor routine, which destroyed him too. A couple of times, he was so convulsed that I thought we were about to come off the mountain without benefit of the road, as we weaved from one side of our lane to the other like a couple of drunken sailors in a stolen motorboat.

\* \* \*

As I tell this, I am reminded of the contrast in our two distinctive personalities, and consider that, indeed, opposites do attract. I am brash, impetuous, sometimes bellicose, too often capricious, and always restless, the kind of guy who stands in front of a microwave oven yelling, "C'mon, c'mon." He is calm, soft-spoken, laid back, peaceful and spiritual, the kind of guy who can see the beauty in a flower, a sunset and probably even a train wreck.

I like folk, he likes Bach, but we both prefer the pop of yesteryear to the noise of today. While he was studying the arts, I was quoting Jim Murray,

Hubert Mizell, Edwin Pope, or Grantland Rice; yet we both would prefer spending an evening chatting with Charles Bukowski, whom we have never met, than with any other living American.

I drink sourmash whiskey, he sips wine, abut we both will quaff a few cold beers on a hot day. I sometimes smoke in the evenings, he detests it anytime. I like the racetrack, he likes the theater, but we both would find something entertaining about any on or off Broadway musical. I take life in large, quick chunks. He savors it in small, tasty morsels. We each eat dinner those same respective ways. I find a ten-minute conversation with this cognoscente to be an education; he probably finds me amusing.

Now, I don't mean to suggest that I would floss my teeth in the dining room at the Waldorf, or that he would be uncomfortable at the Super Bowl either, but okay call me Oscar and call him Felix. But we have spanned that gulf and our friendship has been bonded by at least one common trait—and maybe a second now: We both are egalitarian idealists with an inextinguishable thirst for Truth, and obviously, we both enjoy writing about it.

* * *

It was after 10 p.m. when we cruised into Placerville, a cozy little hamlet that rolls up its sidewalks at dark-thirty. Previously known as "Hangtown" because so many men were strung up there during the gold rush days, today it reminds you of a sleepy Swiss village. The old-time residents brag that "anything will grow in Placerville" and their large produce crop attests to that fact.

About a third of the way up into the Sierra Nevada mountains, the climate at two thousand feet elevation is warm enough in the winter and cool enough in the summer. It lies just south of what one survey chose as the most desirable spot in the United States in which to live. I was impressed with its clean and quaint beauty and a little late, its gracious people. What a great retirement place, I thought from the first time I saw it. Just a little less than a couple of hours from Reno one way and a little more to San Francisco the other.

Kevin and Linda Wilson were delightful hosts and even gave me a bed for a few nights, which was welcome space and comfort for me as well as for Jim in the motor home. Aaron Vanderman dropped over the second night and later pulled out the guitar. I began to strum a few tunes and we all sang along.

After I had a couple of beers, Jim insisted that I do my Pryor routine, and it ended up becoming one of those unforgettable magic nights—a living room variety show where everyone had a funny song to sing or story to tell. It is still what I think of first when I reminisce about Placerville.

The next day I asked Jim about Aaron Vanderman and another couple who had come over the night before, Ted and Katie Lundy.

"Ted and Katie live in southern California, are good friends of the Wilsons, and have become good friends of mine. They travel up this way several times a year and Kevin lets them park their travel trailer on the property whenever they want. So we're old neighbors. They don't know who I am although they almost did shortly after I got here last year. Strangest thing. We were riding in his car and Ted remarked how much I looked like a guy he knew in Tennessee named Tupper Saussy. I almost popped and dissolved right on the spot. He asked if I knew him and, of course, being true to my new code of keeping everyone on a 'need-to-know' basis, I said 'no.' Well that was truthful because what man really knows himself? Anyway, I have no doubt that he could be trusted, but why burden him with a load that he doesn't need to carry?

I knew he couldn't have known Saussy very well, because I barely remembered him. It turns out that he attended one of our 'Seminars on the Mountain' back in Sewanee. Unbelievable. What are the odds of Jim Gordon going 2,000 miles and settling in a place that he has never been and in a matter of weeks, not only meeting but unwittingly becoming close friends with someone who knew Tupper Saussy? Let's have Thorp compute that one. No, never mind. Someday we'll tell Ted and have a big laugh together, but not now.

"Aaron Vanderman is actually the only guy in town who is aware of my background. He never knew Saussy before but is close friends with my friend in Dallas who relocated me when I was in Phoenix. Aaron asked the Wilsons if I could park my motor home here and Lord has since let everything fall into place. Aaron and his whole family are wonderful Christian people, and I have really become close to all of them. His two little girls call me 'Uncle Jim.' He and I have spent many a midnight hour sharing with each other on the Bible and law, and we have helped each other immensely. I hope you can get to know him well. He really is a great friend."

Towards the end of the week, it must have been Thursday, we drove over to Lake Tahoe and Carson City following Ted and Katie in their Lincoln. "Kate needs to feed her habit at the slots and I have a business arrangement that requires some discussion with my partner there," said Ted. For Jim and me, it was another opportunity to talk and maybe take a minor shot at the tables.

En route to Tahoe, a few particles of snow came down like samples, but by the time we arrived, the skies had cleared in typical Tahoe fashion as if the gods of tourism were trying to accommodate both the late season skiers and us ordinary tourists. On the way, Jim had begun to level with me concerning the tolls of being on the run.

"It's driving me crazy not to be able to communicate with Freddy and the boys." He had married Frederique, a Puerto Rican blue blood, in 1973. They had two sons who appeared to be about eight and twelve now, from the pictures he showed me. He carefully replaced them in the glove compartment, rather than carry them in his wallet. I knew why without asking.

"I think about my family hourly, every day and night," he said. "I miss them terribly and pray everyday that they are all in good health and happy spirits ... not to mention that I am also successfully meeting the challenge of celibacy.

It was then that he confided to me that he had spent last Christmas when his motor home was parked in Utah, with his family at her father's home in Puerto Rico.

"But it was awkward," he said. "Freddy was paralyzed with fear. She had to introduce me to everyone as 'her friend, Jim Gordon, the minister.' I had been wearing a clerical collar when I arrived at the airport and we agreed that it would make a nice ruse. Scripture tells us that we are called to be ministers, so what's wrong with wearing the outward sign? It almost backfired on Freddy, though, when one of her lady friends, recently divorced, came by to visit and took a liking to me. She asked Freddy, when I was out of earshot, if Reverend Gordon would mind being asked to escort a divorced lady to a dinner party. Freddy, hoping to head this off before it went too far, told her, 'Father Gordon doesn't date.'

"I wonder if he is celibate," her friend said.

Jim snickered as he repeated Freddy's retort, "He damned well better be."

I howled double hard at that situation because it reminded me of Lenny Bruce's story of his posing as a Catholic priest on the streets of Miami as a fund raiser. He said that he never got laid so much as when he dressed like a priest. He had a Cadillac convertible and would visit the rich Catholic women to raise money for a leper colony and they would give him a nice donation in more ways than one.

After a lull in the conversation, Jim said, "Freddy is coming back to Sewanee next month to ship some of her fine things to Puerto Rico, clean out the office and prepare the house for rental. I wish you would giver her a call and check her pulse."

I thought for a second as a light bulb went on in my head, then said, "I can do better than that," I said. "I know how you can communicate with her without any risk of detection."

"How?"

"Have you ever heard of a voice mail system?" I asked.

"No," he said, "How does that work?"

"It's ideal for someone who is transient like me or one who wants privacy like you." I went on to explain how it is nothing more than a computer programmed to answer multiple lines, but the scope of it is multifold. Two people on the same system can talk to each other through the computer, and you can use it as an office phone because it is answered with your personal voice. The messages can be picked up and cancelled or the message changed at any time and as often as you desire, even from halfway around the world.

"Freddy can call me," I said, "and leave whatever message she wants. Then I can send the message over to your box with the simple pressing of a button on any touchtone phone. You can then reply by pushing your answer back through my system which she can dial up and activate the next day or at any pre-decided time. That way, there is never a record of her having called your number.

"Fantastic. How much does that cost?"

"Less than an answering service," I said. "Here's the number of my system in Phoenix. Get on the program and not only can you and I communicate with it but you will have a permanent number that Jim Gordon can use for whatever business you wish. If Freddy wants to use it later, let me know and I will instruct her on how to enter my system for messages. I can put her on my number as a 'guest' and she can get her own messages without having to sort through mine, and vice versa.. I can punch into the system from anywhere in the world as long as I have a touchtone phone. It's high tech ... as least for someone as low tech as I am. Drop me a message after you get on line and let me know your number?"

"Man, I love it," he said. "This sounds like the answer to my communications problem."

The next night we were drinking a late night cup of coffee in the motor home and discussing some of the in-depth subjects we had covered the year before in Phoenix. Now I could not only understand where he was coming from, but with my newfound knowledge, discuss it with him semi-intelligently. Although I did understand that with control of the "money" a faction could capture anything, the most confusing of all—if indeed there existed a conspiracy to control—was the control of the churches. I was becoming an experienced interviewer though, and, after turning on the recorder, I led Jim into the subject the easiest way I knew—with a question.

"When did you first know that you were a Christian?"

He leaned back and rocked his straight-back chair for a moment, searching the corners of his mind for this provenance and slowly said, "Like many, I was reared in the traditions of institutionalized Christianity as organized by the Episcopal Church. That meant learning dogma, ritual, and fear of wrongdoing. I learned catechism, not scripture.

"I thought I was a Christian because that's what I was told I was. (This sounded familiar to me.) I lived my first forty years without being persecuted. Then, for reasons I thought purely legal and rational, I questioned the monetary powers and found myself persecuted from all quarters. Not until several years later did I discover that's what makes you a Christian—being persecuted for loathing lies."

"Just what is a Christian, anyway?" I asked.

"A Christian is anyone who follows and does the words of Jesus Christ, believing in Him. In America in the 1980's, no one can follow and do the words of Jesus without being persecuted. Wasn't the U.S. Attorney emphatic to the jury in condemning me for my views on money? Aren't most of the IRS press releases about me careful to link me to my book calling for monetary reform, as though to chill any inquiries into the money system?

"Remember, it was Jesus' excoriation in the temple of the church's participation in a commercial monetary system that accelerated the process of His execution. It is not an exaggeration today to say that anyone who claims to be a Christian, but who is not persecuted, is probably not following and doing the words of Jesus Christ, but rather complying with the dictates of some false prophet. How can there ever be separation of Church and State when the states incorporate all the churches?

"I don't welcome persecution and I am not willing to be persecuted for beliefs that are un-Christian. I would do everything in my power, for example, to avoid being persecuted for holding atheistic views. Why? Because there is no reward for suffering persecution for such beliefs, except perhaps applause and recognition from those who admire human courage. But to be persecuted for practicing the words of Jesus Christ is the greatest pleasure I have every known. For this reason, I do everything in my power to expose myself to persecutions from anti-Christians. Of course, it creates inconveniences and brings certain pains, but that's where faith comes into play.

"If you are asserting rights against Caesar's trespass, faith is everything. I acknowledge three kinds of faith: faith in self, faith in Satan or false gods, and faith in Jesus. I've seen self faith win against government prosecutors and I've seen it lose too. Self faith is humanistic and humanism always ends in despair. I've seen faith in Satan or false gods win too. But after the victory, the winner destroys himself carrying out his devious savior's commands to do evil. Only faith in Jesus Christ—the God of the Bible—brings unerring victory. I mean epic victory. But the faith must be unwavering.

I sat staring at him, drilling holes into his mind as he continued.

"Three years ago, the TV stations showed Freddy and me joyously stepping out of the Chattanooga Federal Courthouse after my single conviction. 'This man has just been convicted," asked the voice-over reporter, "so why is he smiling?" The media and those under its influence viewed the government's victory as my loss, but we saw it as God's way of spreading the issue out over a greater population, stimulating wider public awareness, elevating concern over the right to due process into higher political circles.

"The U.S. Constitution bars government from prying into the private lives of those who wish to remain faithful to the God of the Christian Bible and independent of the civil authority. As more and more Christian ministers come to realize that their expansion projects and glistening steeples are the result of their having bought Satan's sales pitch atop the mountain overlooking the world, there will be more repentance. With repentance comes the awareness that, by the terms of our written Constitution, the civil power has no authority over churches. When leaders are gifted with this awareness, the gospel of Christian liberty will begin to make sense to those who need it most."

Everybody that I got to know in Placerville, I liked. The Lord, through his legions, surely did appear to be taking good care of Jim, even though his fortunes seemed to change like the desert wind. After we spent a couple of more days in Lake Tahoe, sleeping in the motor home, we went back to Placerville for a wonderful Easter dinner with Aaron Vanderman's whole family—parents, uncles and aunts, cousins, and "Uncle Jim" and me. It reminded me of some of the family reunions my family held at various places around the country forty years ago. Plenty of fried chicken, cherry pie, potato salad, iced tea and conversation.

Aaron, a real student of the Bible who had attended seminary, was fascinated with my diatribe on Romans 13 and the corruption of Truth by the modern publications. Incredulous that a nightclub entertainer could be aware of this when he wasn't, he stepped to the bookshelf and pulled down the King James version and a New International version to see for himself, and there it was in black and white: One set of rules telling us that we are "subject to the higher powers," and the other, masquerading between the covers of the "Holy Bible," instructing God's people to obey the government." Having spent much of the past, counseling back and forth with Jim Gordon, he already knew that government is one of the lower powers, and only Jesus Christ, God Incarnate, is a higher power to man. AS we ambled towards the kitchen for another plateful of his mother's delicious potato salad, he vowed to research the two editions for more discrepancies.

"The potential ramifications of this are mind blowing," Aaron said, shaking his head.

On Monday, I flew out of Sacramento to Phoenix feeling that I was leaving Jim in good hands. With his faith and friends like these, who could harm him?

*Whoever controls the volume of money in any country is absolute master of all industry and commerce.*

—President James A. Garfield

*The wicked flee when no man pursueth; but the righteous are bold as a lion.*

—Proverbs 28:1

I t was Monday morning when Deputy U.S. Marshal James Karnath, who was directing the search for Tupper Saussy, sat in his Nashville office talking on the phone to his comrades in California. When he cradled the receiver back on the base, a secretary was startled out of her seat to hear him scream from the other room, "We've got that slick sumbitch now!"

She knew what had been occupying his mind nonstop the last 14 months and went charging in asking expectantly, "Mr. Karnath, do you mean the elusive Mr. Saussy?"

"I damn sure do," he sneered with a half-whisper, his eyes glowing wildly like a child's on Christmas eve. "We're gonna' pick him up tomorrow or the next day in California. He has literally let his mouth overload his ass this time. He couldn't resist calling his wife. I knew if we kept that bug on, he'd show up from somewhere while she was here. We've got a positive I.D., and the poor sucker doesn't even know we're coming. I'll get that promotion now. Get me on the next available flight to Sacramento, and if it's not available, tell 'em to boot somebody off and make it available."

Before dark that extra long day he would be drinking Chivas Regal in the California offices of the CID and back-slapping with fellow agents as they made their barbaric plans for the capture which, it was decided, would take place on Wednesday, June 1st.

"Tomorrow, I want to fly over the place," said Karnath to his west coast peers, "and get an exact lay of the land. We don't want anything to go wrong. Line up your best photographers for Wednesday. We want the weekend papers to put the right kind of fear in the next one who tries to pull this number."

\* \* \*

It was Wednesday, June 1st, 1988, when I drove to Sewanee, Tennessee from Atlanta—about a three hour trip for sane people, slightly less for me. I had just spent the weekend in Philadelphia at the wedding of the daughter of a close friend. Prior to that I had done two weeks in Washington, DC after winding up my four week gig with Juan in Phoenix and would spend a week at "Banks & Shane" in Atlanta before heading back to Phoenix again. Another blazing summer in the desert. Would my agent ever get my schedule right?

I had called Freddy the night before and made an appointment to see her at 1:30 p.m., Central time, at the Spencer Judd publishing office in Sewanee, where the famous *Main Street Journal* had been published since July of 1981. The time of day would be significant because that would make it 11:30 a.m. in California.

### WED. NOON C.D.T., 10:00 A.M., P.D.T.

Earlier that same morning in Placerville—about the time the stores were opening—Federal Agents in three-piece suits began to call on business owners in the downtown area and flash the picture of Tupper Saussy. "Have you seen this man" was always answered with a "No." The people were then warned that "... he is known to be in the area," and "... this man is armed and dangerous." At that moment, I was a continent away, steaming up Georgia Interstate 75 towards Chattanooga.

### WED. 1:30 P.M., C.D.T.

Frederique Saussy is a striking brunette—one who could have taken Leslie Caron's part in "Gigi" or Talia Shire's in "Rocky"—ten years younger than her husband. Multi-lingual, she has home-educated their two boys perhaps better than any public or private school could hope to. They, too, are multi-lingual. Of French and Spanish extraction and speaking with only a slight, charming accent, her genteel countenance reflects aristocratic class, but if there is one dagger that can penetrate this, it is the mention of government agents.

Once, she told me, a few years ago, two agents from the bank came to the house in Sewanee to enforce a bank levy against her husband, who wasn't there at the time, and demanded to be let in. Everything in the house belonged to Freddy. When they persisted on wanting in, she demanded a warrant. They had none but kept insisting to be let in in order to inventory and confiscate her property. Finally, she told them, "You may come in, but first you will have to kill me. Then you will have to step over my body and kill my ten year old. After you step over his body and kill my six year old, I guess you will be able to take anything that you want."

When they still didn't get the message fast enough, she chased them off the porch and across the yard to their car with a broom. Needless to say, when the agents reached the safe harbor of their automobile, they hastily beat a path back to Nashville.

Sewanee lies in the mountains forty miles north of Chattanooga and just west of Monteagle. The temperature was warming close to ninety degrees by the time I arrived, but the mountain breeze made it far more comfortable than humid Atlanta. I was struck by the architecture and ancient beauty of the ivy-covered buildings on the campus of the University of the South, Sewanee's long time and only claim to fame before Tupper Saussy came along.

The "business district" of downtown Sewanee consists of a cafe, a service station, a post office, a couple of incidental shops, and one pub, "Shenanigans," which has a monopoly on all the college trade as well as the locals. Most of the streets are paved. I arrived a little early, and, as I was parking the car, Frederique hailed me from a friend's shop across the street as I walked toward the office door.

Freddy doesn't look much like a "Freddy" to me; but more like a "Gina" or a "Maria." We chatted for a few minutes before entering that hot office— the electricity inside had been turned off for more than a year—and I detected an attitude of frustration as we continued inside. She believed in everything that her husband had stood for, and run for, but the results had produced a much more drastic effect on her lifestyle than she relished having to face ... even for another week, let alone indefinitely.

I also found her to be unreasonably paranoid. She was convinced that not only was the office bugged, but every phone in town was suspect. "The boys need a father, and I need a husband at home," she said. "I do not intend to spend my life with my hair dyed blond, using a false name and living in a trailer." I concurred but pointed out that that lifestyle should, somehow, be only temporary.

She argued, "But *how* long," and, of course, the argument was over.

"Where is he, Pat? Do you know?" I nodded my head in the affirmative.

"Where?," she demanded.

"Binghamton, New York," I lied, mainly because of my promise to "Jim," but partly because she just could have been right about the office being bugged. If someone else were listening, it would make a nice smokescreen. I could visualize the goon squad converging on every known "protestor" in western New York.

"They're going to kill him, Pat, oh, I know it. I can feel it." I charged off that comment more to "wifely worry" than clairvoyance. Neither of us could have known that, at that very moment, Tupper Saussy was only seconds and one timely decision away from becoming a bullet-riddled body.

Jim had asked me to help her sell his car— a '79 Saab—and send him the funds, if possible.

"Impossible!" she said. "That car is parked outside the repair shop in Winchester, and they are watching it every minute. If anybody tries to move it, they will be arrested on the spot."

"On what charges", I wondered. We had the title. If she signs the car over to me, it was legally mine. The Feds couldn't prevent her from selling it, and they damn sure would need more probable cause than that to even interrogate me, let alone arrest me. I tried to diplomatically explain that she was not placing herself at any risk. If anybody was, I was, and I really wasn't concerned. At worst, I figured I might be detained for a few minutes, no more. But she was immovable. She was so terrified of agitating Caesar that she had become completely neutralized. I backed off.

"Oh Pat, I just don't know which way to turn. Tupper called here a couple of times last week, at the friend's house where I am staying, and the agents have been tailing me ever since. They follow me wherever I go. I guarantee you they are running a check on your tag number right now!  And they probably will follow you when you leave here."

I chuckled to myself at the thought of them chasing down that license plate number. I had borrowed the car for the day from a fellow entertainer who was working with me at "Banks & Shane."  It was registered to his recently deceased uncle in New York City.  That might give them further cause to check out Binghamton, if they really were listening and watching.

"Tupper wants me to call back at the number in Arizona and tell him what time I will be at a phone booth where he can call me back, but I would have to go to Nashville or Chattanooga to find a tel fono that I could trust, and then I still couldn't be sure. I called that answering system once, and it told me to push this button for this and that button for that, but all I had was a dial tel fono, so I just hung up.

"Tupper didn't plan this very well," she went on, "and he has made a fine mess of our financial affairs."

"How do you mean," I asked.

"Well, he made this decision to leave, and acted on it, all in twenty-four hours or less, you know."

"No, I didn't."

"Yes, he told me later that something just told him not to go into prison because he would be killed. He didn't consult with me. I was visiting my parents with the boys in Puerto Rico and the first thing I knew about it was when my friends sent me the news clippings, or maybe he called me first, I can't remember now. But now it's a year later and his goddamned brother" .... (she paused and looked at me the way a lady does when she knows she has slipped and is wondering if you are offended. I showed no reaction) ... "has stolen all the books from the office and has sold them. He had a yard sale here before I returned and sold the typewriters and computers and furniture. Look around you. This is all that is left. The bastard (her Latin blood was really boiling now) even stripped out half of the stuff in our house.

I am going to have to get a divorce so I can legally sell the house and cars that are in Tupper's name. The lawyer says that I will have to sue him for desertion, and I know he hasn't deserted me, but what else am I to do?"

I didn't respond at the moment but that "divorce" remark hit me like a hammer. I knew that was more than Tupper had bargained for.

She rambled on at forty knots as she continued to pour out her frustrations. I politely listened because I could tell that she needed someone to just listen. She had had no on—at least no one who knew her husband's side—to talk to for months. I asked that she please consider that decision carefully before taking divorce proceedings. I told her that Tupper loved her and the boys deeply, and a Caesarian divorce from the State would probably please him very much, but he felt that they would never be divorced under God.

"What else am I to do?" she repeated. "I have no money, and I cannot convert any of these few assets that are left to cash unless I sue him for desertion and have this property declared legally mine." I felt as helpless as the owner of a sick goldfish. I had no solution to offer.

But I did remind her of the perspicacity of her husband, how I had been educated to truth in the last year, and that I had not believed that his life was in danger at first, but now I wasn't so sure. I did know, and told her so, that if he lost her and the boys, he might as well be dead, because he wouldn't have anything else to live for anyway.

*      *      *

### WED. 11:00 A.M., P.D.T.

That Wednesday brought along a typical California morning as the sun quickly burned through the cool fog. It was at this time yesterday that Jim had heard an airplane circling overhead but decided it wasn't important. This day he slept a couple of hours later than usual because he had been up writing until the early morning hours. His motor home was parked in the usual place; in the vale about 150 yards down the hill and across the creek from the Wilson's house. Everyone else had left early that beautiful summer morning to meet other colleagues at the Buttercup Cafe for breakfast before going to the office at 8:30. He had turned the computer back on in preparation for completing what he had begun the night before and was warming the water for his second cup of instant coffee.

The clock on the wall at the main street offices of MBA showed 11:05 a.m. when the receptionist looked up to see a herd of armed men in blue jackets come charging into the vestibule. A few seconds after the initial commotion, Kevin came out of his office to see what the problem was. He and his partner, Burl Stewart, were pushed around and frisked, and a shouting match ensued. Stewart is a bantamweight, but Kevin Wilson, at six foot six, although in his mid-fifties, is not an individual that one would choose from a crowd to rough up. He yelled at the team leader to have those fools put their guns away and to "show me the warrant."

During this skirmish, an "angel of mercy," as Jim later described her, slipped out the back door to the parking lot, jumped into her car, and sped out of town on the ten-mile jaunt toward the Wilson property.

A month or so earlier, Jim had traded his editing services for a few gold coins which he then traded for an old Eldorado Cadillac. He had spent a few bucks tuning it up, in preparation for a trip across country; a trip which would, he hoped, include a rendezvous with Freddy. Except for being a gas guzzler, the car was in tip-top shape and was parked outside his motorhome at 11:30, ready to roll, when he heard a vehicle come roaring up out front. Before he could look outside, he heard pounding on his door and a familiar voice calling his name. When he opened the door, he recognized the face as one of the ladies from an office down the hall whom he had befriended, and greeted her with a warm, "Hi!"

Without returning the greeting, she said, "Get in your car and get yourself out of here! They are in the office right now with guns and a warrant for your arrest talking with Linda and Kevin, and they are probably coming here next!"

Fortunately, he had already dressed. Fortunately, because that is all he left with—only the clothes on his back. His cache of gold and silver, his clothes in the closet, his computer, his toothbrush, *everything* he owned, his life savings, were left behind. He did, however, escape with the most important thing—his life.

At 11:40, while the half-consumed coffee was still warm in the cup, a 20-man SWAT team, armed with automatic weapons and wearing bullet-proof vests, converged on the Wilson property with guns drawn, surrounded and entered the motorhome. Upon finding no one there, they hooked it up to a tow truck and hauled away all of the worldly possessions of Tupper Saussy/Jim Gordon.

One of the young agents held the half-filled cup of coffee in his hand as he strode towards the passenger side of one of the unmarked Chevrolets wherein sat James Karmath. "We just missed him Mr. Karmath, the coffee is still warm. If we had come here first, I believe we'd have found him."

"You moron!" screamed the disgusted Karmath. "I *believe* if my aunt had balls she'd be my uncle. Take your belief and stuff it. And while you're at it, take a dozen men and comb those woods and hills."

The subservient lackey said, "Yes sir," and quickly turned on his heel to do as he was told in order to escape further wrath from his boss. Karnath turned to his driver who had the hand-held radio and said, "Tell that chopper to circle low and see if they can spot him. The sumbitch is probably up one of them trees laughing at us right now."

The capture of an unarmed misdemeanant requires this show of power? Was this the Sundance Kid they were stalking? Or was this, more likely, a repeat of the Gordon Kahl scenario in North Dakota and Arkansas five years before? The premonstration earlier in the day by the visits to the town's business people certainly set the stage for "legalized murder," and the site in the country, with no witnesses, could hardly have been more private. In any case, Jim frustrated their efforts by escaping in the nick of time. There would be no stories about the capture of Tupper Saussy in the papers this weekend.

* * *

He was in a panic; walking through a surrealistic nightmare. If they were that close behind him, he had to get out of town. But where to? And how? They undoubtedly already had a make on his green Cadillac, he thought. He probably wouldn't even get to the state line. And money. He couldn't go anywhere without some cash. Listening to the better angels of his nature, he realized that Aaron Vanderman was his only hope. He damn sure couldn't contact the Wilsons. They would hang up on him at this moment.

He stopped the big Cadillac at a supermarket and prayed all the way across the parking lot as he attempted to walk casually to a telephone. It must have taken a titanic effort to remain nonchalant at this point, but he managed it. He had seven bucks in his wallet and, fortunately, some change in his pocket. He felt for a quarter and slammed it the coin box, quickly dialing the memorized number. His prayer was answered when Terri picked up the phone but denied when she told him that Aaron was not there. Then he was encouraged again when she said that she was sure that he would be at the Buttercup Cafe because he had a noon appointment there for lunch. She noticed the consternation in Jim's voice and asked if there were anything she could do.

"No, Hon," Jim said, "But I may not see you again for awhile so please give the girls a hug and a kiss for me. Gotta' run. Goodbye."

The few seconds Jim fumbled the yellow pages seemed like minutes as he scurried through the listings for the Buttercup Cafe. It was now 11:55 and maybe, just maybe, Aaron had arrived early. He had him paged and a minute later, Aaron answered, and Jim quickly told him what had happened.

"Stay where you are, I'll be right there," said Aaron and then quickly called the MBA office to confirm the problem. Yes, indeed, the agents had been there, but most of them had quickly left when they discovered Jim Gordon was not there. Aaron already knew where they had to have gone.

In a few minutes Jim and Aaron were sitting together in Aaron's station wagon discussing strategy. Both being strong believers, the first thing they did was say a prayer for guidance. Jim began to calm down, and they dissected ideas back and forth as soberly and precisely as if they were making corporate boardroom decisions. After several ideas were rejected by one or the other, they came up with the best spur-of-the-moment one they could conceive on the spot.

Aaron is a real estate developer and, in preparation for the first of the month payday, happened to have his payroll stashed in his toolbox in the back of the station wagon. He gave his friend three hundred bucks and they embarked on the two-hour trek to the Reno airport. Aaron then bought him a ticket to Seattle and Jim flew away with nobody waiting for him. It was Tupper Saussy against the world all over again. Aaron returned to Placerville to take care of the Cadillac and try to remain as calm as possible.

### WED. 4:30 P.M., C.D.T.

At about the same moment that Aaron was sending Jim on his way in Reno, I was bidding adieu to Freddy in Sewanee, both of us still ignorant of the goings-on in California. She would be heading back to Puerto Rico in a few weeks, and I promised to stay in touch with her. Outside, she gave me a hug, a sisterly peck on the cheek, and thanked me for coming and for my concern. I felt frustrated because there was nothing I could do to help her, help my good friend, or help them get together again. Opening the car door and thinking of the song, "Elusive Butterfly," I lightheartedly sang her a line from the lyrics, with a slight rearrangement, as I sat down behind the wheel... "You may wake up some mornin,' to Tupper's silent whisper blowing past your window in the wind." She just smirked a smile, shook her head, and waved goodbye. A lady of mysterious sorrow.

While taking a circuitous route out of the little town, I hummed and sang to myself as I often do when I am driving. "Don't be concerned, it will not harm you. It's only me pursuing something I'm not sure of." And then slowly mumbled: "It's only him pursuing something he's not sure of. Across his dreams ... hmmm hmm of wonder, hmm that elusive butterfly of love."

As I turned north onto Interstate 75, I thought the car which followed me down the ramp a furlong behind might be suspect. I went to the next exit, flip-flopped, returned to the first one and exited again, this time turning east and cruising through the shopping district of Monteagle. When no one followed, I returned to the Interstate and headed south towards Chattanooga and Atlanta.

\* \* \*

With all my traveling on Wednesday, I just hadn't gotten around to checking my messages. I usually check the voice-mail box every night when I am on the road, but I didn't return to my hotel room until nearly eight, and I had to be on stage at nine. On Thursday night when I finally dialed in, Jim's was the first voice I heard.

"Hi! I am in New York and uh, uh, probably going to Europe. Call Aaron Vandermann, and he will tell you the details." He sounded shook. What was he doing in New York? I couldn't imagine at the time what could possibly have flushed him from his comfortable nest and have him suddenly talking about going to Europe. This had to be a smokescreen. I waited until after eleven o'clock when it was only eight o'clock in California and called Aaron at his home. He was vague and would only give me a number of a phone booth that I should call in five minutes. I waited ten and dialed him back.

"What the hell is going on, Aaron?"

He went through the whole story, and I was aghast.

"Sheeeit," I screamed, "He tried to tell me a year ago that they were trying to kill him, and I didn't believe it. Those bastards were going to take him out, weren't they?!"

Aaron is one of those lovable Christians who doesn't use the scatological Billingsgate, but isn't offended by it if you do. "It sure looked that way to us, Pat, but we got him out, and he's safe now."

"Praise the Lord," I heard myself saying, "Where is he now? Is he in New York City?"

"I'd rather not say over the phone. It's not that you can't be trusted, but I am concerned about who else might be listening."

"10-4. How did they find him?"

"Who knows. You know there was a gumshoe snooping around here in November, so maybe they just checked back on a lucky hunch and followed him from the office. But let's not talk too much about it right now ... and let's refer to him as 'Sam' from now on. I don't trust any phone in town."

I gave him the number at "Banks & Shane" and suggested that he call me from a "safe" phone booth any night before Sunday. I gave him my schedule in order that he not waste a call while I was on stage. Before we hung up he remembered that he had to be in Sacramento on Saturday and would catch up with me then.

When Aaron called on Saturday at the prescribed time, I learned that "Sam" was now in Seattle in a twenty dollar a night motel and quickly running out of money. I got the number, gave him a call there, and found him in his room relaxing and watching a rickety old TV with a semi-clear picture.

"Where are you?," he asked.

"Just strummin' my guitar and singin' to the drunks in Atlanta," I replied. "Life ain't too bad if you don't sting Caesar with your cattle prod. I heard you almost met the firing squad this week."

"What do you mean?"

Apparently, Aaron had not yet told him what had transpired at the motor home site after he flew the coop. I repeated what second-hand details I had and told him, "You were being set up, and they damn near gotcha.' You're no Carl Lewis, but you run pretty good for a Caucasian."

"Well, maybe so, but the Lord promised that if I would obey Him, he would protect me. He confused them long enough for me to escape their net."

We talked for awhile, and his main concern seemed to be his shortage of funds. I told him that money was like sex in that it was only important when you don't have any, but that I could help with that—the money, that is—and that I would call a friend of mine the next day who would give him an advance on my word. If he could wait until Monday, I would have time to arrange it.

He said he had plenty for now, but three hundred bucks wouldn't last long with motels and restaurant meals, and he didn't feel it was prudent to be out looking for an establishment job right now. I agreed, but thought playing the piano in an out-of-the-way pub would not be too obtrusive. George might know a spot.

"What name should I give him?" I asked.

"Schott. James A. Schott is my new name," he said. Hmmm, I wondered. Wasn't that the name of the General played by Burt Lancaster who was instigating a military takeover of the government in "Seven Days in May?" No, that was James Mattoon Scott. How the hell did I remember that?

"Okay, Mr. Schott. What does the 'A' stand for, 'Almost?'"

"What?"

"Never mind. If you don't hear from me by Monday, it means that everything is in hunkeydorey order, and you can give my friend a call Monday night. Write down his name and number. And, by the way, since we're going to be doing all this surreptitious, clandestine stuff, let me teach you a code for providing new phone numbers to each other over the phone."

I remembered a John McDonald novel that I read many years ago in which "Travis McGee" had used a factoring system which, when known by both parties, can transmit in normal conversation a number to which any eavesdropping parties cannot become privy without the code. It can be used for addresses, telephones, anything with a number. In two minutes "Jim Schott" had it memorized.

"That's great! I love it!," he said. "Be sure you teach this to Aaron the next time you talk." I agreed to, suggested he find a job at a piano bar, and told him to drop me a message at the voice-mail box if he needed me because I would be traveling across country by car starting tomorrow, and there would be no planned place he could reach me.

Thanks to my Atlanta friend, Rod Gibbons, who had a dealer's license and could get us in the car auction, I had gotten a great buy earlier that week on a Nissan 300-Z, a car that I had been lusting after for years, and I was actually looking forward to my trip across country. I had sold my 450 SL before leaving Phoenix the last time and had enough to pay cash for this one. I had already decided that I was going to shop for a "Z" while flying around the country on this jaunt, and, if I couldn't get the deal I wanted, I would pick one up when I got back to Phoenix. This one, at one year old, with only 13,000 miles and priced at less than wholesale, was a deal I couldn't refuse.

The first time I had made this cross-country trip was way back in 1959 in my '54 Bel Air Chevy. This passage would have to be more fun.

It was after noon on Sunday before I got my "Z" gassed up and departed "Hotlanta," a year-round sobriquet which is most appropriate in June for that southern city. I grabbed a sack full of heavily mustardized Krystal Burgers and fries in Jackson, Mississippi at dusk, filled the gas tank again, and continued zooming across I-20. Pausing only to call some old friends in Monroe, Louisiana who did not answer, I was on the outskirts of Dallas before midnight and got a cheap room at the Motel 6 on the east side.

There were no messages at the box, but before I crashed, I called George in Seattle and told him that my friend, Jim Schott, was in town, down on his luck, needed a job, and that I would appreciate anything he could do to help him, and even if that were nothing, I was still sending him $500 to pass on to him when he called. George and I were good enough friends that he knew he could advance that amount meantime and agreed to do so.

By Monday night I was in Las Cruces, New Mexico, having burned up more miles that day than the first. Thanks to the Interstate system, one can now motor from coast to coast without seeing anything. I was tempted to go on in to Phoenix, but I was too pooped, and I had long ago learned that by driving all night, I only have to waste most of the next day with sleeping, so what was to be gained? I found another Brand "X" motel and flopped down. The next morning I had three messages in the voice-mail box. One was from Aaron Vanderman.

When I called him at home he greeted me warmly and asked that I call him back at the same phone booth, if I still had the number. I did, which saved him from having to repeat it over the suspect phone lines.

When we made new contact ten minutes later, he asked if I had been in touch with "Sam." I told him I had and passed on the fact that I had made arrangements for "Sam" to have some provisional funds, and that he was looking for work. Nothing else was new. "He sends his love to Terri and the kids and asks that you please not worry. He's getting along okay," I said. "Bored as he'll ever be in his life, but okay."

"Pat," Aaron said, getting around to the real reason for his call, "Can you to come back to Placerville one more time."

"What for?" I asked.

"To pick up Sam's car. I've got it stashed on a friend's property up in the country, and I don't know what to do with it."

"So what do you want me to do with it?"

"Use it. Sell it. Run it off a cliff. I don't care. Just drive it out of here. Nobody around here can use it. I'll buy your plane ticket if you will come up here and drive it away. All of his friends are afraid to touch it. Take it back to Phoenix and sell it for Sam. He could use the money. I've got the title."

"Well then, why don't you just put it on a lot in Sacramento? That would be simpler, wouldn't it? And cheaper?"

"Of course it would, but I don't want to drive it. Everybody that knows him is already involved more than they want to be, and I don't want to involve any of my other friends. We've all decided that you are the only man for the job."

Holy Jerusalem. What the hell kind of sentence do these people think they would get—the electric chair— for selling a car to which they held rightful title? There could be no Aiding and Abetting charges here. They never knew Tupper Saussy, the fugitive; only Jim Gordon the mild-mannered reporter, friend to all mankind. (When I had traveled with him in the motorhome, he was helping me, not I him. And, come to think of it, technically, I didn't even send him any money; I sent it to George Corbin.) Can the Feds really attach such a stigma to an individual that his best friends will deny even knowing him? From the Apostle Peter to modern times, I guess human nature hasn't changed much at all.

I was in the middle of a 2,000 mile trip now and surely wasn't relishing the idea of being a car courier again so soon, but on the other hand, if Aaron was willing to buy my ticket, it must be awfully important to him that we move that vexatious Cadillac, and I knew that Jim could surely use the funds at this time in his hectic life. I relented and told him to pre-pay the ticket in the name of 'Jimmy Carter' from Phoenix to Reno on Wednesday afternoon because that would give me Tuesday to rest and wash clothes and Thursday to drive it back before opening Friday night at the Casa Loma.

We said goodbye after he told me he would call me back at my apartment in Phoenix that night with the flight times. I had a great lunch in Tucson at my favorite Mexican restaurant in the world—a much needed fix for my habit from which I was about to suffer withdrawal pains after so many days in the East—and had a leisurely drive into Phoenix Monday afternoon.

* * *

It was late afternoon on Wednesday, exactly a week after the motor home hit, when Aaron met me at the Reno Airport. During the two-hour cruise back to Placerville, he gave me the blow-by-blow description of what had happened the previous week.

"Why in the world did those dummies go to the office first instead of the motor home?" I wondered out loud. "They obviously knew where it was." We were rattling west across I-80 in Aaron's old pickup towards Sacramento. Placerville would be a 30 minute shot south on State Highway 49 about half way down the Interstate.

"Jim and I decided that the Lord just confused them," he said.

"Either that or they just naturally assumed that he would already be at the office with everybody else," I pointed out, and then reached for a pad and pen on his dashboard. "Oh, by the way, Jim thought it would be a good idea for you to have this." As I wrote down a few particulars, I told him about the factoring code for discussing phone numbers over the telephone. He grasped it and wrote down the instructions in his calendar book.

"We will use this from now on," he said. We pulled into his driveway in Placerville in the early darkness. It was a beautiful, modern, ranch style home. Just the type I would expect one in his profession to own. His wife, Terri, whom I had met briefly on my first trip there, had dutifully prepared all the vegetables and trimmings for supper, awaiting Aaron's arrival for him to display his culinary touch in the final grilling of the steaks.

I was still tired from the previous scamper across country and wanted to get a good night's sleep before tackling the fourteen hour trek on Thursday. Aaron, a teetotaler knowing that I wasn't, took care of that problem by uncovering a bottle of delicious Chianti to enjoy with my steak, which I summarily beheaded and pulled on while he cooked. I filled three glasses from it during the meal and polished it all off following dessert. "This stuff will spoil, you know, once it is opened," I said, and I think Terri believed me. I retired to the guest room and slept as if I was embalmed until 7:00 a.m.

When I walked into the kitchen, Aaron was already up, drinking coffee, and reading the paper. Some of the weeks's activities were tending to make Aaron Vanderman a little paranoid, too, I noticed. He was saying things that were not as way out as Freddy, but his nervousness tended to remind me of her.

I said, "Look, stop sweatin' it. They are not hovering overhead in helicopters waiting for your next move. They don't know anything about you or me. You're giving them more credit than they deserve. Where's the car?"

"Up the road about ten miles from here. I thought we'd go up to the Buttercup for breakfast and head out from there."

"Okay," I said, "I'll be ready in five minutes."

We both had the cafe's sausage, egg, and pancake special, and with all that on top of the previous night's meal which had not worn off yet, I was stuffed. As we got ready to leave Aaron said, "Listen, Pat, I think it would be better if I gave you directions and called a cab for you."

I knew it. He was getting frazzled. "Why would you want to involve someone who keeps records?" I asked.

"Because everybody up there knows me, and I think it would be better if I were not seen in the area where the car is. I've still got to live around here, remember."

"Aha," I said, 'Velly old Chinese pwahvub: He who rides the tiger is afraid to dismount!' "

He wasn't amused at my facetious attempt at humor, so I got serious. "Dang it all, Aaron, we have come this far with privacy, don't screw it up by involving others. I've always said that if you want to keep a secret, you don't involve *anybody* else. We both are already trusting one more than we need to. Just drop me off down the road and point me towards the car. Nobody is going to see you do that or care."

But Vanderman was adamant. This was the end of the line for him and me. He intended to give me ten bucks for the cab fare, but, after buying breakfast, he was caught short, and I would have to take care of the hack driver on my own. He did supply written directions for the driver, a quarter to call the cab company, the car keys, and said goodbye, before heading his pickup down the hill toward his sanctum of home. In another week, the feds would have him singing like the proverbial canary.

When the cabby arrived, I directed him to the correct turns and then had him drop me a hundred yards down the road—on the left side instead of the right. After he drove away, I lugged my suitcase and shaving kit the added distance back up the hill and found the green Cadillac backed up amongst the pine trees where Aaron had said it would be. His friend, Pete, who lived there and worked as a carpenter, came out as I was getting it warmed up and confirmed that he was expecting me. I thanked him for taking care of it for me, told him I was on my way to Denver, and lit out for Phoenix.

Exiting California, I avoided U.S. 50 by using some unmapped backroads which Aaron had pointed out. A couple of hours later, going south on US 95 in northern Nevada, I stopped at some of the same joints that Jim and I had "raided" on the way up the road back in April, and made a few more small hits. That experience, my innate cupidity, plus the lure of Las Vegas night life forced me to stop and spend the night there. What the heck, I rationalized, as I wheeled the big Eldorado into the parking lot at Caesar's Palace. I could drive on into Phoenix tomorrow and still get there in plenty of time to rest, freshen up and be at the club by eight. The sun hung without heat low in the western sky as I locked up the Caddy and walked across the warm asphalt towards the registration office.

My eighty buck room came with everything but a seraglio of showgirls. There were bottles of both red and white wine in the small refrigerator and a gurgling hot tub just a step or two from the king-size bed. The room service menu said I could get a fifth of Jack Daniel's for only thirty dollars or a lilliputian shrimp cocktail for twelve dollars. I decided to eat in the coffee shop and limit my contact with John Barleycorn to the free drinks provided by the casino while I played blackjack.

After I won a little more than enough to pay for the trip, I was back in the room before ten o'clock and decided to try to track down Jim. There was no answer at my friend George's home, so I tried the motel. The fugitive was there, and I could hear the sounds of television in the background.

Knowing full well who must be calling, he answered with: "Is this the troubadourious singing bard, weaver of Irish folklore and great benefactor to the poor and persecuted?" It sounded to me like he had made contact with our Seattle connection.

"The one and only, I guess. What's happening? Got a progress report?"

"I'm just resting and reflecting," he said. "Reading the Scriptures and waiting for guidance. If I didn't have this Gideon Bible, I would be bored silly. Have you seen the disgusting junk they put on Donahue lately?"

"No."

"Garbage. Just garbage."

We yakked the usual small talk. I told him that I had the car, and it was running like a sewing machine. He told me that he had spent quite a bit on it in the last month with a tune-up, new radiator hoses, a completely new exhaust system, and brakes. "It's a great car for its age," he said, "and I believe those low miles are true. The mechanic thought so after working on the engine."

"Did you catch up with George Corbin?" I asked.

"Yeah, I met him for lunch on Tuesday, and we hit it off okay. Afterwards, I went for a long walk, and the Spirit led me to a music store where I met the owner and made a deal for a sales job on commission only. He has just gone through a divorce himself and is sympathetic to my needs for privacy. I start work on Friday selling pianos and band instruments."

"Sooopercalifragilistic!"

"It looks pretty promising ... for now, anyway. If not, the Lord will provide somewhere else. "But I've got some even better news than that," he went on. "Your buddy, George, has got me some living quarters, too."

"Fandoubletastic!" I yelled.

I had already decided to stop trying to mask my pathos and get rid of my fears and worries for him altogether. If he could hold such faith and maintain such a remarkably positive attitude while on the hot seat, then I, as merely his cheerleader, certainly could too. I was just glad his butt was out of the wringer. "Positive thoughts are God's; negative thoughts come from Satan," he had once told me. "The product of Faith is Hope; the product of Satan is futility."

"It's exactly what I'm used to; all the comforts of home. He has a small trailer parked in his driveway and said I could use it for awhile until the owner comes after it. And, I've got a whole new wardrobe. You just wouldn't believe how far fifty bucks will go at Goodwill Industries. I've got shirts, socks, underwear, even a sportcoat. This is working out so well, I can hardly believe it myself and, hey, thanks."

"Oh, baloney. Forget the thanks. I've got it, you need it. You always said that God does the providing; I was just the tool this time. Just stay out of hot water for awhile, will ya?" I almost said, "God takes care of drunks and fools" but thought it inappropriate, and considering my luxuriant surroundings and what must his meager ones, I didn't have the heart to mention that I was currently unwinding in the hot tub myself while we spoke.

"Don't worry. I feel real good about Seattle. I'm going to like it here."

"How fortuitous," I said sarcastically, "considering you are married to it for the next little while or more. I'll be in Phoenix all month, maybe longer. Call me at home in a week or so and give me a progress report. Or, better yet, I'll just keep track of you through George."

"Good enough ... and thanks, again, Pat. See ya.'"

As I zoomed south over Boulder Dam and Lake Mead the next morning, I felt good about his security. Then I remembered that I felt the same way, too, about things when I left Placerville back in April, during the calm before the storm. I began to hallucinate with some wild fantasies about the feds rubbing out George Corbin's whole family while Jim Schott escapes. Satan's negativism attacking again.

* * *

The following Tuesday morning my phone was ringing before I was ready to spring back into this world, and, after the fourth firebell, I heard the machine answer, followed by Aaron's Vandermann's voice telling me that there was some more activity in Placerville that I needed to know about and would I please call him tonight. I picked up the phone before he could get away and then punched the "off" button on the recorder. Well, I'm up now, I thought. Let's talk on his nickel.

"Good morning," I said, but I really didn't think it was yet. "Good Morning," he responded. "I had a visit from the Gestapo yesterday and thought you ought to know about it." It wasn't a very good morning for him, either.

"What did they want?"

"What do you think they wanted? They've been talking to everybody in town who knew uh ... Sam so it was only a matter of time before they got around to my house. A couple of gumshoes showed up late yesterday afternoon. They probably suspected I was hiding him here."

"What did they ask you?"

"Uh, somehow they knew about the car. They had already talked to the cabdriver, and he described you perfectly. Six-three, 200 pounds, and dark hair."

His insinuation hung in the air like a bad smell. Tell me another fable, Aesop. "That's a lotta' crap, Aaron. They couldn't have tracked me with a random search of cab records; not without knowing what to look for. They had to know either where I was picked up or where I was dropped off. Your buddy at the house in the woods never saw the cab, so he doesn't know how I got there. Only you and I shared that information, and I know I didn't tell 'em."

"Well," he sheepishly admitted, "they cornered me up at the MBA office on Friday and made me tell them that I had stashed the car up at Pete's place up the mountain."

"They made you tell them, huh." I was getting sarcastic now, and that always precedes my getting loud. "I suppose they hung you up by your wrists and beat you with a cat-of-nine-tails."

"Well, suffice it to say, they got it out of me. Then they went to the cab office, checked the records, and talked to the driver. He told them about picking you up at the Buttercup. They had already talked to Pete before they came back to me yesterday; scared the dickens outta' me when they read me my rights in front of my wife and kids."

"They read you your rights, and you still talked to them? Didn't you hear the part about 'You have the right to remain silent and anything you say can and will be used against you?'" I was just below a yell now. "Don't you know that the First Amendment right to free speech also protects your right not to speak? Have you ever heard of the Fifth Amendment? Those outlaws can only learn what we are stupid enough to tell 'em!"

"I am sorry, Pat. I just don't have any experience with this sort of thing. They had already figured out that I was trying to hold out on them and they came down hard on me ... accusing me of everything but the crucifixion."

"What did you tell them about me?"

"Well, they wanted to know who you were; were you a friend of mine, and where did you live. I told them that I only knew you as 'Pat' and didn't know where you came from or where you were going. When they pressed me for the last name, I told them I thought it was Schalli or something Italian like that. They don't know that you stayed here or that I flew you in from Phoenix, or that you went back there with the car."

A world class criminal he ain't. He had told them all of my first name and most of my last. Only a cretin would do something as stupid as that. First he flies me in to help him out of a jam, and then does everything but take out an ad in the paper to let them know what went on. In my nightclub life, I have some nonchristian friends who would break his legs for less. "Jiminey, Aaron, I could tell better lies than that in grammar school. What is the matter with you? Why didn't you just give 'em my phone number too. I'm damn glad you don't have my address."

I shouldn't have been so hard on him. I began to realize that a year earlier, I was just as ignorant and probably would have told them too much too, but I doubt that even then I would have folded up like an accordion. Every cop knows that questioning a suspect is a one-shot deal; no shot if he invokes his rights. I cooled off a little as he apologized again.

"I screwed up, and I regret it, Pat. They won't get any more out me. I've come to my senses now. Terri was a lot sharper than me. She just kept saying, 'I don't know, I don't know' to everything they asked. Wish I had thought of that."

"Well sure. You don't have to be nice to them, and you don't have to tell them anything. If you do, throw 'em a red herring. And if you don't, they learn nothing. You haven't broken any laws, but they will dang well make it look like you have if they can. Fear is their biggest weapon and 'Conspiracy' their favorite accusation. But don't worry about it. The Good Book says the Lord will guard you. He knows you were helping out a brother Christian. Just don't talk to them any more. It's a good thing we didn't book that ticket in my name. Of course, if they are smart, which they aren't, they could check your credit card records and see that you prepaid a plane ticket from Phoenix to Reno."

"No, I covered that one," he said. "I went to a travel agency in Tahoe and paid cash."

"Good," I thought. Maybe he wasn't a complete idiot after all.

"If they somehow find out, which I doubt they will, they will want to know what that was about and who 'Jimmy Carter' is. On the outside chance that they come back with that question, you want to tell them that it had to do with 'church business.' No, it had to do with 'Christian work,' which is true, and that's all they need to know."

"Right. Good answer. That's what I'll tell them," he said. "It's just that I'm not a very good liar."

I told him of the Scriptures I had learned on that subject, and he remembered them. He was going back that day to his Bible Concordance to see what other characters of history had been protected and blessed because they lied to protect the righteous. I reminded him of Corey Ten Boom and Giorgio Perlasca, the World War II champion deceivers.

Finally, I said, "Hey Aaron, I'm sorry I yelled at you ... but just stay cool, will you?"

"I will. I will. I'll call you if I hear anything more.

"You probably won't," I said, "They were just fishing—wanted to frighten you and the family. But I'll call you in a week or so just to get a progress report."

"Fine. I'll talk to you then."

I did talk to Aaron a few more times and even had occasion to stop through Placerville in August and visit with him for an hour; not at his home, however. He was still gun shy about inviting me there although his paranoia had, so far, proven to be ungrounded. There were no more visits from the feds, but he had acquired quite an education. I left feeling that he still was a pretty good guy who was caught off guard, and one who wouldn't wilt under pressure next time. He also, I was certain, would do his dead-level best to make sure there never is a next time.

We spent the night at the "Motherlode" in Carson City, and a friend with whom I was traveling dropped me at the Reno Airport the next afternoon. I caught a plane up to Seattle to spend a couple of nights at George Corbin's house and visit with Jim. He had since acquired more comfortable living quarters than the trailer George had so graciously provided. He now had a cabin on the water some distance from the city, loaned to him by another sympathetic government fighter.

That's all I learned about his personal situation and all I wanted to know. With the potential heat that could come down on me now, I did not want to know too many answers. George met my plane and took me to a prearranged meeting place where Jim was already waiting. I gave him the dough from the sale of the Cadillac, and he handed me back five $100 bills.

"Thanks for the loan," he said.

"Anytime."

George had told me on the way in that Jim had confided in him a few weeks before, so I wasn't surprised when the three of us sat down to dinner that Jim told George and me the details of his final morning in Placerville. He already missed all his good friends but acknowledged that it would be a long time before he ever went back there.

"By the way," he said, "I now know how they pinpointed me at Wilson's house."

"How? I've been wrestling with that one myself," I said.

"I met an ex-cop here in Seattle who has some knowledge of phone company technology, and he explained to me what undoubtedly happened. It is not necessary for them to tap a phone anymore in order for them to learn where a call is coming from. Apparently, it is still somewhat difficult—at least, time-consuming—for them to obtain a warrant for a legal tap to horn in on a conversation, so they circumvent that law with something called a 'Pin Register.' *(Author's note: We later learned it is a 'Pen Register.')* I was so frustrated at Freddy for not cooperating with our voice-mail system that I broke my own rule and called her in Sewanee two or three times from Wilson's house.

"Anyway, let's say that you were the one they were after. They would put a 'Pin Register' on your wife's phone, your best friend's, your business associate's, and your parent's, for instance. It is not required for them to notify the owners; the phone company cooperates because the FCC controls them, and all government agencies cooperate with other government agencies—especially the IRS. They are not eavesdropping on the conversation, so they don't need to go to the trouble of getting a warrant.

The 'Pin Register' simply tells them where the call is originating. Now whenever a call comes into any one of your close contacts more than once from the same location—particularly a location that has never phoned there before—the odds are astronomically in their favor that they have your new location.

In my case, it turned out to be the Wilson's house, with a motor home parked on the premises when they checked it out. A quick look at their files reminded them that the Wilsons just happen to own MBA, coincidentally, the office where they had thought 'Jim Gordon' might be found six months ago. Then, they knew they had a positive ID and contacted Nashville."

George said, "Do you mean they can nail it down with only a couple of calls?"

"Sure. How many people in the world are likely to have reason to call your wife and your business, best friend, or parents? The odds are prohibitive. It's a better bet than the Seahawks against Sewanee High."

It was then that I leaned forward and butted in like someone had stuck a pin in my arse. "*That's* why they went to the office first. They knew you were camped in the country but thought the office was more likely at that time of day. The motor home was their second choice but by that time you had skedaddled."

"Thanks to one divine angel to whom I shall leave all my accumulated riches at the end of this life," said Jim, with a big smile.

"Think about this, George," I said. If they can drop a man on the moon, talk to him the whole time going and coming, drop him back in the ocean within a square mile target and retrieve him in a matter of seconds, don't you think they have the equipment to beam in on us right now and hear every word we are saying?"

"I never thought about it before, but I guess they do," George said.

"Disregarding, of course, some very interesting material that suggests, maybe proves, that man has never been to the moon," said Jim.

"Oh shit, what have you been reading now?"

"Learn all about it in my next book."

"Oh, by the way, guys," I said, as George was lighting up a cigarette. "I've got a riddle for you:  Who is a beautiful, 36-24-36, leggy blond currently dancing in the follies with Salman Rushdie on the Las Vegas strip?"  They both paused thoughtfully and then shrugged.

"Tupper Saussy!" I said, and George nearly gagged on a mouth full of cigarette smoke. Har! Har! "That's very funny," said Jim Schott, without mirth.

* * *

On Saturday morning, Jim and an old friend from Oregon with whom he had made contact since arriving in Seattle came rolling up to George's house in a travel van.

"Pat, this is Roy Richards. Roy, Pat Shannan," said Jim. He then introduced George, and we sat around his hot kitchen, with its warm odor of mellowing apples and brewing coffee, planning a day trip north of the city to see "some of God's most beautiful work."  Part of the early laity, Roy had been designated by Tupper a few years before as his "West Coast Bureau Chief" for the *Main Street Journal*, a title that Roy claimed surely could have been bestowed on someone more productive than he, but, nevertheless, it was a mantle that he wore proudly.

Roy said, "I thought the best thing to do to take the spotlight off Tupper was to put out the rumor that he was dead. So after a meeting last month in Portland, I made mention of that fact in conversation to a friend. He asked how it happened, and I said I didn't know, I had just heard that he had died. When I walked away the man was crying like a baby. Maybe we better think of a different ploy."

We took a seven hour drive around the area in Roy's travel van and, indeed, did see what must be the best kept secret in the United States. "We discourage the Chamber of Commerce from advertising this too much," said George. We've got too many people here now."

I left there after a three-day visit and flew to Chicago for a new gig on the near North side. As far as I know, Tupper may still be in that cabin. I haven't seen him since then, and, whenever I talk with him, I don't ask where he is anymore. When he wants me to know, he'll tell me.

Larry King, the talk show host, once interviewed Chief Parker of the Los Angeles police department. Larry later said that he was one of those typical old cops who seemed to be as tough as they come and everything was going well until he asked the chief about working with the F.B.I.

"Phoniest organization I ever met in my life," Parker said.

"They're all PR. Dubuque, Iowa probably has a better police force than those guys. I'll take any cop walking a beat in Los Angeles and stack him up against any agent of the FBI in a criminal investigation. All they know is how to ask for funds. They investigate only the cases they think they can crack; they never take the really tough cases. J. Edgar Hoover is a phony and a fraud."

Larry said that the next day two FBI agents who came to the studio, asked for a copy of the tape, and he never heard from Chief Parker, who is now deceased, again.

*Paper money may be deemed an aggression on the rights of other states.*
—President James Madison

# CHAPTER ELEVEN

## BANKERS, LAWYERS, DOCTORS, AND PREACHERS

*Now I beseech you, brethren, mark them which cause divisions and offences contrary to the doctrine which ye have learned, and avoid them. For they that are such serve not our lord Jesus Christ but their own belly; and by good words and fair speeches deceive the hearts of the simple.*

—Romans 16:17 and 18

What can a man believe? The government incarcerates for multiple-life sentences men like Bob Berdella and John Gacy for murdering young boys during satanic homosexual rituals, yet pursues relentlessly those who attempt to expose the similar satanic practices by government. Today, men are pilloried for telling the Truth, if that Truth in any way threatens those in control.

Can a little bit of roach poison be good for us? A quick check at Walgreen's of the labels on their recommended roach poison reveals:

ACTIVE INGREGIENT:

Sodium Fluoride.....95%

Inert ingredient.... 5%

May be fatal is swallowed. Do not contaminate food or foodstuff. Keep out of reach of children and domestic animals. Rinse container thoroughly before disposal. Do not inhale; keep away from cuts, scratches.

Are we to believe that the same government which fights the use of natural cancer preventives like vitamin B-17, decimates us with free abortions, sterilizations, lethal Swine Flu shots, Agent Orange, radiation, chemotherapy, syphilis & AIDS experiments, and phony wars we are forbidden to win, actually puts a deadly poison in our water and toothpaste *in order to protect our teeth?*

Sodium Fluoride is what your dentist keeps telling you is *good* for you. On the other hand, our consideration of that advice might be altered somewhat if we were aware of a little publication by the New York Federal Reserve Bank called *Keeping Our Money Healthy* which tells us that their unlimited money would keep its value ... "if there were fewer people bidding against each other."

Some iconoclastic doctors have testified in court and written in medical journals that fluoridation in the human system inhibits thinking and makes us docile. Can you think of why we are taxed when government prints all the "money" it needs to do whatever it wishes? Or has your thinking become gradually more difficult?

Do not drink a glass of tap water before thinking about this: In a June, 1968 national magazine, McDonald's ran a full page ad that headlined, "ON ANY TRIP, McDONALD'S FEEDS A FAMILY OF FIVE FOR ABOUT $2.55." Then it detailed: "Three cheeseburgers, two hamburgers, five french fries, one shake, two small drinks, two coffees. Total about $2.55." This makes today's prices seem excruciatingly high, doesn't it? Or does it?

In June of 1968, prices were still measured in lawful money. It was on June 24th that year that the Fed and the federal government conspired to renege on their obligations to pay silver on demand for their notes outstanding. Now, over twenty years later, the ratio of fed tokens (FRTs) to silver is about 5:1, in other words, one dollar of silver can be traded for five fed farts.

So to compute how much the cost of eating today has increased through "inflation," we need to say 5 x 2.55 = 12.75 and then take that amount down to the local McDonald's to see how much of the above order can be bought. I did. I could get everything on the above meal for five, and the total would come to 9.86 in today's "dollars" leaving me 2.89 in change before the sales tax. Question: Is the cost of living really going up or is someone playing with our minds?

Gasoline in 1968 was about 30-35 cents a gallon. With the same 5:1 ratio, and even following the so-called "Desert Crisis" in the Middle East, are we not paying less today? The public screwing has come at the other end (no Freudian pun intended). There are more efficient and less costly methods of deriving petroleum from the ground today, but jobs that paid X in 1968 do not pay 5X now. They pay more like 3 to $3\frac{1}{2}$X. This is legerdemain by greater professionals than Houdini. With speeches as long as roller towels, the politicians continue to use fig leaf phrases to cover naked ignorance, and the people keep believing them.

Dr. Susan Rosenberg, a convicted felon who described herself as "another political prisoner," was recently interviewed from prison on CNN. I was one of the most interested watchers as I happened to be typing some of the earlier pages of this manuscript at the moment it was on. Her parents were in a Washington, D.C. studio on satellite and revealed some very interesting facts about her case before the scene flashed back to the prison and Dr. Rosenberg. After only a couple of minutes of an intriguing story that had been previewed as their "Feature Story of the Day," the interviewer suddenly and awkwardly said, "I am sorry Dr. Rosenberg, but we have run out of time," and nothing more was mentioned of the story.

I wonder if the average watcher and listener noticed, as I did, that at the very moment that this "Feature Story" lost its importance was when Dr. Rosenberg began giving testimony to the fact that there is, indeed, an American Gulag in existence, and she was one who had spent 20 months in one of those secret prisons which torture people with such things as burying them underground in severe heat or cold for 23 hours a day. She had been forced to shower without a curtain under constant surveillance of the TV cameras as well as having to submit to degrading body searches by male guards.

At this time, the commentator's ear plug obviously began to crackle with instructions from behind the scenes, and the interview was terminated. I would like to know more, even talk to Dr. Rosenberg myself, but will have to come up with a better method than just writing a letter to her in prison. I fear that my reply might likely come as a personal visit from someone I did not invite, and right now, I would rather not have my apartment ransacked, and my computer and papers confiscated. Maybe later, thanks.

Lt. Col. James "Bo" Gritz was one our most decorated officers of the Vietnam "war" (War is called "war" when it is never declared by Congress) with 62 citations for valor over his 30-year career, including three Silver Stars and the Vietnam Medal of Honor. When the government needed a real-life "Rambo" to go after the MIAs, Col. Gritz was the likely choice of the National Security Council at the White House in 1986.

Then Vice President George Bush, former head of the CIA, had received information that General Khun Sa, czar over the Golden Triangle, was holding an undisclosed number of American prisoners of war. Bo Gritz accepted the mission despite the knowledge that Gordon Liddy states in his book, *Will*, that no American has ever gone into the Golden Triangle and come out alive. George Bush must now wish that Bo Gritz had suffered a similar fate.

*U.S. News and World Report*, in an article dated May 4th, 1987, described General Khun Sa in these terms:

"In the rogues gallery of world-class criminals, Khun Sa is unique—a cutthroat freebooter from a 'Terry and the Pirates' comic strip, with the brooding menace of a character in a Joseph Conrad novel. The spiritual father of narco-terrorism, Khun Sa rules his remote domain in the rugged 60,000 square mile Golden Triangle area of Burma, Laos, and Thailand with feudal brutality. Deserters from his army are tracked down and shot; informants buried alive.

One tale has Khun Sa ordering wrongdoers hanged and drawn and quartered in the marketplace of Ban Hin Taek, his former Thai headquarters village. Another has him killing a barber who had given him a bad haircut."

From here it is a long story—350 pages long in Gritz's 1988 book, *A Nation Betrayed*, of clandestine intrigue, danger and his ultimate betrayal by his own employers. When I met Bo in Las Vegas in September of 1988 and heard him speak, I saw what could best be described as a "metamorphosis." He had gone from another just-following-orders livery who refused to buck the judgment of his superiors to an astute patriot who in the course of one year or less had had a tremendous curtain lifted and was overwhelmed with what he saw backstage. A fitting subtitle to his book might have been: "The Education of Bo Gritz."

Bo and a small, but highly trained, rescue team went to Burma, Thailand and the Golden Triangle and, strangely enough, befriended Khun Sa. They learned that five Americans had been lost when Khun Sa's men were trying to help them cross the swollen Mekong River. They had drowned, along with several of his own men and their horses. But, in what must be the most shocking saga of the decade, they also learned that Khun Sa was moving some 1,400 *tons* of opium into the United States annually *with the cooperation of the US. State Department* and in particular, Richard Armitage,[1] the Assistant Defense Secretary. Khun Sa was willing to stop "every ounce and disclose all U.S. officials" who have been his best customers for more than 20 years. Colonel Gritz returned with some 40 hours of video-taped documentation and called his contacts in the White House to confirm same. The response was: "Bo, you don't understand. We don't want to know about that. *Destroy the tapes.*"

There is little likelihood that the now President of the United States, then Vice President in charge of the "Stop Drugs" campaign and former head of the CIA during a part of that twenty years, could not have held some, if not full,

---

[1] After George Bush was elevated to the Presidency in 1989, Richard Armitage was one of three on his list to be nominated to Secretary of the Army. Possibly out of fear of not being able to pass muster of the scrutiny of a Senate Investigation and interrogation which always precedes such an appointment, Armitage, instead, withdrew his name and resigned his position. He was last seen standing next to President Corazon Aquino as she attempted to explain away the murders of the two Americans shot down by terrorists in May of 1990. He is said to be the NOMFIC of the negotiations with the Philippine government to keep our Air Force base there—still in the employ of the State Department.

knowledge of what was, and is, going on. A long letter from Gritz to George Bush went unanswered. A two-pager from Khun Sa to the U.S. Justice Department, naming names and requesting prosecution, was fruitless. While Nancy Reagan was chirping her "Say No to Drugs" banality, those in her husband's employ were screaming, "Yes, yes, yes."

A year after his return, Colonel Gritz was prosecuted by the U.S. Justice Department for traveling overseas on four bogus passports. These passports were intentionally issued by the U.S. State Department for the sole purpose of helping Gritz travel undetected while attempting to rescue the missing U.S. prisoners of war. It was a U.S. Government mission! Although Gritz was acquitted and the trial was exposed as a travesty, the message was clear: Do what you are told—regardless of what is true—or the same hand that feeds you will slap you down. Gritz was the Populist Party's candidate for President in 1992.

What is Truth and where does one find it? The one source, the source that this nation was born on, the source of Truth for literally billions of people for nearly two thousand years, has been the Holy Bible. It was the text that God used to raise America above all other nations. That it must be the *sole* source is strengthened by the fact that it was barred by the Catholic Church during the Dark Ages.[2]

For hundreds of years only the priests were allowed to read a Bible. What better way to keep the people in the dark than to deny them their source of Truth? The people just didn't know any better. There was a time when if you were caught with a Bible, you were dragged out of your home, hung up on a pole and burned alive in your front yard. It makes you wonder, with our

---

[2] In the Council of Toulouse, the church leaders ruled: "We prohibit laymen possessing copies of the Old and New Testaments. We forbid them most severely to have the above books in the popular vernacular. The lords of the districts shall carefully seek out the heretics in dwellings, hovels, and forests and even their underground retreats shall be entirely wiped out." Council Tolosanum, Pope Gregory IX, Anno Chr. 1229. In more recent times when Bible societies were formed, the Catholic Church classed them, unbelievably, with communism. In an amazing decree, Pope Pius, in 1866, said in his encyclical Quanta Cura, "Socialism, Communism, clandestine societies, bible societies ... pests of this sort must be destroyed by all means." The church Council of Tarragona ruled that: No one may possess the books of the Old and New Testaments in the Romance language, and if anyone possesses them, he must turn them over to the local bishop within eight days after the promulgation of this decree, so that they may be burned." D. Lortsch, Histoire de la France, 1910, p. 14.

suppression of Truth today, if our Bibles will not be the next thing to go. I am only reading the label that been put there. This premise is strengthened by the tremendous influx during the last twenty years of the dozens of "new" truths that have been our accepted source of Truth since 1611.[3]

Certainly, as learned men would argue, there were some translation errors there, too, but the Truths are being distorted and discarded by new versions.

Evidently, someone in a very high place has heeded the advice of George Bernard Shaw, who said, "Religion is a great force—the only real motive force in the world; but you must get at a man through his own religion, not through yours."

This story was not written necessarily to talk about religion. However, during my research of Constitutional facts, I found our whole history and founding documents to be permeated with Biblical Truths. It is a matter of fact that this author finds organized religion to be a malediction to Truth. The recent scandals surrounding PTL, later their accuser, Jimmy Swaggart, and other religious heroes of television have caused the average man in the street to turn his back on Christianity. Could this be by design? It is surely the religious corruption of Christianity that should be shunned. Indeed religion is the greatest enemy Christianity has ever had.

The Truths of the Bible have withstood the test of time, but most people who call themselves "Christian" today do not know the difference between Christianity and churchianity. Professors of Christianity have deserted the faith. They have denied the Divine Sovereignty of Christ and proclaimed instead divine sovereignty of the State. If a person (or a nation) does not obey the laws of Christendom, will he (it) really be recognized as a Christian in the eyes of God? Or will he (it) be spewed out like warm vomit?

The IRS and the legal profession have now suckered churches into incorporating. A corporation is a creation of the State. Anything that you create, you control. As Pastor John Lewis says, "How can Jesus Christ be head of that church when the State is making all the decisions? The churches have prayed to Caesar for the privilege of their utter existence." The IRS has issued 501(c)[3] status to those incorporated churches which means that they are now

---

[3] The most obvious and most quoted example in Romans 13:1: "Set every soul be subject to the higher powers." God Almighty is the only power higher than man, especially in a nation such as ours where the bureaucrats are, supposedly, "public servants." However, most of the new versions of that chapter instruct us to "Obey the government," or something similar. How can both of these versions contain the Truth? Pastors John Lewis, Bob McCurry, et al say that they have no problem obeying the higher powers. It's these "lower powers" that they, in good faith, cannot follow.

required to file tax forms each year to Caesar. Any church could have resisted
(as over 5,000 have), but most of those establishment churches who are
registered dare not speak out against anything government chooses to do.

Yet those churches are admonished by the Scriptures to obey only the laws
of man which do not conflict with the laws of God. Exodus 23:32 instructs
God's people to not make any covenants with government. With this law in
mind, is it a bona fide or counterfeit Christian who attends and financially
supports a 501(c)[3] State institution? Jesus said, "So then because thou art
lukewarm, and neither cold nor hot, I will spue thee out of my mouth" (Rev.
3:16).

Now we don't profess, by any stretch of the imagination, to have a monopoly on truth and knowledge. We would like to know, as "Red" Beckman
asked in his pamphlet, *"In our Hour of Need, Where are our Preachers?"*

In the days preceding the American Revolution, many of the ministers were
preaching freedom. The King was taxing his subjects at a rate of fourteen
percent. Ministers spoke out against such outrage and motivated many to join
the fight for freedom."

Today we are harassed by a government which devours over fifty percent of
the people's wealth. Where, oh where have those preachers gone? That
question is being asked, and we need an answer. We are desperately needing
the blessing of churches upon the Freedom Movement now exploding across
the nation. The church should be supportive of the people, but that is not
happening. Let us look at some reasons why the preachers are out of step
with what is happening.

First of all we must realize that most churches are incorporated. The churches
have been deceived into asking the State for the privilege to operate as a
church. In other words, the articles of incorporation are granted by the State
as a privilege to be a church. Does that sound like separation of church and
state? If the State grants a privilege, it also has strings attached. One of these
strings is that the State has the right to examine all records. The State can
also withdraw its privilege as it sees fit. What has really happened is our
churches are State churches if they incorporated under State law. Tax
exemptions become a carrot on a stick to entice the church to come under
control of the State.

Now, if you belong to an incorporated church, and you have had no
problems, I can tell you what your pastor is teaching from his pulpit. He is
teaching a lie, and the State will not bother him as long as he continues to
extol that lie. Any pastor who will preach and teach that we have a Caesar,
will have no difficulty maintaining corporation and tax-exempt status.
Preachers love to preach on "Render unto Caesar" around April Fools Day
each year. Not only is such a preacher telling a lie, he is also guilty of
treason. If he is teaching that we have a Caesar, he is also misquoting
Romans 13: 1-7. He is teaching we have a Caesar who is our higher power.
These pious hypocrites believed everything they were taught in the
government schools, and they believed their professors at seminary. They

were programmed, not educated. They did not check their teachers as to the accuracy of what was being taught.

Let's put the blame where it belongs. "We the People" believed a lie, now we must pay for our mistake. Confront your minister with this Truth and try to get him thinking. This is not a nation conquered by the Roman Empire. If he continues to promote a Caesar and government over man, you should find another church. There are a few churches that preach Truth, and that is where you and I belong.

* * *

When it comes to the Constitution (the supreme law of the land) and government, the same ignorance abounds, and our captors have the power to continually keep the apparent cost of revolt higher than the cost of submission. If you have not graduated from the mass media (as I hadn't before being reunited with my old friend), revolt is the most ridiculous thing that could enter your mind.

But if you have been trying to decode the news; to filter through the web of confusion, then you may understand that men like Tupper Saussy—and the list is getting longer every year—who have learned the Truth and don't fear it or its consequences, live only for the day when the cost of submission is more expensive than that of revolt. It is their belief that then, and only then, will there come a semblance of true freedom in this country again. Meanwhile, maybe all of us are captives in our own land.

So I suppose that if we think we still have the country that we pretend to have, we are operating under a delusion; living in what the author Saussy once called the "kingdom of artifice." I have spent a long time looking for that Constitutional Republic under God and cannot find it. It's been erased like a blackboard. As I type these words, Senator Ted Kennedy is being shown on CNN concerning the "Flag Burning Amendment" debate saying in a public speech, "... and to the democracy for which it stands." If you can find that word in our pledge to the flag or in any of our founding documents, you can win a lot of prizes from a lot of people. (And while we are on the subject, Dave Wilber says that if you can only describe the "money" that our government "spends"—and of which we supposedly have a deficit, he will send you one hundred pounds of it.) What a bizarre turn of historical events it is that office holders can now use such anti-American words in public speeches and be cheered by Americans. Where we once elected Statesmen to the distinguished office of U.S. Senator, today we have only politicians; professional deceivers. I now make this statement unequivocally because even the so-called "good guys" who get elected cannot challenge the source of destruction of our liberty—the money system—without fear of complete annihilation.

(Remember Congressman Larry McDonald.) Yet all who remain quiet are deceivers. By living with it in repose, they condone it.

*When bad men combine, the good must associate, else they will fail, one by one; an unpitied sacrifice in a contemptible struggle.*

—Edmund Burke

It is not the Constitution that is the problem, nor has it ever been a problem except to those evil men who desire to circumvent it in order to achieve their nefarious goals. The problem shared by all of us who are known as "We the People" is the corruption of that Constitution by those it was intended to restrict. Our Constitution lies brain dead in a hospital room beside what they call "Freedom." The two haven't been buried yet because the physical bodies have been kept alive with lie transfusions to the people. There are those, more astute than I, who would say that the Constitution was created by the same special interest groups that still control it. Nevertheless, former Congressman Ron Paul of Texas and Jim Jeffries[4] of Kansas found that forcing government to obey the Constitution as written is next to impossible today. With any and every attempt by government to pass further amendments, there will be an underlying plan to grab more power over the people while attempting to maintain a patina of normalcy.

Incidentally, when God passed down the Ten Commandments, He didn't mention anything about amendments. Whenever the rumblings of a "constitutional amendment" to do thus and so raises its ugly head, we are reminded of Patrick Henry of Virginia who walked out of the 1787 Convention and refused to sign the completed document *because of the inclusion* of the Bill of Rights. He believed that free men had "all God-given rights" and therefore we should not attempt to enumerate them. Can you imagine what he would have to say about a Constitutional Amendment to stop desecration of the flag? We can hear his vituperation right now:

"You bloody fools! I told you two hundred years ago! What will you attempt to do next? Give away your weapons so your government can march right over you? Let us punish everyone who cannot sing the "Star Spangled Banner" because that has been such a great American tradition, and after all, it

---

[4] To his credit, Congressman Jeffries, quit and refused to run again for what would have been practically a guaranteed lifetime seat in Congress, rather than participate in that "disgusting, ungodly system." When we last talked, his prime goal in life was the repeal of the 17th Amendment. Ron Paul, after a losing bid for the Senate in 1984 and a dismal run at the Presidency in eighty-eight on the Libertarian ticket, still dabbles in politics uttering foolhardy absurdities to the masses who like to be massaged with his rhetoric about "balancing the budget." If you can't whip 'em, join 'em.

is the national anthem. And what about baseball? This is America's pastime now, so anyone who doesn't like baseball and attend at least thirty games a year should spend thirty days in jail. You bloody fools. Will you always allow tradition to override law?"

\* \* \*

Banking can be pure and honorable or a government-sanctioned, giant, multi-level con game, depending on who is operating it. Today it is a pyramid scam that makes all the others seem small time. At the top of the pyramid is the Federal Reserve Board and their owners. AT the bottom are all the little branches of all the different state and national banks. As in all these type schemes, the small branches at the bottom will topple first, taking most of the heat off those at the top.

What most people don't know is that the system was designed to fail and enrich certain people (families) in the process. That process is called usury. Banks loan us ten dollars and repay eleven dollars. But because banks are the only ones who created the money and loaned it into circulation, we have nowhere to turn in order to get that elusive eleventh dollar.

We are faced with two options: One, live without credit, which is God's way and means that you would never go into debt to the banks, or two, borrow an extra dollar, either from another banker or from another victim, with which to repay the banking system. Since there is never enough money in circulation to pay back that eleventh dollar, we are forced to compete with each other for survival, to try to wrench away from our neighbor some dollars with which to repay that eleventh dollar debt, even though it will make it impossible for our neighbor to repay his. This must be why God forbade it.[5]

The premise of this game is that some must fail. There are three players: you, your neighbor and the banker. Of the three, the banker is the only one who is assured of a profit without borrowing any money  so it is pretty obvious which will survive the longest. The banks lend nothing in order to foreclose on something.

\* \* \*

In January of 1986, the Internal Revenue Service published a secret book (for their eyes only) that sets down guidelines under which most Christian churches can be targeted by the IRS and their beliefs determined to be spurious. This book, labeled the *Illegal Tax Protester Information Book*, was written by the IRS National Office Criminal Investigation Intelligence Analyst, Ruth E. Schweizer.

---

[5] Please reread the author's second conversation with Dan Hoffman in Chapter One.

No government agency, least of all the IRS, should be deciding which religious beliefs are spurious and which are valid but when former IRS agent turned whistle blower, Paul DesFosses[6], exposed this atrocity, his house was destroyed by arsonists. The case has never been solved.

Not much has changed. If people lived for three hundred years instead of seventy or so, maybe they would realize that this control struggle has been going on for generations. One of the great pluses for the conspirators is the educational advantage they now enjoy over young minds. Control of the money gave them eventual control of everything else, for instance, public education and the news media.

Some people seem to believe that there is a conspiracy of sorts but that it only goes so far. When they are presented with the proposition that the conspiracy is so far advanced that political action has become a farce, they fall back in disbelief. Educated, articulate, intelligent people still believe that we achieved something by electing Bush over that disgusting Dukakis or Reagan over the incompetent Carter.

When we point out that the Machiavellian principle of dualism—that which requires that the perfect plot have two opposing sides, the good guys and the bad guys, both striving for the same goal—their eyes glass over and my credibility is jeopardized. They cannot cope. The brainwashing has been so total that when the idea that both sides or all sides are controlled are phony opposition, they either scatter like rabbits running from a prairie fire or, more commonly, just change the subject and treat us as though we must be some near-future candidate for the local funny farm. But nobody has any plausible alternate explanation for the stories presented here. The enemy has been very patient, indeed, and has done its job very well.

We are bound by tradition. My own mother, a near octogenarian, a well-read, intelligent woman in complete control of her mental and physical faculties who plays golf in Florida four days a week, read Chapter Eight of this manuscript prior to its publication. Concerning the part about John Voss and the lawfulness of traveling without a license, she asked me, "Do you drive without a license?"

I replied, "No, Mother, I don't drive at all, so I am not one who is required to have a license."

She said, "But you drove in here yesterday. That's your car out front."

"No, Mother, dear, I traveled here in that car. Didn't you read the Supreme Court decisions defining that?"

---

[6] Paul DesFosses is president of National Coalition of IRS Whistleblowers, P.O. Box 7750, New York, NY 10116.

"Yes, but you still can't break the law."

"What laws am I breaking, Ma?"

She paused thoughtfully and said, "The laws of the United States."

Oh, well. I guess woman's irrationality was forever confirmed when she took dietary advice from a talking snake.

Almost everyone has a mental block beyond which they will not inquire. This is how the system holds us in check. Only a very few get through this vast net of belief systems and escape into objective reality. These few are allowed to babble all they wish and print newsletters because the authorities well know that not enough people will listen to them for them to be a threat to the system. This point is driven home many times in the conspirators' rule book (our term), *Protocols of the Learned Elders of Zion*[7]. Listen to some of their instruction:

> Those fools who will think they are repeating the opinion of a newspaper of their own camp will be repeating our opinion or any opinion that seems desirable for us (page 53).

> In order to put public opinion into our hands, we must bring it into a state of bewilderment by giving expression from all sides to so many contradictory opinions and for such length of time as will suffice to make the goyim (Ed. note: that's you, gringo) lose their heads in the labyrinth and come to see that the best thing is to have no opinion of any kind in matters political, which it is not given to the public to understand, because they are understood only by him who guides the public. This is the first secret (page 34).

> We shall destroy among the goyim the importance of the family, its educational value, and remove the possibility of individual minds splitting off; for the mob, handled by us, will not let them come to the front nor even give them a hearing (page 44).

> Beg you to note that among those making attacks upon us will also be organs established by us, but they will attack exclusively points that we have predetermined to alter. Not a single announcement will reach the public without our control (page 51).

We see people advance to different levels of understanding and then stop cold when they come face to face with a challenge to their belief system ... it could be even your own mother.

While most Americans do not approve of either socialism or communism, if they are called by those terms, they have been tricked into these alien concepts by masters of deceit. Almost all of the foundations for this shift in our basic form of government have not patiently been planted, built upon these foundations of socialism is the high private and public "debt," while

---

[7] Victor Marsden. Britons Publishing House, United Kingdom, 1968. Available through Christians Awake, P.O. Box 110013, West End Station, Birmingham, Alabama 35211.

patriotism and morality is at an all time low. Under Democracy, all this ins not only perfectly acceptable, but worth fighting for. Everybody wants to eat from the government table, but nobody wants to do the dishes.

Understand, those who brought the famine, starvation, and death to Cambodia do not have any moral restrictions about bringing the same upon America. They know no loyalty to any nation. Socialists, by whatever name, control the American government at all levels right down to the local police and sheriff's departments. The confiscation of citizen owned firearms will be one of the final blows to our Constitutional safeguards that must be near the top of the enemies' list. These guns are obviously not needed to defend ourselves, militia-wise, against a foreign invasion. They are necessary to protect Americans from complete capture by the federal government. Have you been to Washington, D.C. lately? Those metal detectors that you must enter before visiting your own hometown congressman were not placed there to protect them from foreign terrorists, as they would like for you to believe.

More aware than anyone of their own legal shenanigans the past many years, the politicians' real fear is that their captives (who happen to be still armed) may learn the facts of their capture before they can be disarmed. Indeed they are terrified and rightfully so. Andrew Jackson predicted "revolution by morning" if the people ever learned the truth. Meanwhile, with the continual injections of paper legal tender and imaginary credit into the society, the deep religious faith, honesty, and powerful sense of honor of the captives continues slowly to erode and degenerate into alcoholism, hard drug addiction, promiscuity, hypochondria, hatred, insanity, and suicide.

\* \* \*

I was finally back in "Murphy's Landing" in Kansas City for a couple of weeks in late February of 1990, and made an appointment to talk with Dan Gibson, the founder and principal creator of the "The School for the Last Days" about whom I learned while in St. Louis but had never made contact. By unusual coincidence, our appointment was in his apartment/office for Wednesday morning, the 28th, which turned out to be less than twenty-four hours after he had been raided by the IRS.

"Welcome to our humble abode," he greeted me with a beg smile.

The place was in shambles, papers strewn on the floor, books pulled from the shelves; video tapes and equipment, computers and printers and boxes of paper had been hauled away. Dan's wife had been nursing their five-month-old baby at the moment they burst in and one of the agents held a gun on her for several minutes until she finished. I had seen and read enough in the last two years to believe these people were capable of anything, to know that nothing was sacred to them.

"They even broke down the bathroom door while Mike was sitting on the pot," Dan chuckled about his paralegal researcher as we ambled towards his "office," a converted bedroom of the five-room apartment. "I knew the IRS was kind of like the Gestapo," he said. "But until you've had people point guns at your wife and baby, you don't really get a flavor of what it's like. We ought to have a token IRS raid on all judges and magistrates, so they'll know what it's like."

Dan would reach his 45th birthday in two weeks. He is a pastor and ex-Marine having seen infantry combat in Vietnam and is a former successful business executive. All this experience has filled him with human interest stories that he often uses in his talks and writings. He explained to me how he became interested in educating others to Truth and the evolution of this School:

"Any discussion of law by laymen, is generally shrouded in mystery, confusion and apathy. If asked, most people will give a vague definition of law such as: 'Laws are the rules made by government by which we all must abide and through which we are punished when we disobey.'

"There is a notion that since laws are made by elected representatives, they represent the 'will of the people.' Therefore, no matter how oppressive, unfair or Godless a law might seem to the individual, he must obey. After all, hasn't he heard that same sentiment preached from his state-licensed pulpit since his youth?

"But the mystery doesn't end there. Can we know and understand a law system that presently contains over 4,000,000 statutes, codes and ordinances at all levels of government and grows at nearly 4,000 new ones each month?" How about the language and procedure of the law? Do you understand the meaning of hundreds of Latin words and phrases commonly used by lawyers and the courts?

"Can even literate men follow the maze of procedures required to present a defense in court? Can they write acceptable motions and briefs, select a jury, present evidence, examine and cross-examine witnesses and write an appeal? Which of us does not suffer anxiety walking into a courtroom where a black-robed high priest sits glaring from his high pedestal, speaking a strange and foreign language.

"Would it surprise you to find out that the conditions I just described were never allowed by our founding fathers," he asked me directly, "that the courts belong to the people and not the lawyers; and that all the mystery has been purposely contrived by the self-serving legal profession?"

"Three years ago it would have," I replied. "Nothing surprises me anymore. But tell me this: What is law and where does it come from?" Both my leading question and my switching on the recorder told him I was beginning the formal interview. He didn't tarry.

"Oh, how I wish the average man in the street would ask himself that question. Law is the expressed will of a sovereign, directed at his subjects," he began. "By very definition, a sovereign is a law-giver while non-sovereigns are 'subjects' or those subjected to the law the sovereign. Most of us claim that we serve one master, Him being Jesus the Christ. We call him "Lord" and "Master" and say that His word is law to His people. Through the Holy Scripture He has given us a model set of statutes, designed to preserve the liberty and free agency of His children while, at the same time, providing for our safety from those who would do us damage."

He went on to tell me that every conceivable crime is covered in God's law. After all, if General Motors can write manuals for the proper care and maintenance of a Buick, dare we think that God would fall short in giving us His instructions we need for leading happy and healthy lives? From his well marked Bible, which he calls his "Owner's Manual," Dan read me some instruction: "Ye shall have one manner of law, as well for the stranger, as fro one of your own country; for I am the Lord your God." (Lev. 24:22 and Num. 15:16). And from Deuteronomy 4:2: "Ye shall not add unto the Word which I command you, neither shall ye diminish ought from it, that ye may keep the commandments of the Lord your God which I command you.

"Judges are to be governed by this and originally in this country, they were. There was a time when Godly men sat at the bench and their only lawbook was the Bible. Our elected representatives break this commandment every time they make 'legal' what God has forbidden, or by making 'illegal' the things that He has commanded. The scriptures are the words of the sovereign law-giver. It has been said that we cannot break these laws but we can break ourselves upon them.

"Many Christians have been caused by the modern day preachers to con-fuse God's laws with the ceremonial ordinances He gave to Israel but anyone can discern the difference between "Thou shall not steal" and the practices of sacrificial offerings."

He showed me where God's people lived His law very happily for many generations. Their relationship to one another was that of individual free men; God protected them and provided for all their needs. They had no sovereign except Him, no king, no rulers. It ended when the people went to Samuel the Prophet and asked for a king so that they could be like "all the nations." The Lord told Samuel that the people had not rejected him ... "but they have rejected me, that I should not rule over them" (I Sam. 8). The Lord had Samuel warn the people that a king would take their sons (like Vietnam?) and daughters (like into the army for the next "Vietnam" in the Middle East or Central America), their flocks and best fields and some day they would be sorry and cry out to God who "will not hear you in that day."

So ended men living God's law. From that point in history until the founding of America, all men lived the arbitrary, capricious and self-serving laws of those who had gained dominion by force. The cycle began again in 1933 when the American people, God's people, once again chose to have a king (government) provide their needs instead of Him. Or maybe it was in 1913, or maybe even July 2nd, 1776. Some believe the high water mark of the American Republic was the day it began.

Dan told me more about "jury nullification" and the story of William Penn, which took place in England in 1670, a full century before our nation's founding. The Quaker meeting hall in London had been padlocked by the authorities, causing Penn and his associates to conduct their preaching in the street outside. They were arrested for "Leading a conventicle, conducting an unlawful and tumultuous assembly ... the disturbance of the peace ... and conspiring and abetting together to do the same." They were placed in the Newgate prison.

"At their trial," Dan said, "Penn's study of the law allowed him to ably present their defense to the jury. He didn't deny holding a conventicle, but pointed out that their right to religious freedom is found in the Magna Charta, and said, 'No law enacted by the Kin g of England can take away those rights.' The judge told the jury that it was clear and manifest that they had violated the law and gave the jury fifteen minutes to find the defendants guilty."

The jury saw tyranny in the judge's charge and returned in thirty minutes with a "Not Guilty" verdict, the foreman stating to the court, "The court has no power in the Magna Charta to dictate the jury's verdict." The judge became so infuriated he put the whole jury in jail."

The judge reconvened the court the next day, even though it was Sunday, and demanded that the jury bring a verdict of guilty. "Not Guilty, for each prisoner," said the foreman. Back in the slammer they went.

On Monday, the same thing happened and, despite the pressure, the jury continued to refuse to yield. "Every man has the right to worship God according to his own conscience," they said. "We shall sit until death on that principle. If we yield, all England will be enslaved. We, as jurors, must stand between religious liberty and governmental control of our conscience." The judge then released Penn et al, but jailed the foreman of the jury and three others who refused to pay a stiff fine for their insolence. Nine weeks later, they were released on appeal when a higher court said, "A judge may try to open the eyes of the jury but not lead them around by the nose."

Dan concluded, "Thus was established forever the independence of the jury and the doctrine—unfortunately unknown to most of us today—of 'Jury Nullification.' In other words, 'We the People,' when serving on juries, can judge not only the facts of a case, but the law itself. Several states still reference 'jury nullification' in their Constitutions, but it is fading away as government grasps more and more control. What the people don't know ... well, tough."

I began to understand more of what Dave Wilber had said; that the jury, and not the judge, is king in the courtroom, but since the judge is in charge of the proceedings, he never tells the jury of their veto powers. It takes a person not only educated on the facts when he/she sits in that jury box, but one with tremendous intestinal fortitude to stand up with Truth to the powers that be. Dan explained that the courts avoid any potential confrontation of this sort by stacking the jury with sheep from their own camp rather than "peers of the defendant." A tax case was recently reversed by the Appellate Court in Denver, Colorado when it was proven that IRS agents were sitting on the jury.

"The law, to American freemen," Dan continued, "was not their master but their guarantee of liberty. We the People understood that rights were inalienable, that is, God granted and uncancelable."

I interrupted with a question. "So how can we separate wheat is really 'law' from legislative acts which a usurpation of power by an immoral government?"

"First we must understand the proper role of government and that the people who have created their government can only grant powers that they, themselves, have in the first place. Obviously, they cannot grant what they do not possess."

"Okay," I said. "Now we are getting to the bottom line. Just what powers properly belong to every person in the absence of and prior to the establishment of any organized government?"

"Well, for instance, in a primitive state, there is no doubt that every individual would be justified in using force, if necessary, to defend against physical harm, theft of the fruits of his labor, or enslavement by another.

"We are told by Bastiat in *The Law* that if every person has the right to defend—even by force— his person, his liberty, and his property, then it follows that a group of men have the right to organize and support a common force to protect these rights; its reason for existence—its lawfulness—is based on individual rights. So we appoint (elect) a sheriff. Then city councilmen, state representatives, and congressmen. But we can't grant right to any of these people that we don' possess ourselves ... such as taking from one to give to another.

"So, how could we have gone from a Christian, independent people who, if they went to court at all, pleaded their own causes, to the legally dependent society we have today? Because we began to love money more than God; to praise more highly the clever lawyer than the truth.

Despite God's admonition in Exodus 23:32 that we make no covenants with foreign governments, we have contracted away our 'freeman' status to that of 'serfs' ruled by government. Although we were suckered into it, nevertheless, the fact remains that we signed everything away with social security, business licenses, drivers licenses, and so on. We surrendered the right to do these things when we applied for the privilege.

"Now do you see why the sentiments and traditions of the founding fathers are only rhetoric from the mouths of modern politicians?" Dan asked me directly.

I nodded in the affirmative, not wishing to speak and break his train of thought.

"... Why each generation enjoys less liberty and more regulation? Can we really hope to out-vote the masses who love comfort and security more than liberty ... prosperity more than God? Right here in Kansas City, the majority lives from the government trough, so how are we to vote them out of it. Franklin said that once the people discover that they can vote themselves largess ...," he paused, smiled, and I remembered the quote.

"Are you proposing that we make the legal profession obsolete by every man learning the law for himself again?" I asked.

"That would certainly be a beautiful thing," he chuckled, "an idealistic fantasy of mine, but I don't expect to get that drastic a result in my lifetime.

"No man can serve a master he does not know," he went on. "For us to serve God we must know both his law and its application in our lives. Likewise, if we are to be freemen and Christian, we must have God's law written in our hearts plus a working knowledge of man's law to both be able to defend ourselves and witness of Christ before men. You may find it interesting that there is no scriptural example of the Lord, or his people, ever hiring a lawyer to represent them. Think of Paul before King Agrippa. Did he have someone speak for him? How about Daniel. Couldn't Christ have taken a collection to hire the best lawyer in Jerusalem?

"You see there is a principle involved in speaking for one's self. This principle is consistent throughout scripture and the common law. It is called personal accountability. The great desire of man throughout the ages has been to avoid personal accountability. He wants insurance policies to put his risk on someone else; he wants someone else to see to good government; he wants a lawyer to 'get him off' when he's accused, and most ardently, he wants to avoid standing before the Great Judge on the day when the books are opened to judge him. Ministers who preach a gospel of "God loves everyone and certainly wouldn't allow anyone to suffer hellfire" can build large congregations of those who cherish the thought of avoiding accountability.

"Which reminds me ... Do you need 535 people gathering together in Washington making new laws? I don't. If government exceeds any law in this book (he waves his Holy Bible), it has gone beyond its lawful function. There was a time when judges were handed a Bible and instructed: "This is the law." Now they just enforce anything the 535 congressmen and senators can dream up to further oppress the subjects. For instance, today not only do the statutes require one to be a member of the bar in order to counsel someone else in the courtroom, but only 'those trained in law enforcement' in most counties, in most states, may run for the office of sheriff, thereby restricting both sections of their 'club' to 'members only.'

"All practicing lawyers are officers of the court. Their duty and obligation is first to the court and second to the client. In other words, all lawyers, in order to keep practicing, uphold the system first.

I once had lunch with a prominent lawyer who had previously served as a prosecutor. We were discussing a layman's brief challenging the constitutionality of the money system. Although the lawyer was in agreement with the principles involved, he said: 'If I were ever to file a brief like that in court, the judge would call me into his chamber and tell me that if I ever did it again, I would be through practicing in his court.' A lawyer knows that he serves at the pleasure of the court. Should he alienate the judges, he will find his motions denied and his cases prejudiced. He could no longer be an effective choice for his clients. I have presented this scenario to several other lawyers since, and all were in similar agreement. Their whole careers would be in jeopardy for presenting Truth to the courts.

"By virtue of the obligations they have to the court and the government— their master—there is legitimate question as to whether one can be both Christian and lawyer. But I choose Tao leave that question to the lawyers and God to answer and I believe that they, indeed, will have to answer to Him for it. The day is rapidly approaching that the few good men still struggling to be Christian lawyers will have to choose God or Caesar, lest both become angry ... for both are jealous masters.

"However, faithful in his duties, another spokesman can never speak *your* heart and mind or give a message the Spirit would give through you. I have lost count of the number of times I have heard people complain that their lawyer didn't handle their case the way they wanted; that he never brought up the things they wanted said. Most of those people never understood that when they hired a lawyer, they granted their personal 'power of attorney' to someone else. The presumption of law is that you must be incompetent to speak, else why would you waive your right to defend yourself and have someone represent you? That's why the judge tells you to shut up and let your lawyer address the court.

"So is there a need for lawyers? Definitely. Common law criminals need attorneys. After all, their desire is not to see justice done or be a witness to a corrupt and filthy generation, but rather to use the cleverest attorney money can buy to evade just punishment. Do they want to face a jury of their neighbors to explain away their crimes? Of course not. That doesn't work. For them, it is better to hope that their 'mouthpiece' can trick and cajole or maybe cause a procedural error that will win on appeal.

"Lawyers can also be helpful to those of us who defend ourselves by giving *counsel* rather than representation. Their many years of study can be put to good use through counseling on matters of procedure, the meaning of statutes and explanations of courts and appeals. There are still good men who will give help and encouragement to those who would fight and defend matters of conscience. Many would like to see us win even if they are not willing to argue the issues we face personally.

"One last thought on our national dependency upon lawyers: When your money runs out, so does your lawyer. The vast majority of Christian families in America cannot afford to sustain a battle in the courts, no matter how vital the issues are to their peace and safety. Some cannot even afford an office visit for advice. It's amazing to see good people 'swat the hornet's nest' by home-schooling their children, protesting abortion, practicing natural health care, fighting the unlawful tax system, or by just generally marching to a different drummer, with no money for defending the inevitable attack from the 'establishment' and virtually no knowledge of how to defend themselves in court.

That's why we put together the school. We not only have found the need, now we are filling it. We have a 102-hour course on video tape with dozens of briefs and one can learn not only the law, but procedure. It's a course that your whole family can use for a lifetime of defense against Caesar's attacks and our total cost is probably less than the next single payment that you will make to your lawyer for whatever he does for you.

"So who should know the law? All men who would live free. All parents who would preserve our heritage of freedom for their children and grandchildren; and, those who are *active* Christians as opposed to the lukewarm, casual observers of events by whom we are surrounded. It is not easy to learn law ... freedom is too precious to be had without price. The establishment has erected formidable barriers to keep you from seeing that the Wizard of Oz is really not so frightening if you peek behind his fa!ade. Not the least of these barriers is the preacher who lulls his flock into docility.

"One of the sad commentaries of our society is that primarily the so-called liberals study law. They have learned an important principle: In the courts, one person can pit himself against the might of the whole government and its citizens. Look what the ACLU has done to destroy our Christian traditions; what Madeline Murray O'Hare did to school prayer. She hates God fundamentally and the courts love her. That faction could never have won such victories at the ballot box.

\* \* \*

Shortly after we met and talked in Phoenix that June day in 1987, Jack McLamb organized a team of twelve lawmen from various states to go to Arkansas in an investigative effort to re-open the Gordon Kahl case. "Since all local efforts had been suppressed (by the District Attorney et al) to have a Grand Jury inquiry," he said, "we decided to do our own with a dozen highly qualified people and present the evidence in hopes of forcing the Grand Jury to act." Not only were their efforts stonewalled, but later that year, McLamb's only source of income, his medical retirement check, was confiscated by the IRS.

Elden Warman is attempting to eke out an existence selling real estate in Canada and put his life back together. Yorie Kahl still languishes through a life sentence in a Federal Pen in Lewisburg, Pennsylvania. In July of 1990, his parole was denied. Frederique Saussy filed a six million dollar lawsuit against the government for the unwarranted assault and battery on her and her children. It was thrown out of court and she has been back in Puerto Rico working and taking care of her children and elderly parents. Former Congressman George Hansen has a new organization and is still attempting to fight, but because such groups are eigher ignored or belittled by the national media, it is difficult to monitor his progress. He was recently trapped in the Middle East with the unfortunate hostages after the Kuwait invasion by the Iraqis, but later released.

Harry Hall is back in the country in Houston starting a new company unrelated to off-shore trusts. In August of 1990, he was finally indicted for "Conspiracy to defraud the United States," accepted a plea bargain on the advice of his lawyer moments before trial, and now is serving a few months in "Club Fed."

Franklin Sanders won his fight in the Memphis courts, but lost nearly everything he owned to the lawyers in order to pay for the longest trial in Tennessee history—over four months. Dwight Snyder is quiet. Gary Beck served time for a while at the Eglin Air Force camp in north Florida and at Maxwell in Montgomery, Alabama.

NCBA has closed the doors of its gold and silver exchange. As we go to press, Dan Gibson is on trial for five years of his life for "conspiracy." Literally hundreds of Christian ministers have been incarcerated for denying government intervention into their ministries. Their crime? Sedition. More than forty thousand people have been arrested in the last two years for peacefully demonstrating to "stop abortion." That is four times the number that went to jail during the Civil Rights movement of the sixties (4,400 babies a day are still refused entrance into this world.).

Indeed, there must be more political prisoners than criminals in the U.S. prisons. Do the American people—and especially jury members—really believe that they have more freedom now because these "criminals" are out of circulation? The government appears to be winning its battle against personal freedom.

What have I learned from all this experience? That I must learn to live privately; that the government is almost never my friend and the less they know about me the more freedom I can enjoy the rest of my life. I have a much stronger respect for things made lawful by God and a much greater repulsion and fear of things made legal or illegal by man.

I have learned that the word "shall" in a legal sense, when used in any statute in this land means "may" and has been ruled so by the U.S. Supreme Court and numerous appellate courts and, therefore, signing up for the scam of Social Security, applying for a license to "drive" and filing income tax forms, among many other things, are voluntary.

I have begun to understand that human beings can be made to believe that black is white if they are fed enough mental doses of gray over long periods of time. And I have learned that any person who trusts his property to a banker, his liberty to a lawyer or his life to a medical doctor is very, very foolish ... and the biggest fool of all is he who would trust his soul to a preacher. I didn't embark on this journey with plans of crossing the Rubicon. But cross it I did. *Alea jacta este.*

Because I now have firsthand knowledge of the devious antiacs of the federal judiciary, many of the names in this book have been changed to protect the "guilty." But who is really guilty of what when there is no victim to a statutorily construed "crime?" Personal courtroom observation and the testimony of others have convinced me that U.S. attorneys and their assistants must be the single most conniving, manipulative, and untrustworthy group of respected people in the nation. As twisters of truth, they may be second only to those godless roabots of the Internal Revenue Service with whom they conspire daily. In recent years, I have become acquainted with many of these disgusting individuals and am yet to meet one who possessed a single admirable character trait.

Where and how did they acquire this mantle of respect in our society? Indeed a homeless street bum or a member of a motorcycle gang about whom I know nothing would be more welcome in my home and at my dinner table to abe trusted with the family silver than would the most heralded, brightest shining star of the of the United States Justaicse Department or Internal Revenue Service. At least the bum has yet to prove himself, but about the others, I have no doubts. Anyone who would cooperate with these federal weasels by "squealing" on a fellow American or attempt to "cut a deal" aby selling out someone else in order to get better treatment for themselves can never stoop any lower in life. May the hottest spots in Hell be reserved for those who do.

This book will not change the world. The more astute reader understands at this point that the world has been changed already without his or her permission. The average reader has probably learned only of another outrageous abuse of power by the federal government in its quiet persecution of a private citizen. Because such abuse has become increasingly more commonplace in recent years, most people will prefer to forget what they have read and will go back to their world of W-4 jobs, ball games, movies, and churchianity. They may or may not thank whatever god they worship that it never happened to them, but they will certainly continue to tell their children about how wonderful it is to live in a free country.

\* \* \*

In the early days of Christian persecution, there was a pernicious individual named Arius who was a thorn in the side of the church. He was teaching that the Lord Jesus Christ was not the eternal God, the second person of the Trinity, but rather was a created being, not of the same essence with the Father. Arius wrote "The Unbegun made the Son a beginning of things originated; and advanced Him as a Son to Himself by adoption." It goes without saying that that foul heresy, if accepted by the church, would have destroyed Christianity.

When over three hundred leaders of the church met with the Council of Nicea in 325 A.D., it was discovered that while many still held to the orthodox doctrine, some had already jumped the fence and were followers of Arius. Arius and his disciples were so eloquent in their defense of their blasphemies that some of those who believed the orthodox doctrine were intimidated into silence. Who would defend the deity of Christ?

A young man, small of stature but great in faith and intellect—Athanasius by name—was in attendance. Technically, he attended as a scribe—a reporter—and not as a leader of the church, but when others were silent, Athanasius arose and delivered a powerful, irrefutable defense of the orthodox doctrine. This courageous warrior stood even much taller in light of the fact that people were abetting crucified for their vituperative outspokenness. In closing, he recited the Nicene creed which epitomized the thinking of all who had been tiptoeing around his same beliefs.

Throughout this colossal challenge to the faith, Athanasius virtually stood alone. Many others believed as he did but none fought as he fought. Before the day's end, a friend said to him, "Athanasius, the world is against you."

The bantam weight giant replied, "So be it. Then Athanasius contra mundum (Athanasius against the world).

*  *  *

I still hear from him occasionally, but I haven't seen him since I left George's house in Seattle. Sometimes he finds out from Juan here I am and we have a midnight conversation. Usually he just calls my recorder and says "Hi" for no other apparent reason than to make contact, abut he doesn't know that each time; I hear his voice, I silently smile with pride that he is still avoiding and frustrating the monster.

His notes are brief and to the point. Once, when he was requesting that I forward some mail, a Cole Porteresque, hand-scribbled missive said succinctly, "In this world of ordinary people, I'm glad there is you." This is his only touch with the outside world. He never leaves a number and asks that I call back anymore. And although I would be happy to, I understand his need not to jeopardize his old friends. Many, such as those in Placerville and Sewanee, would be petrified of his leper touch.

A fugitive cannot become too close with new friends and must dissolve all ties with old ones. In the story books, when you save a man's life, you are richly rewarded. A fugitive chased by the furies must save his own life first and his reward is one more day out of jail.

Like Tupper Saussy, Richard Kimble was an innocent victim of blind justice, freed by fate en route to the death house, freed to hide in lonely desperation, to change his identity, to toil at many jobs, freed to run from the relentless pursuit of the police officers obsessed with his capture. Unlike Richard Kimble, our fugitive does not have Hollywood scriptwriters to invent a new escape for him each week. But there is no desperation anymore now either. Not even in what would be desperate moments.

"When there is loneliness, it is wonderful because the Lord has me to Himself and His strength is made perfect in my weakness," he said to me once. Unlike most of us entertainers, he does not need an audience to thrive. A piano in the woods would keep him perfectly content; especially if there were a diversionary typewriter and packet of paper nearby.

Remembering Dan Gibson's words: "If we are to be freemen and Christian, we must have God's law written on our hearts plus a working knowledge of man's law to be able to both defend ourselves and witness of Christ before men." I realized that Tupper Saussy probably possesses more of that combination than anyone else in the United States ... if, indeed, he is still in the United States.

"They were just doing their jobs," he says about those who prosecuted him and harbors no ill will. "They prosecuted someone who thought he was a Christian, but wasn't. In my exile, I have become a scriptural Christian rehabilitated by God."

So it is in 1991. Tupper Saussy contra mundum. Tupper Saussy against the world .. but with God on his side. I reckon that gives him a better advantage over his enemies than having ;any Hollywood writers. God is a playwright and a "play right" who, with His *deus ex machina* creates His own scripts too.

Maybe another shabby, another reaching out to fetch someone he has met along the way and the play goes on. Maybe he is still in that cabin by the lake, or maybe by now he really is in Binghamton, New York, or is a priest in Puerto Rico.

Sewanneans are always spotting him riding in a car, walking down the street, or somewhere on campus. These "sightings" are never confirmed. Someone jocularly reported seeing him with Elvis at the K-Mart in Kalamazoo. Another claims he was dealing blackjack in Atlantic City. In my opinion, the ultimate "moon" by him to the establishment—the perfect ending to this story will be when he is found, thirty years from now, as an upstanding, distinguished, eight-five-year-old president of a small town Federal Reserve bank, who forgives all the farmer's loans.

The hard times America is experiencing these days is really nothing more than Divine punishment, he believes. "For my children's sake, I must obey God, not terrorists." For his wife and children's sake, wherever they are, I hope and pray he has found a way to be with them again.

"Events in recent years have proved to me beyond any doubt that God had raised me up to be an example of Christian liberty, not Babylonian enslavement. His protections have been miraculous thus far. To imagine their withdrawal would be blasphemy."

The fugitive game is a lonely one ... seemingly without end.

*If ever again our nation stumbles upon unfunded paper, it shall surely be like death to our body politic. This country will crash.*

—President George Washington, 1789

If your ears can hear the sparrow,
if your eyes can see the sun,
if your lips can go smiling
when you've lost instead of won;
Though the shadows may be frightening,
if a voice within you sings,
through the thunder and the lightning
you can walk alone with Kings.
'though today may hand you sorrow,
one by one your plans fall through,
if your heart can  say, "Tomorrow"
all your dreams can still come true.
When you're stumbling through the dark night,
If you have a faith that clings,
soon you'll walk alone with starlight;
soon you'll walk along with kings!"

—Roy Hamilton Album, circa 1955

(W.B.)

It's a rainy and chilly December 28, 1991 and Pat Shannan and I have just seen Oliver Stone's production of "JFK" together. Currently we are relaxing around the warm fireplace, enjoying a libation in his living room in northern California. I invited myself over following the matinee to get a brief update, show him a copy of the final manuscript, and to see a letter which he had told me about some time ago. Because we still are so immersed in the movie, it is some time before we get down to business.

Our conversation returns to Chapter Six, and he has shown me the Zapruder film for the first time. I, too, am aghast at the ramifications of what I have seen. Surely Oliver Stone and his film editors could not have missed the actions of driver William Greer during the thousands of times they must have looked at it . . . unless, maybe, it was already spliced out.

We speculated as to why "Conservative" columnist George Will attacked Stone and his movie as "a three hour lie."

"Why is actor Kevin Costner lending himself to this libel of America? ... 'JFK' will give paranoia a bad name," he said. Four days earlier, "Liberal" columnist Tom Wicker of the *New York Times* said, "The Warren Commission was under time pressure; its report was hurried out, and it contains errors, omissions, and debatable interpretations,"... and called the film's premise "contemptuous of the very constitutional government Stone's film purports to uphold."

*Time Magazine* blasted the movie, also, but may have slipped up when they admitted that Warner Brothers and Time Life are owned by the same conglomerate.

As a docudrama, I find "JFK" troubling because the genre makes it impossible to separate the "docu" from the "drama." But for a moment, forget the facts. This is a work of art. Like any art, "JFK" stands or falls on its power to disturb viewers, to make them think and rethink. It bothered me before I saw it. It bothers me more now. Writer/producer Stone's theories lionizing Jim Garrison may or may not hold water, but they make one consider the possibilities.

There is still some strong, but circumstantial, evidence that Carlos Marcello, then the Mafia boss of the South, might have called the shots, no pun intended, and, of course, the unfounded rumor (which must have begun about an hour after the assassination) that Lyndon Johnson engineered the whole thing. Has the blatant evidence of the shot from the front finally become so obvious that by vociferously denying the possibilities of a shot from the grassy knoll, everyone will believe it; thereby taking the spotlight off Bill Greer forever?

We had another glass of wine and threw all of our saved-up speculation on the table, having fun playing "devil's advocate" with each other and never reaching any conclusion.

Finally, Pat arose, disappeared for a few moments, and returned with two letters in his hand. The following words, just as everything since the beginning of Chapter One until now, are his.

* * *

(J.P.S.)

Shortly after seeing him and George in Seattle and then playing the gig at "Easy Street" in Chicago, I spent two weeks in Hawaii at a fabulous club called "Polynesian Hideaway." It was October of 1988. I had left him a message on the voice mail system as to where I could be reached. A few days later, a letter arrived at my hotel requesting that I call Freddie in Puerto Rico and relay some answers to a list of questions when he called me the following week.

A few days after that, Tupper did call me from wherever he was (I didn't ask), and I read him the notes I had taken from the phone call to Puerto Rico. I told him that during my conversation with her I had told Freddy I was in Honolulu and had just seen Tupper, and that he was doing fine. This, of course, was not to placate her so much as to confuse anyone else who might be listening. He was amused at the diversion but was a little concerned that Freddy might be slightly jealous if she thought he were living a life of luxury in the Hawaiian Islands. In his next letter to her, he made a particular effort to clarify the fact that he was not.

When I returned to Phoenix at the end of the month, there was a large envelope in my mailbox with a long letter to Freddie and instructions for me to please read it before sending it on. Why he wanted me to read such a personal thing, I don't know, but what I read has to be the most beautiful love letter since Browning to Barrett; a declaration of his Christian commitment to her filled with Biblical instruction. I never knew that such powerful phrases of Jesus Christ could fit so perfectly into a love letter from a man to his wife, but they surely did.

Except for an occasional phone call or a request to forward an enclosed letter that came in an envelope, I had little contact with Tupper in all of 1989. In early January of 1990, I received a letter from him outlining a five-point plan. He wrote in longhand:

1. We now know that the special agent that prepared the information against FTS for the Criminal Tax Division was authorized by letter of delegation to investigate nonresident aliens only. We can put him on the stand and demand his delegation of authority.

2. We now know that none of the computer codes on the IRS material for FTS indicate that he failed to file. Instead, the codes show that he did file. Wayne Bentsen could testify expertly on this, and I believe he still has copies of FTS's IRS printouts.

3. We now know that the Code of Federal Regulations 1.1441-5 removes a declared citizen of the United States (having only income derived from sources within the U.S.) from the jurisdiction of the IRS. CFR is positive administrative law, binding on agencies and courts.

4. The problem is: How does FTS present this without risking arrest and incarceration until the issue becomes academic? Perhaps submit it through a next friend in a jurisdiction that is less vengeful than the Eastern District of Tenn. FTS might be willing to appear provided execution on the Order of Mandate be stayed until all appeals on the newly discovered evidence are appealed, and that no "escape" charges be filed.

5. In your travels and conversations, please mention these things to the people from whom you have been acquiring your education. No one has ever seen a warrant for the arrest of FTS. We wonder: does one exist?

* * *

Once back in Phoenix just a few days later, I received a copy of the following three-page, handwritten letter with the request that I visit Don McPherson in his Phoenix law offices and talk with him about the prospects of being an intercessory between Tupper and the Federal Court. I also had a letter of introduction portraying me to McPherson as "Bill Maitland." I was becoming a "medium;" Tupper Saussy's window to the world, and I wondered if that were illegal. I didn't care. I knew by now it wasn't unlawful and stepped into the breach.

January 24, 1990

Re: U.S. vs. Tupper Saussy

Dear Mac,

Greetings! On April 10, 1990, I shall have been out of circulation for three (3) years. During this period, I have been separated from my beloved wife and children, my friends and relatives, my home, my livelihood. You have seen firsthand the degree of devotion between my wife, children, and myself; you can appreciate it when I say that I suffer hourly being apart from them.

The court had demanded one year of penitentiary service on the 7203 verdict, and it has thus far received *three*. "Whosoever shall compel thee to go a mile, go with him twain." The court demanded my coat, and I gave it my cloak, as well.

I have done three years of penance not under federal case workers but under God. He has completely repented me of any willful attitude toward taxing authorities, and has led me in ministering to the attitude problems of others. My various guardians, if they could be granted immunity from prosecution for "harboring and concealing," would account for just about everyday of existence since April, 1987, that I lived a simple, honest, and prayerful life. These people are solid citizens, many of them outstanding members of their communities. I believe that federal law permits a defendant to choose this form of custody in a sentence of one year or less. It certainly makes sense: if I had consented to federal penitentiary, the public would have had to pay (at $80 per day) some $30,000 to rehabilitate me over a year's time. As it has happened, my repentence has cost the public nothing. Truly, the ends of justice have been served.

I'm ready now to get on with my life. I haven't talked to my family in two years. No matter how tempting it might be for me to say that they are suffering "irreparably" from my absence, I know they are well because I have committed them to the Lord's care. Nevertheless, they need the guidance, love, personal presence, and spiritual ministry I am now able to give them. It is my duty to return to them and resume being their husband and father. I have a son-in-law and grandson that I've never met!

Mac, I want you to contact John Littleton and John MacCoon and the court (probably Thomas Hull in Greenville, Tennessee) and negotiate disposal of this case on the grounds that the sentence has been 100% effective. I am no longer "unrepentant," no longer a tax activist advising Constitutional challenges against IRS.

I know that the main concern is not my rehabilitation but rather the public's perception that my stance was wrong, and that justice was done. No one familiar with my case would ever want to try the Fifth Amendment challenge, and my repented position is to advise against any such challenge. Nor could anyone in his right mind perceive that my three-year separation from my family has been spent cheating the justice system. This time has been spent rendering to Caesar exactly his due, and to God His. This is what is meant, I guess, by "all things work for good for those who love God."

I will not be the government's slave, and I don't believe the government wants me to be its "voluntary servant," because I would only be rebellious and difficult and that would get neither party anywhere. I want, simply, to be left alone to conduct my ministry of loving one's enemies.

I have nothing left. All my material wherewithal has been taken from me. I will be starting on square one, at age 53. I will not be asking for any government subsidies or entitlements. My only source of energy and deliverance will be the Spirit that has so faithfully led me over these past years, and now leads me to send this letter to you.

If you will be my intercessory, Mac, you'll be richly rewarded, although that should not be your motivation for involvement any more than I should be able to identify the source of your reward. A friend will be contacting you in a few days. His name is Bill Maitland. Please alert your receptionist to put Bill through to you when he calls.

Your brother in Christ,

Tupper

P.S. A friend is remailing this letter from San Antonio. To protect him, please destroy the envelope, especially if it bears his logotype. Also, please remail my note to my son also enclosed. Thank you.

* * *

I had an eye-opening meeting with Don McPherson the next day. After the receptionist finally got him on the line following my first call, I had a little trouble communicating exactly who I was. Eventually, after decoding my telephone hieroglyphics, he understood the reason for the call because he had received the letter just a few days before. However, only the first two pages were included in his envelope, which accounted for our initial communication problem. He could not know that an intermediary would be contacting him nor any of the letter's conclusion and requests. Knowing that Tupper is much too precise to commit such an error, we both thought this to be a rather strange twist of events and wondered out loud if someone were tampering with McPherson's mail. He suggested that I come over, bring along my copy of the third page, and talk in person.

Although he knew me only as "Bill Maitland," I enjoyed becoming acquainted with Don McPherson. A West Point Graduate, scholar, athlete, and still a weight-lifter, he reminded me of Ryan O'Neal with more androgynous features. We chatted for two hours late one February morning and through the lunch hour, and for the first hour it was about everything except the subject at hand. I was very familiar with "Mac" and his work by this time, and we discussed several of the tax cases he had defended around the United States. Although he has had some disappointing losses, he is more successful than any other attorney with defending Tax Evasion/Willful Failure cases in the United States. He gave me a copy of each of his two books and autographed one with a quote from John Adams: "Fear is the foundation of most governments."

In the opening statement on page one of his latest book, *Tax Fraud & Evasion—The War Stories*, McPherson, now an Army Reserve Major, admonishes himself for being a gutsy Airborne Infantry Captain in Vietnam at age twenty-four and then coming home to tremble at the thought of being tailed by Treasury Agents. "If you are afraid of your own government, Major Mac, you might as well move to Russia," he says to himself in the very first line.

"Mac" and his wife and three children attend church in the protestant establishment tradition, and he teaches a weekly Sunday School class. He embraces Christianity and is not ashamed to discuss it in conversation or his writings. However, he also holds a government-issued license to practice law and must wrestle with that quandary often; or ignore it.

When we finally got around to talking about Tupper's plight and flight and rehashing the possible scenarios of the missing page, he asked for my copy. After rereading the whole thing, Mac peered over the top of his reading glasses from behind his desk and asked me what I thought about it.

Seldom disingenuous, especially in private, I didn't hesitate to tell him, "Personally, I think he is suffering from delusions of grandeur if he believes Caesar is just going to roll over, but he has tremendous faith that God and Truth will prevail. I have to believe the same, but, somehow, I just don't think it will be this easy. Otiose, I think, is the word. However, he doesn't need my opinion, he needs a legal opinion."

Mac smiled a nodded agreement and, while seeming to not hear or just ignore the two pleas for help—mine just spoken and Tupper's written— replied, "You are right on. I believe in God, too, but my legal opinion is that this is a waste of time. He's made monkeys out of them, and they're not going to let him get away it without some time plus maybe five years extra for 'escape.' They want their blood sacrifice."

We talked about it some more; and, as he thought out loud about all the ramifications, I could tell he was not reaching any positive conclusions. Finally, he said, "Bill, I have too many clients who value their privacy, and I've already got red flags all over me down at the Justice Department because of the type cases I have defended the last decade.

By taking this on, I'm just going to end up with a phone tap, and I don't want to risk compromising all my other clients; especially when I know this one is a loser anyway. It's just not worth it. In fact, now that I think about it, I wish you would take this letter that he asked me to forward to his son and drop it in the mail box. I think I would rather not. I don't need to be placed in any position of having aided a federal fugitive. By the way, do you have a dollar on you? In order to make you a *bona fide* client, I must charge you a fee, and you must be a client in order for me to protect our private conversations today or in the future."

I looked in my wallet and found nothing smaller than a ten, but in my pants pocket I found a Kennedy half and placed it on his desk.

"Will this suffice?" I asked.

"It will," he said, handing the letter, and we shook hands and bid farewell.

"Good luck," he said, "and keep me up to date with any happenings." He handed me the letter addressed to Puerto Rico in Tupper's poorly disguised handwriting. On Tupper's behalf, I thanked him and left wondering who else in recent history has escaped the clutches of a lawyer with such a bargain.

When I went charging down the steps from the law offices to the flower-draped, horseshoe-shaped patio, I fantasized the enemy everywhere. A burst of machine gun fire went by my ear. A hand grenade exploded in the flower bed destroying a section of the parapet a second after I scooted by. Rounding the corner and sidestepping like O.J. Simpson up the sidelines of the asphalt parking lot, I saw the cloudless sky filled with helicoptors echoing with cannon bursts as the Fighter Jets dropped napalm all around me.

An exploding land mine would have finished me had it not been for Rocky Blier appearing out of nowhere and shielding me by covering the blast with his helmet. Wearing complete combat regalia covered by a white, black, and gold Pittsburgh Steelers jersey with #20 on front and back, Rocky then sprang forward and threw a crushing block which cut down all three bayonet-wielding gooks who were about to impale me. Darting through the smoke and fire, I finally spotted my four-foot-high, two-foot-wide, dark blue and white-trimmed destination.down at the corner near the stop light, a straight shot still a hundred yards away. Carl Lewis appeared in the lane next to me and, nine seconds later, was still one step behind as, somehow having dodged the conflagration, we sprinted by the finish line. I stood proudly on "Mailbox Hill" and planted the small "flag" inside the blue box.

Suddenly, all was quiet, and after John Wayne and Audie Murphy showed up for a brief ceremony to award me the Congressional Medal Of Honor, I calmly strolled unmolested through the solitude of the Arizona sun, not at all out of breath, climbed into my "Z," and headed through the streets of Phoenix toward Tempe.

It only hurts when I laugh.

# APPENDIX

## HUMAN LIBERTY—THE OPPOSITE OF PAPER MONEY

All the talk about human liberty, the Constitution, representative government, etc, is just so much hogwash. There is no such thing as human liberty in a system of paper money. It just cannot be possible.

If we commence our search for understanding of how and why we continue to have diminished liberty premised upon the above, we could achieve a shortcut to knowledge and save a lot of lost motion and valuable time. It all seems so simple, but yet it is fundamental, complicated by professional deceivers.

Paper "money," including, of course, non-paper "money" computer symbols, is non-production owned by a monopoly. The government and the banking money monopoly "buy" whatever they want with this nonproduction ("money") including your thoughts and your religion. This is awesome power, and it is the explanation of the chaos that we live in today, and it is worldwide.

Every day that you work, you exchange your production for government banker non-production ("money"). How is it possible that you are not a slave when you are required to exchange your labor (production) for government nonproduction? Their "money" is acquired for nothing. It is, therefore, theft and fraud.

The IRS does not collect money. How long will people believe that hoax? How long will we believe that there is a national debt? If there is no money of account of the United States, you cannot owe or pay a debt with anything but credit. Since gold and silver were designated in the Constitution as "the money of account of the United States" and this has never been rescinded, **there is no money of account**, and there has been no money of account since 1968 when all the silver was removed from our coinage. If there is no money of account there is no tax liability. This is exactly why the IRS has to have police power to reduce our consumption and gather information, under the pretext of "collecting taxes." Hocus Pocus!

If we understand paper money, we can see the great hoax called a "federal budget" and we can see why nothing is ever done to "balance the budget." It is all deceit and propaganda to keep us from finding out that government gets its wealth and power for nothing and that we are slaves. Ah, yes, as paper money makes us slaves, it also makes us happy and contented slaves.

No matter what a government calls itself, whether democracy or communist, it is a slave system of paper money. This makes all the propaganda about Eastern Europe going to Democracy so much bunk. It is all still a paper-money-debt slave system. Paper money is slavery. Only the gangsters who create it change from time to time.

—BOB LIVINGSTON, Editor/Publisher of *Christians Awake*
Newsletter Ministry